THE SOUND OF THE HOUNDS

GREGORY BART NATION

D1528496

Published by Dog Days Publishing
 ISBN: 9780615854915

Printed in the United States of America

THIS BOOK IS DEDICATED IN
MEMORY OF MY BROTHER AND MY
FATHER WHO ENJOYED HEARING
A GOOD HOUND RUN AND TREE A
COON.

TABLE OF CONTENTS

THE MEASURING STICKS
1

Coon Hunting with hounds became a part of my life when only barely old enough to get around in the woods. My Father was first to take me on a hunt with the Plott Hounds he owned and hunted at that time.

On our first hunt the hounds were loaded into the box and we then drove to the river bottoms for some easy hunting. I suppose my Father didn't want to make the first hunt too hard on a beginner. The hounds were released and we sat on a log waiting for a strike - which quickly came. The hounds swiftly put a tree at the end of the track and we slowly walked to them. Following a few minutes of shining a big ol' coon was spotted high in the tree and given to the hounds. This was my first hunt, my first coon, and I was hooked forever.

I hunted with my Father off and on until family, work, and business brought his hunting to a halt. He quit hunting but encouraged me to continue running the hounds with a couple of his friends. I hunted all night every night if someone would hunt with me. If no one wanted to hunt I would often go alone near my home, only I didn't hunt all night. Many nights when hunting with other hunters I would return home just in time to get ready for school. I went to school, came home, rested a little and prepared for another night in the woods. My Father always said, "Don't stay out all night tonight, and I hope you are keeping up your school work or there will be no more hunting." I worked hard at that too so my hunting could continue.

The first hound that I called my own was a Bluetick female named "Kate" which my Father bought for me. Kate was a young hound but treed lots of coon for me. She was a registered hound with bloodlines consisting of ancestors from a famous line of hounds still being promoted today.

Some of the fellows whom I hunted with worked regular jobs and were unable to hunt all night, every night. One of the hunters was a barber and had to run his barber shop, but he liked to hunt as much as me and would many nights hunt 'til daylight. A couple others whom I hunted with farmed and raised cattle and would much of the time hunt all night. I never stopped looking to add more hunting buddies to the list, for the purpose of having someone with which to hunt every night.

While one day listening to the radio there was a call-in from a man advising that someone had stolen his Bluetick Hound. He was informing everyone that he had posted a reward for the return of the hound. I phoned this man only to talk, relating to him that I knew nothing about his dog but that I also owned and hunted a Bluetick. As our conversation continued I asked if he would like to go hunting sometime and gave him my phone number. Following this conversation a friendship that would last the remainder of his life began. My new friend "James" possessed more knowledge pertaining to hunting dogs, and was one of the hardest hunters I have ever known. He was a die-hard Bluetick man but was not color blind to a top hound of any breed or color. My Father was acquainted with James and stated that he would probably hunt harder than I would, or could.

I was raised in the North Georgia area where coons were scarce at that time. Our area had all types of terrain ranging from river bottoms, swamps, cutover, to steep mountainous territory. Much of the terrain was very rough with an abundance of deer and fox. James and I began hunting together and our terrain of choice was the mountains. Hunting the mountainous terrain was often tough, but it was home to more coons and an abundance of off game too. Shortly after James and I began hunting on a regular basis his Bluetick Hound that had been stolen was recovered. He phoned to ask if I wanted to hunt that night. Sure I did, as I wanted to hunt with the hound I had heard so much about.

As darkness approached James arrived at my home and we headed for the mountains. He was hunting only the blue male he called "Tiny" and I had "Kate", my blue female which had made a pretty fair coondog. We arrived at our hunting territory, removed the hounds from the box, and as I looked Tiny over I realized he was one of the best looking dark blue hounds I had ever seen. Both hounds were released from the mountain top into a deep hollow that ran to the base of the mountain. It was in the dead of winter, very cold, without leaves on the trees. In a short period of time a hound opened way deep with an extremely loud bawl mouth. I thought there was no way it could be Tiny as he had gotten so deep, so fast.

James casually stated, "Well, he barked 3 times and he will tree that one somewhere." Tiny drifted deeper as we walked to stay within hearing range; there were no roads in the area where he was trailing, so there would be no driving around. Kate never opened and I thought maybe Tiny was running off game, but was proven wrong when he located with a big pretty bawl and shortened it down to a bawl and chop before being backed by Kate. As we walked in to the tree I saw this dark blue hound stretched high as possible on the tree, looking straight up paying attention to nothing else. The hounds were leashed back and the tree shined.

James soon yelled, "Here he is," and a big boar coon hit the ground. This was the first coon I saw Tiny tree, but I would get to see him tree several more that night and many more during his life. We hunted all night as Tiny treed coons in front of, behind, and all around Kate. He was only a young hound at that time but dead broke from off game, and when he treed there would be a coon in the tree. Over the years I have thought back to this hound and realize there is no reason for a hound to make a lot of trees where a coon is not seen.

James and I hunted all night every night for the next month until my Dad said I was going to have to slow down or get me a hound that would not keep me out all night. He assumed my hound was running trash and I couldn't catch her when ready to come home, and I was staying out until she was caught up. This was not the case as we were just hunting all night, or most of it, anyway. Dad asked James if he knew where we could purchase a better hound than I now owned, one which I would not have to stay out all night attempting to catch. My Dad offering to buy me another hound, in no way, hurt my feelings as I was all for the idea.

At the time there were four or five top hounds in the area, other than Tiny, that we knew about. There was a top Plott, a Redtick, a Black and Tan, and a Walker colored part bird dog owned by one of my old hunting buddies. We spoke to the hunters who owned these hounds but none wanted to sell, so I began asking James to sell Tiny. He finally agreed and put a price on him. I advised my Dad that James had agreed to sell Tiny and quoted him the price. He replied, "That's a lot of money, but I guess if that is what you want you'll be doing a lot of work around here." The following day I owned Tiny.

James still owned a female that treed lots of coon so he was not without a good hound and we continued to hunt most every night. Even though we hunted nightly James was not content at the end of our hunts because he was not taking Tiny home with him. He asked to buy Tiny back and offered me a considerable profit on him. I really liked Tiny as he treed coon anywhere and anytime turned loose. I had owned him for a year and taken 125 coons with him during coon season. Warm weather was approaching and we had lots of work to be done around the farm, managing 1200 hogs, several hundred head of cattle and the farming along with a couple family owned businesses. With these thoughts in mind I spoke to my Dad about the possibility of selling Tiny back to James. I also told him that James had offered a considerable amount more money than I had given him. Dad said if, in fact, I did sell Tiny back to James that I should sell him for the same price I had given for him.

After all, he had been generous enough to let me have him to begin with.

I still owned my female Kate and she was bred to Tiny; I wouldn't be without a dog to hunt. After some thought Tiny was sold back to James, and we still hunted almost every night, just not all night as it was summertime and very hot. I was also working most of the day and couldn't hunt as hard as I previously had.

My female Kate delivered 10 pups but experienced problems with them and only 2 lived. The two pups had to be bottle fed because Kate developed an infection and died only a few days after giving birth. I was now without a trained hound to hunt, even though James and I still hunted. It just wasn't the same hunting without a dog of my own. James made the offer to sell Tiny back to me but I said, "No" as I knew how much he meant to him.

My hunting slowed almost to a standstill in the next couple months and when fall rolled around I was once again ready to hunt. I heard that the man who owned the good Redtick hound in my area had quit hunting and sold the hound back to his original owner, who was an older Gentleman whom I knew from the coon club. I phoned the Gentleman to inquire if he would sell the hound. He answered, "Yes. I'll sell the hound, but he might be too much hound for you to handle. I'll show him alone or with whatever you want to bring along. He will speak for himself, he trees coons and runs nothing else and is only 3 1/2 years old." A hunt was arranged for the coming Friday night.

I phoned my hunting buddy James and asked him to accompany me on the hunt with the Redtick. I also asked him to bring Tiny along for me to make a comparison.

James and I traveled to the Gentleman's home on Friday night and were met by several other hunters who wanted to see the two hounds go together. Neither James nor I had ever seen the Redtick hound and when the Gentleman loaded him in the box we looked him over. He was a dark colored, open ticked hound with one large red spot on his side. He weighed 60 to 65 pounds, had a big flat head with good ears, dark eyes and good feet and legs. "If that hound is anywhere near good as he looks, he will fill the bill," James stated.

On the drive to our determined hunting area, the Gentleman rode with James and I while a couple trucks of other hunters followed to observe the two hounds hunted together. The area we were going to hunt was atop the mountain where the terrain was rough and there were plenty of coons, deer and fox.

The hounds were released into an abandoned orchard and both left the leash in a hard run. Fifteen minutes passed without a bark. Tiny then struck directly ahead of us, but very deep, and began to open here and there on an old bad track. A few minutes passed before the Redtick called "Spot" struck deep to our right on a separate track near an old lake. He had one of the biggest horn bawl mouths ever heard on a hound and he was running the track to catch.

In the meantime Tiny continued to trail deeper into the country, opening as he drifted the track. After only a couple minutes the Redtick slammed a tree with a roaring locate that would make your hair stand on end and then shortened it up to a hard, hard chop so loud it rang all over the hills.

As we walked in the direction of Spot's tree we heard Tiny locate and put a tree on the end of his track, in the opposite direction. Arriving at Spot's tree he was found to be on a large oak that had a coon sitting in a fork near the top. James and I stood back and admired this tree dog.

James stated, "That is some more tree dog there. Even an old man can hear him." The season had yet to begin and the coon was not taken. The Gentleman leashed Spot and we walked in the direction of Tiny's tree. After walking 100 yards or so the Gentleman released Spot and within minutes he was struck again and quickly slammed another tree, directly in front of us. The tree was shined on our way to Tiny and another coon was quickly found. Spot was leashed once again but was led on to Tiny's tree this time. We shined Tiny's tree, an extremely large oak that was difficult to shine but one of the spectators found the coon lying flat on a large limb. Tiny and Spot were both led from the tree and released back in the direction of the trucks.

James said, "Two for the Redtick and one for the Blue dog. That Redtick can sure go home with me if you don't want him." As James spoke the words Tiny opened and was joined by Spot - they were together this time. Everyone commented that we should get to see the hounds work together on this track.

They were in a big wooded section on the flat part of the mountain which contained lots of standing water and swampy areas. They worked the track, drifting, cutting and slashing until they had it up and running. Spot suddenly slammed the tree with Tiny only half a bark behind him. Walking in to the tree both hounds were found stretched high as they could reach on the tree, paying no attention to the other. They were leashed back, the tree shined and a coon quickly spotted. All the accompanying hunters stated, "They had just seen two coondogs tree coons the way they were supposed to be treed." The Gentleman said he had to call it a night as he had a hard day ahead of him. Both hounds remained on the leashes as our group walked back to the trucks.

The Gentleman spoke very little on the drive back to his home. As he exited the truck I said, "Just take your collar off Spot and leave him in the box." As he took the money he replied, "I sure hate to see him go but you will get more use out of him than I will. I'll tell you this; if you live to be my age you will never buy another dog that good for the price you gave me for him." He removed his collar from Spot's neck, petted him on the head and slowly walked toward the house.

I climbed back into the truck one happy young man. James said, "Boy, I've hunted many years and have never seen or heard a tree dog of that caliber, and he is not mean around the tree either. If you ever decide to sell him, I'll give you a nice profit on him."

I went home and was unable to sleep the remainder of the night. I was thinking about turning Spot and Tiny loose again the following night. James and I hunted these two hounds together almost every night during coon season and up into the spring. They treed almost every track they struck, were split treed a lot and missed very few coons.

I had let James have the two pups I raised from my Kate female and Tiny. He had named them "Bigun"' and "Littleun"'. As spring began we were hunting them and they were really turning it on. The water did not get too deep or the going too rough for either pup. They were usually hunted separately with the older hounds, but sometimes turned loose alone. Both were outstanding young dogs that improved every night in the woods.

One summer evening James phoned to ask if I wanted to hunt a place on the river where the coons were destroying a farmer's corn. I said, "Yeah, sure." About dark we headed out. James brought along Tiny, Bigun' and Littleun', and I had Spot. It was a rare occurrence when James hunted the two young hounds together, but he wanted to get them on a few cornfield coons.

We drove to our hunting area and cut the hounds loose. They stayed together with Tiny getting the strike followed by the young hounds and Spot. Bigun' grabbed the tree and was backed by the other three hounds. We walked to the tree, leashed the hounds back and swiftly spotted two coons in the tree. Tiny and Spot were kept on the leash as we walked back in the direction of the truck. The two young hounds remained loose and caught a coon on the ground along the edge of the cornfield. We hurriedly walked to them and I put Littleun' on the leash with Spot. James tried to catch Bigun' but he was so hyped up that he couldn't get his hands on him. Bigun' started up a farm road and didn't slow down until he hit the highway. He attempted to cross the river bridge and was struck by a vehicle while on the bridge.

James and I had made it back to the truck, loaded the other hounds and drove toward the bridge in an effort to head Bigun' off, but we were too late. He had already been struck by the vehicle but was still alive. James picked him up and placed him in the truck bed but he died almost immediately following. For a long period of time James never spoke. When he did finally speak he said he was

14

not going to hunt anymore; that he was quitting. He went on to say he had someone who wanted to buy Littleun' and if I wanted to buy Tiny that he would sell him to me.

James stuck to his word and quit hunting for a short period of time. I purchased Tiny from him and was very happy to own both him and Spot, but sad that my old hunting buddy was so down and out. I continued to hunt - I think even harder than I had in the past when James and I hunted. Eventually James began to hunt again but it wasn't the same. He never asked to buy Tiny back, even though he could have gotten him back. He started from scratch but told me many times that Tiny was the best hound he had ever owned. He also told me he was glad that he had given his friend the opportunity to own him. He knew I would appreciate him. James and I remained friends until he passed on. I owned Tiny and Spot until they both passed on - at around 12 years of age.

These hounds were used as measuring sticks to gauge future hounds I would own. They were the total package - completely balanced from strike to tree, with nose and brains to use it. One of the most important facts is there would be real live raccoons in the trees at the end of their tracks. These two hounds were never in a point hunt, but they won many poundage hunts and were only pleasure coon hunted. They will always be remembered by me and anyone who hunted with them.

I went on to own hundreds of Nite Champion and Grand Nite Champion hounds, some that would win many of the larger hunts. Some were even coondogs whose performance compared to Tiny and Spot. I used these two hounds to judge what I was hunting at any given time. I was hard to please and always wanted and was always looking for something better than I had on my leash, but that's how most coon hunters are.

I learned from my friend James not to be color-blind as to the breed of hound hunted. Yet, I have always been partial to the Bluetick and English Hounds even though I have owned many good hounds of other breeds. This is a tribute to these two great hounds that are buried out by the barn in the North Georgia clay, alongside many other greats to include such hounds as Grand Nite Champion, Grand Champion Fuller's Hopsing, Grand Nite Champion, Grand Champion Davis' Blue Scooter, Grand Nite Champion, Grand Champion Sugar Creek J.R., Grand Nite Champion Rock 'N' Roll Rowdy and many, many more. My favorites were always kept, regardless of the offering price - they always had a home and were never sold.

THE GIFTS OF TIME

2

The ears of the two mules pricked up as they heard the bawl of the hounds on the distant ridge. Mr. Bill was riding the older mule called "Molly" and young Ben rode the one called "Jenny'. Bill and Ben pointed the mules toward the sound of the trailing hounds; and they trotted in that direction. Both mules were well trained for coon hunting and knew to follow the barking dogs.

Mr. Bill and his young neighbor Ben had met at Bill's kennel for an early morning coon hunt, just as the eastern sky begin to lighten. They had released two of Mr. Bill's Plott Hounds, "Grady" and "Granny" from the kennel, directly onto Dry Branch, pointing them in the direction of the rolling ridges.

The men had then proceeded to the barn and readied the mules for their hunt. Their plans were to catch a live coon for young Ben, to possibly have for a pet. Mr. Bill knew how it was to once be young and want all animals one came in contact with; now only a faraway memory. As the two mounted the mules and rode across the pasture they heard the loud bawl of Grady followed by the chops and bawl of Granny, far up Dry Branch. The mules were now trotting toward the trailing hounds.

Mr. Bill, given name William but called Bill or Mr. Bill by one and all was a man of indeterminate age; he could have been fifty or seventy. Bill had been a hunter, houndsman, and outdoorsman since old enough to get around on his own. He hunted and fished for food and sport, but wasted no game; as he had been taught. He hunted all game, but enjoyed hunting raccoon with his Plott Hounds most of all. He had even run and treed a few bear with his hounds in his younger years. Bill raised and trained the hounds he hunted He mostly hunted alone, until only several months back when a young man and his mother moved into the country home adjoining Bill's large land holdings. Recently, Bill with no children of his own had become friends with the young man "Ben" and begin letting him help around the farm and also hunt and fish with him. He was progressing slowly with the coon hunting as he didn't want to break the young man before he was "hooked".

Young Ben, given name Benjamin but called Ben or Benjy by one and all was a city kid in his early teens, only recently moved to the country. Ben's mother, a single parent, had relocated to the country for Ben to mature in a better environment, with a better quality of life. Several years before, Ben's father had gone away to a foreign war, and like so many before him, had failed to return. Ben was now the man of the house and had been for some time; he was mature for his age. After moving to the country he had taken a liking to Mr. Bill, the farmer next door. He worked on Mr. Bill's farm and also hunted and fished with him. He liked working with the animals and really enjoyed coon hunting with the hounds; he would go hunting any time given the chance. "This country life is okay," he thought.

The mules slowed to listen as they heard Grady and Granny locate and begin to tree, far up Dry Branch; almost out of hearing range. Mr. Bill and Ben had been riding alongside the branch, across the pasture, into the timber and up the hollow, following the trailing and now treed hounds. They rode on until they came upon the barbed wire fence that divided the upper and lower woods and pasture.

"I guess we will have to leave the mules here or go back through the gate to get closer to the dogs," said Ben. "Nope, that fence is not a problem," stated Mr. Bill. "Just watch and learn."

Mr. Bill hooked his dog lead to the top and bottom strands of barbed wire, pulling the top strand low as possible, removed an old blanket from his pack and threw it over the fence at the lowest point. He then raised and secured the stirrups to the top of the saddle on both mules. Crossing over the fence with reins of Molly mule in hand he clicked a couple times and Molly squatted low and jumped high, easily clearing the fence. He then repeated the process with Jenny mule.

"Wow, they didn't even have to get a running go to clear the fence!" Ben exclaimed. "As I said, watch and learn," replied Mr. Bill, who then explained why he had done the things he did, such as tying the top strand of wire to the lower, putting the blanket over the wire, securing the stirrups to the top of the saddle etc. He wanted Ben to understand all he had done, and why.

The two remounted the mules and rode on up Dry Branch in the direction of the treed hounds. As they rode to within good hearing range of the dogs, and the terrain begin to level off, the water in the small branch disappeared.

"Notice how the water in the branch dried up? That's how it received the name Dry Branch. The water flows under the ground for a couple miles before resurfacing, it never actually becomes completely dry," explained Mr. Bill to Ben as they followed the dry creek bed. "Just something I thought you would be interested in knowing about the area you now live."

Approaching the treed hounds, they found Grady and Granny stretched high on a large hickory tree. Upon further inspection the tree was found to be hollow to the base, from a hole in a bend, ten feet above the ground. Looking the tree over no game was found on the outside and young Ben climbed up to the hollow to attempt to look inside. He soon saw the coon sitting at the base of the tree and advised Mr. Bill of such. Mr. Bill removed a short handled axe from his pack and cut a leaf covered limb, which he passed up to Ben, telling him to stuff it into the hole to prevent the coon from running out of the hole and up the tree.

"Climb back down and we'll cut a hole and try to catch Mr. Ringtail," stated Mr. Bill. Ben climbed to the ground and leashed Grady and Granny back from the tree while Mr. Bill chopped a basketball sized hole in the tree, a few feet above the ground.

Mr. Bill made quick work of chopping the hole and soon said, "Here he sits at the bottom of the tree and he has some size on him too. Get the catcher and that burlap sack and let's see if we can get the scallywag into the sack."

Ben held the sack open while Mr. Bill slipped the noose of the catcher over the head of the coon and pulled him from the hole. He then put the coon into the sack and advised Ben to pull the drawstring tight before he released the coon from the catcher. "This coon must weigh twenty pounds," proclaimed Ben, as he held the burlap sack above the ground.

No sooner than the words were spoken the large coon busted the seam in the bottom of the sack, hit the ground and ran up the ridge side. Grady and Granny went into a frenzied state as the coon ran passed, and Ben stood in a shocked stupor.

"Do you want me to turn the dogs loose on his trail?" The dazed young Ben asked Mr. Bill.

Mr. Bill smiled and replied, "No, it's really hard to re-tree a coon that has gotten away like that one just did. He would probably go into a hole in the ground or into another hollow tree where we would possibly be unable to get at him again. Besides he destroyed your burlap sack so we have nothing to put him in even if we caught him again. I think that coon was way too big and old for you to have tamed anyway; don't worry we will get a young one for you, eventually."

As the two slowly rode back towards Mr. Bill's with the hounds in tow, Mr. Bill described the origin of Grady and Granny. Both had been raised and trained by him; same as all the others in his kennel. His foundation stock came from dedicated Plott men, many years in the past. He had purchased a male and two females, trained them, and later raised what he hunted from the three. He only occasionally utilized outside studs.

The original three hounds came from the bloodlines of, if not directly from, Bennie Moore, Berlin King and Dale Brandenburger. Mr. Bill explained that these men would always have a good hound on their leash and were not afraid to hunt their hounds against other hounds of any breed. They knew the caliber of their hounds and were proud to show them in competition or otherwise.

Ben was pleased to hear the origin of the hounds, and the facts about some of the breeders of the Plott Hounds. He was also eager to go on their next hunt and asked Mr. Bill, "When are we going to hunt again? At night I mean." He preferred the night hunting over the early morning hunts. Mr. Bill answered, "We might try it tonight if the weather remains nice." This brought a big smile and an, "Okay!" from Ben.

That night Mr. Bill and Ben loaded Grady, Granny and a young hound called Hogg, with intentions to hunt some flat river bottoms. The bottomland was scarcely ever hunted by houndsmen. All three hounds were released onto a slough which ran into the river, and soon had tracks going in two directions. Granny was first to strike with Hogg joining her on a good moving track that was taken up the creek that fed the slough. Both Granny and Hogg were moving away from the river.

In the meantime Grady started a track of his own; one not as good as Granny and Hogg's, but he steadily moved it toward the river.

"Listen to Granny and Hogg run that track," said Mr. Bill. "Notice that Hogg is a solid chop mouthed track dog and that Granny also chops the majority of the time, bawling only occasionally. Those two can move a track of any kind and put a tree on the end of it; with the groceries in the tree. They will put a tree on the end of that one soon. Now it could take old Grady a little longer, as his track is cold."

Mr. Bill and Ben stood listening to the hound music, admiring the track work of all three hounds, when suddenly Granny and Hogg loaded up on a tree. "Sounds like they just put that one up a tree," stated Ben. "Yep, you're catching on real fast," replied Mr. Bill. "Guess we better head in that direction."

The two hunters walked in the direction of the treed hounds, relishing the sound of the hard treeing chop mouthed hounds. On arrival at the tree, a large hardwood, the hounds were leashed and the tree searched. A coon was quickly spotted and dispatched to the two deserving hounds. Walking from the tree, leading Granny and Hogg, the hunters heard Grady's long, loud locate and the hard chops began, far down the river.

"Well, Grady is down towards the river and it's going to be a long walk in to him, there is no way to get closer. I think we should drop the coon, Granny and Hogg off at the truck and walk down the slough to the river. I believe Grady is on the riverbank or near it," said Mr. Bill.

They dropped the coon, Granny and Hogg off at the truck and proceeded in the direction of the treed Grady. On arrival at the tree it was found to be a leaning tree on the riverbank, with limbs reaching over the water. Grady was leashed, the tree shined, and a large coon spotted on a limb far out over the river. Mr. Bill said to Ben, "Turn Grady loose as he will have to swim out to get the coon if I'm unable to walk it down and have to just put it out where it sits."

With that Mr. Bill begin to shoot at the coon, which walked back toward the river bank to a fork in the tree and refused to move any further. Mr. Bill then solidly hit the coon and it bailed out. Grady swam out to retrieve the coon and the fight was on.

Ben had never seen the likes of what was going on with the coon and Grady. The coon was attempting to get on Grady's back or actually his head and Grady was trying to grab the coon around the neck. Following several minutes of dog and coon warfare Grady was able to dispatch his foe, but by this time he was thoroughly exhausted. The coon was extremely large and Grady was having trouble getting it back to the river bank. Rather than let loose the coon, Grady was slowly drowning himself because the coon's weight was pulling him underwater. Seeing this and without thinking Ben suddenly jumped into the river to save Grady. The big Plott sprang forward using Ben as a stairway, and onto the riverbank he went.

Mr. Bill watched in disbelief as Ben jumped into the river to try and save Grady. Watching the outcome, and swiftly acting, he picked up a long, thin limb and extended it out to Ben while yelling, "Grab the limb and I'll pull you in." Ben grabbed the limb and was pulled to the bank by Mr. Bill.

"Guess we better start back to the truck and get you out of those wet clothes before you get sick," stated Mr. Bill as he leashed Grady and retrieved the coon. A smiling Ben replied, "I've never had so much fun in all my life. I can't wait until our next hunt."

On the walk back to the truck, and on the drive home, Mr. Bill talked to Ben about the dangers of him having jumped into the river. Informing him of the dangers, yet trying not to scold him too badly.

Ben only smiled and said, "All's well that ends well." Over the following months Ben hunted with Mr. Bill every time he turned the hounds loose. He was learning more and more about hunting and dogs as the time passed. He was also learning how to get around in the woods without becoming lost or turned around. He was developing into a pretty good woodsman and becoming tough as a pine knot.

Granny was soon bred to Grady and halfway through coon season she gave birth to a litter of fine puppies. Mr. Bill and Ben continued to hunt Grady and Mr. Bill's other hounds, but Grady remained Ben's favorite. Watching Granny's pups grow Ben secretly wished he could have one of the pups for himself, but said nothing to Mr. Bill.

One night while hunting Grady alone, Mr. Bill and Ben after making several turnouts without a bark were about to call it a night as a storm seemed to be moving into the area. "Let's make one more turnout, I know Grady will tree a coon before the storm arrives," said Ben. "We'll try a quick drop. If Grady doesn't get one going on this drop we'll go home and try it another night," answered Mr. Bill.

Grady was then released into the woods where they had run and treed several coons before. Shortly after Grady was released a terrible rain storm commenced. Grady had struck a track just as the rain began and Mr. Bill stated, "We have two choices, either we sit in the truck and wait the rain out, or we follow Grady."

"I think we better follow Grady as he could get way deep in those big woods and get out of hearing in this rain," said Ben.

Grady did an outstanding job running the trail in the pouring rain. He pushed the track hard and soon his loud locate and hard chops were heard, deep in the section of woods. Mr. Bill and Ben trudged through the rain storm and arrived at a small pine with Grady stretched high on its side. A coon was quickly spotted and given to

Grady. Ben then put the coon into his game bag and leashed Grady, stating to Mr. Bill, "I'll lead Grady back to the truck."

Once back in the warmth of the vehicle Mr. Bill told Ben he wanted to talk with him. "I have a few things I want to talk about, first I want to say if you want them I'll give you a couple of the pups from Grady and Granny as a gift, your pick. You might not want to always hunt Plott Hounds but I've found them to satisfy my needs in a dog in every way. They are cold nosed, good track and tree dogs and most important you will see game at the end of their trails. They are a versatile breed of dog that can be hunted on an assortment of game, both big and small. There are good dogs in all breeds but I have stayed with these old Plotts because they satisfied me, and I'm the only one they have to please. You have hunted with me for some time now and I think you are going to be a tough coon hunter who will stay in it for the long haul. With the gift of time comes a wealth of knowledge, you learn as time passes and with age comes wisdom. Hopefully these hounds will please you too. Come over tomorrow and pick your pups if you decide you want them."

"I definitely want the pups and have wanted one since they were born. This coon hunting has gotten into my blood, and yes I'm in it for the duration. I'll come over first thing in the morning to pick my pups, and thank you for the pups and introducing me to this great sport," responded a delighted Ben.

Not the end, but the beginning!

COMPETITION FEVER

3

The point hunts were becoming a big thing all across the country and everyone was beginning to participate in them. The young hunter knew nothing about them but had always hunted the weekly poundage hunts at the local coon club. At these hunts, the coon was actually brought in and weighed with the heaviest coon winning for the night. Usually, the weight from every weekend was combined and at the end of the season there would be an overall winner. The poundage hunts were hard on the coon population and only conducted during hunting season. The point hunts took place year round and only trees were made and scored without the coon having to be taken.

The young hunter was considering trying his hand at the point hunts. At the time, he owned a couple of good older broke coonhounds, a young English Redtick that he had been hunting hard and two English Redtick pups. The young Redtick, "Joe", was almost a finished hound, but still a handful. Joe had been hunted hard all winter but he was hard headed, and was not completely broke off fast game and might never be. He had been given the medicine for running deer and fox on numerous occasions and it worked for only a short while before he would break back over.

A friend of the young hunter, "Randall", was going to attend one of the point hunts, a U.K.C. event in the adjoining state, and asked if he would like to accompany him. Randall told the young hunter that his young Redtick, "Joe", should do really well in the hunts as he was quick to strike and quick to tree and have a coon in the tree. Randall then explained how the hunts worked, "All you have to do is strike Joe when he barks and tree him when he trees. Ain't nothing to it. Real easy" he stated.

On the day of the hunt Randall came by to collect the young hunter for the one hour drive to the hunt location. On arrival they signed up for the hunt and patiently waited for draw-out time, hoping to draw out together - which didn't happen. The young hunter drew a couple of Walkers and a Redbone, with the handler of one of the Walkers guiding and judging.

Randall stated, "That guy judging your cast only hunts that big swamp a little ways from here, it's rough and you are about to get wet, so be prepared." The young hunter was accustomed to hunting rough country so that wasn't a problem. He only hoped that Joe didn't get out of pocket where he would be unable to get him caught up at the end of the hunt.

The young hunter rode to the woods with the judge who asked if Joe ran deer. He casually stated deer were thick as fleas where they were going to hunt; and yes, it was the big swamp. The cast arrived at the swamp, removed the dogs from the boxes and listened as the judge explained the rules and talked about the area they would be hunting. Following the brief discussion, the four hounds were led to the water's edge and released into the swampy area.

The four hounds immediately struck and everyone called their dog at the same time. The young hunter ended up with third strike but learned that he needed to open his mouth quicker in a situation such as that. All four hounds were running hard when the track broke down and they split up. Joe was a chop mouthed track dog, and because of all the water, he was barking much more than usual. The judge said he thought that Joe was treed, so unfamiliar with the rules the young hunter treed him, even though he knew Joe wasn't treed solid. Joe was minused almost fast as the young hunter had treed him. The young hunter was learning fast.

The other three hounds were now back together and treeing on the same tree. All were treed and put on the scorecard and the time started. As the cast walked to their tree, Joe treed on a separate tree. The young hunter immediately treed him, knowing that he would stay treed, as that was one of his strong points. A coon wasn't seen up the tree where the three hounds were treed; the tree was big and leafy, so it was circled. Joe had a coon up his tree that was scored plus points and put him leading the cast. The cast walked a short distance from the tree and released the hounds once again. They quickly struck with Joe being called for first strike and the others put on the card accordingly. They again split, with Joe and one of the Walkers going one direction and the other Walker and Redbone going the opposite way. Joe was running his track to catch and the young hunter thought maybe he was running a deer, but the track was treed just as the thought occurred. The Walker swiftly backed Joe, but not before the young hunter had treed Joe for first tree. The other two hounds had also treed their track and all were put on the scorecard. As time on the tree expired the young hunter was thinking he sure needed to see a coon in Joe's tree. Joe did have a coon, but the other two hounds also had one in their tree and plus points were received by all.

The cast was still being led by the young hunter at this time, and the end of the hunt was near, so he hoped one more turn loose and it would be over. They walked only a short distance and cut the hounds loose. The two Walkers and the Redbone were struck and put on the scorecard. Joe did not open on this track and the young hunter was wondering where he was at. The other three hounds were soon treed and the time started on them. The cast walked to the tree just as the hunt ended and the young hunter surmised if they had a coon he was beat, but if not, he had done well in his first hunt.

The tree was small and there was eyes swiftly spotted in the tree, only they were possum eyes and all points were minused. Joe had done well in his first hunt and the young hunter was proud of him. He realized that Joe might occasionally run fast game, a hard deed to catch him at, but he definitely would not tree a possum and it had paid off. Back at the clubhouse, Randall's cast was already in and he had cast win with more plus points than the young hunter. As it stood with the cast so far in the young hunter had second. Minutes before deadline, a cast returned with the winning score. Randall placed second and the young hunter ended up with third - not bad for his first hunt.

On the drive home the young hunter advised Randall that he liked the point hunts and intended to start participating in them. Joe was entered in several more hunts but he failed to earn the first place win required to make Nite Champion. The young hunter was lucky when Joe competed in competition, as he ran no off game, or if he did he got treed off of it. While one night hunting the Wildlife Management Area, Joe was lost and never recovered. The young hunter was pleasure hunting with friends who owned a young hound that ran deer. It had been a long while since Joe had ran any off game, but when the young hound started a deer he joined in and showed him how it was supposed to be run. Over the mountain he went to never be seen again. The young hunter looked far and wide for his hound, but he was never found.

Joe was the first hound hunted in competition by the young hunter; the first of many to follow. He now had the competition fever but he knew that his other two Redtick pups were not yet ready for competition, and his two older hounds were too old. He was now in the market for a hound he could competition hunt and win with. After hunting and trying numerous hounds that did not suit him, he finally found what he was looking for. This hound was hidden away in the Tennessee hills just waiting to be competition hunted.

A friend from Tennessee phoned to say he knew of a top hound that could win in the hunts. He said the hound was the kind everyone was looking for; the hard to find kind. He explained that the hound had it on both ends; he was a go hunting outstanding strike dog, a good track dog and a fast locating, stay put tree dog that absolutely would not pull. It all sounded good and a hunt was arranged to try this hound the following night.

The young hunter drove to Tennessee to hunt the hound alone with hope that it would not be another wasted trip. On arrival he looked over the hound before he was taken to the woods, and a hound he was, as he had long ears, a big head, big feet and loose skin under his neck. If he had been red he would have been a Bloodhound, but he was solid red headed and blanket backed with nice red trim. He was a Treeing Walker with some of the best breeding known to the Walker breed. The young hunter had his doubts as he thought, "This hound is sure ugly."

A short time after dark, they prepared to release the hound into an excellent looking heavily timbered creek bottom, "a very cooney looking place." The hound named "Tom" was cut across a field toward the distant woods. Tom left the leash in a hard run and was struck before the hunters could get situated for the hunt. He ran the track for ten minutes before locating with one loud bawl and turning it over to a hard, solid chop. The hunters listened to him tree for several minutes then walked to him. On arrival at the tree, Tom was up on the tree with his toenails dug in and slobber running down his sides.

The young hunter shined the tree and spotted the coon before looking Tom over some more; he was sure-nuff a tree dog. The young hunter didn't really care about all the hard barking but it was a must that he stayed put once he was treed. Three more drops were made and a tree made on all three. A coon was seen in two of the trees and the third was a big hollow tree with nothing found. It was getting late and the young hunter had seen enough, but he now wished that he had brought along one of his older hounds to have made a turnout with Tom. Even though the hound was a little older than the young hunter preferred a deal was negotiated nevertheless. Tom now had a new owner.

Tom had never been in a competition hunt and had been hunted alone most of his life. The young hunter wanted to hunt him with other hounds to see how he performed before entering him in a hunt. A pleasure hunt with friends had been planned for the following night after purchasing Tom. He chose to take only Tom and the two friends each had a hound of their own, so this would be a good opportunity to see Tom work with strange dogs.

Late that evening the young hunter loaded Tom into the box and drove to the home of his friend "Tim" who loaded his hound "Sport" and looked Tom over in the process. On the short drive to collect the other friend "Jimmy" the young hunter explained to Tim how the hunt with Tom the previous night had turned out. "That hound will have to be good in the woods because he sure isn't going to win any shows, as he is the houndiest dog I have ever seen," replied Tim.

Jimmy was waiting in the front yard with his hound "Fred" on the leash. As he started to load Fred into the box he began to laugh and said, "That is the ugliest thing that I have ever seen. I bet he is slow as molasses; he probably can't get through the woods for his ears dragging the ground. Where did you get that thing? He looks like "Flash" off the 'Dukes of Hazzard."

The young hunter, not knowing what to say, looked at Tim who had a big grin on his face and answered, "He came from the dog pound, but he could be good for something." Thus the discussion about Tom's looks ended and the hunters proceeded on to their hunting area. They were going to hunt a large river bottom with soybeans growing in the fields and a good creek running into the river. They parked ¼ mile from the river and cut the dogs toward the creek from the field road that crossed the soybeans.

Tom left the lead same as the night before, as if shot from a gun. Tim and Jimmy's dogs were still wetting the bushes when Tom struck; barking only a few times on the ground, located with that one big bawl and began to chop. Jimmy said, "Someone else is hunting in here," as he started to catch his hound. A smiling Tim replied, "I think that might be the houndy looking Walker dog. Jimmy countered, "No, he is probably hiding under the truck."

It was now the young hunters turn to smile. Tim's hound Sport quickly backed Tom on the tree, and Fred soon joined them. To the tree the three hunters went. It was a small tree with the coon sitting in plain sight. Tom had his toenails dug in and the slobber slinging, same as the night before. An astonished Jimmy said, "Bet he won't do that again, let's turn them on down the creek and we will see."

Four more trees were made, three which had coon in them and one where there could have been a coon. Tom mostly had first strike and first tree on everything. Both Tim and Jimmy's hounds were above average hounds and consistently treed coons anytime turned loose, but Tom had made them look pretty bad.

On the drive home Jimmy stated, "That long eared, loose skinned Walker put it on us tonight." He then asked the young hunter what the price would be for the dog-pound dog. With this, Tim and the young hunter had had their fun and told Jimmy the truth about Tom. Jimmy became one of Tom's biggest promoters and never missed a chance to hunt with him or handle him in a competition hunt.

Tom was an outstanding, balanced coondog and a top competition dog. He was very quickly made Nite Champion in three different registries, winning over 90 percent of his cast in the process. He was coon hunted hard and hunted in competition when time permitted and rapidly made a name for himself. Many hunters who hunted with Tom wanted to breed their females to him, and did so, but good as he was he never sired a pup anywhere near good as him. Tom was a coondog but was not a reproducer, as the majority of his pups were worthless. Even so, Tom was a great competition dog that showed the young hunter, and many others who hunted with him, what it would take to win in the hunts.

Considering Tom's age and other factors involved he was sold to a pleasure coon hunter, to be enjoyed in the woods. If the young hunter was going to spend the time and expense involved in promoting a hound in competition hunts he wanted one that would reproduce some good hounds. The search then began for the ultimate competition dog that would also reproduce his likeness or better.

The young hunter still owned two young Redtick hounds he was finishing out and two older finished hounds but he felt he needed something more to win big. His search for a top competition hound had intensified. Breed or color did not matter, but performance was the key factor. Word soon traveled throughout the coon hunting grapevine that the young hunter was in the market for a top competition hound. It seemed everyone he spoke to owned what he was looking for, and it was for sale. The long weary task of trying some of these hounds now began.

The young hunter had his mind set on being very picky with the hound he chose. Everyone had made fun of Tom's looks and he'd had to prove his worth in the woods. The young hunter didn't want to listen to all the laughing and joking again. This time he wanted something that had looks backed by ability and good breeding. When inquiring about a hound he asked about ability, age, breeding and looks. He preferred that the hound have everything he was looking for in one package. Male or female made no difference, but an accurate, stay-put coondog was a must. The young hunter wanted a hound from an area with an average to thin coon population and a variety of rough hunting terrain. He didn't want a hound that had been trained in thick coon with easy hunting. He preferred a balanced hound that would go hunting, was quick to strike; a track driving open mouthed hound that was a quick accurate tree dog. He didn't want a mean hound but the hound would have to stay put once treed. He also wanted the hound to have a loud bawl on track and a chop on the tree. But could he find what he was looking for? The first hound the young hunter tried was located in Alabama and was supposed to have all the tools. The hound was a good looking, open spotted, three year old Walker female called "Bama" that had been hunted hard and alone. Bama had never been entered in a competition hunt but was said by her owner to be ready to win. She had the looks and the breeding; and the young hunter would soon see if she had the ability he was looking for. A two night hunt was arranged, and the young hunter brought "Jim" one of his young Redticks along to see how he compared to Bama.

The first turnout, Bama was released alone in some rough hilly terrain with a lot of cut over timber. She went hunting immediately and was not heard for 20 minutes until she exploded on a tree with a couple of loud locating bawls and turned it over to a hard, loud chop. Bama had a coon which was easily found, and was an outstanding tree dog, but she had not opened on track. The young hunter thought there was a possibility she had treed a lay-up or possibly just ran across the coon.

The second drop was in a wooded section similar to the first, only Jim was released with Bama this time. Both hounds went hunting in a hard run. A few minutes passed before Jim struck with a loud squall bawl then drifted through a rough cut over, located and treed with his never ending machine gun chop. Bama did not come in to the tree, and Jim had a coon. Jim was cut loose off the tree; he went hunting and was soon struck and treed again with another coon - and still no Bama. Jim was cut loose off of this tree and again went hunting. Suddenly, Bama was heard with a couple bawl locates and then treed solid. She was quickly covered by Jim and a coon was seen in this tree too. The hunters decided to call it a night following this tree. They would try it again the next night.

On the drive home, thinking back on the hunt, the young hunter thought about Bama treeing two coons, yet she had not covered Jim on either of his trees. Jim had treed two coons alone and backed Bama on the coon she had treed when they were hunted together. The young hunter assumed that Bama was probably silent on track as she had not barked on the ground on either coon she treed. He was still going back for another hunt the following night as he wanted to see Bama go one more time. He was going to take Jim along too. The following night the young hunter and Bama's owner met for another hunt and decided to hunt a rough swampland. On the first drop Bama and Jim were both released and went hunting. Bama located and treed within a few minutes and was swiftly backed by Jim. A coon was seen in the tree and both hounds were cut loose off the tree. Jim quickly struck a hot track and treed again with a coon found in the tree, but no Bama. Jim was cut back into the swamp while the two hunters talked and waited.

The young hunter and Bama's owner stood at the water's edge waiting to hear the hounds open, while discussing the two hounds. The young hunter asked Bama's owner if she ever barked on track and he answered, "Well, maybe sometimes, but she always has a coon when she trees." About that time she located and treed again and was immediately backed by Jim, and another coon was seen in the tree. This ended the hunt for the night.

On the walk back to the truck the young hunter told Bama's owner that Bama was not what he was looking for, as he wanted a more balanced type hound. He explained that Jim was only a third strike dog when hunted with good strike dogs and that he had out struck Bama and had treed coons alone. He had also gotten a piece of her coons. Bama's owner apologized for the wasted time, he then tried to buy Jim, but Jim was not for sale.

Several months passed with the young hunter trying a hound every weekend, with much the same results as the two hunts with Bama. They were not what he was looking for. The young hunter always took Jim along to compare what he was trying and it seemed Jim always looked better than the hounds he was hunted with. As time passed, the young hunter gave up on finding another hound for the hunts. He decided he would start hunting Jim in the hunts as he was better than anything he had tried and was much younger too. If Jim did not work out the young hunter also owned Jim's younger brother "Country" that he liked even better than Jim.

Jim was out of the first litter of pups sired by a hound that would prove to be a winner in the larger hunts and a great reproducer too, as time would tell. His mother was also a top hound with looks, breeding and ability and already a proven winner in the larger hunts. Jim was colored more like his mother, being red and white and lightly ticked. Jim started young and was easily broke from off game and seemed to improve every time taken to the woods. He was a little tighter mouthed on some tracks than the young hunter preferred. But, he had the uncanny ability to get off by himself and tree coons, and it seemed that he would have a coon that could be seen most of the time.

The young hunter and the owner of Jim's sire and dam were friends and hunted together occasionally. Even before the young hunter began to hunt the competition hunts, he hunted with Jim and Country's sire- a young hound at the time and a total pleasure to hunt with. The young hunter tried to buy him numerous times but he was not for sale. The young hunter was allowed to take his pick of the first litter sired by this hound, thus came Jim, and subsequently had the pick of a later litter too. This second litter is where the young hunter's other hound "Country" came from.

Without the burden of looking for another hound, the young hunter began putting Jim and Country in the woods together, and separately, preparing them for the upcoming hunts. Jim was a quick, hard hunting, tireless hunter that hunted with his head up and became a lay-up specialist. On the other hand, Country was one of the rare ones. He was a hard, deep hunter and an outstanding first strike dog, a track driving brute and a loud one-bark locating tree dog. He was cold nosed and did not pick his tracks, yet he was good as Jim on lay-up coon. Country was the total package with more brains than a hound should have. It seemed he learned from every good hound he was hunted with, or against. He only became better every time he was hunted.

The young hunter thought that both his hounds were ready for the hunts but began with Jim because he was older. The first hunt Jim was entered in was in a drizzling rain, the perfect weather for his style of hunting. Jim drew a four dog cast. The judge and guide said they were going to hunt a large farm that had cattle feeders the coons were eating out of. The hunters loaded into two vehicles and drove to the hunting location. The hunting area was excellent, consisting of a secluded tract of land with rolling pastureland and a good creek around the perimeter. There were heavily timbered rolling hills adjoining the creek.

The four hounds were released across the pasture toward one of the large cattle feeders. Jim turned and crossed the creek heading into the timber in the opposite direction. The other three hounds proceeded in the direction of the cattle feeder and were soon struck in for first, second and third strike. Jim was heard in the timber and struck in for a fourth strike on a separate track. Jim then located and treed, he was put on the scorecard and the five minutes started. After the time expired the cast went to Jim's tree, found the coon and plussed the points. Jim was then released back onto the track the other three hounds were working and struck in for another fourth strike. In short order, Jim was again treed and put on the scorecard and time started. He was swiftly backed by the other three hounds. The hunters walked to the tree, quickly spotted another coon and plussed the points.

The rain was beginning to heavily fall and the hunters agreed to call time out and wait for the rainfall to pass. The rain continued to fall and after an hour of waiting the hunters decided to release the hounds anyway. Two of the hounds did not want to hunt in the downpour and were hunting only enough to avoid being scratched. Jim and the remaining hound had disappeared.

During a short lapse in the pouring rain Jim let out a couple squall locates. He was called struck and treed and put on the card and time started. The other hound was at the tree when the hunters arrived but he had not been struck or treed. A coon was seen in the small tree the hounds were on and Jim's points were plussed. The hunt ended with this tree and the young hunter was congratulated by the other hunters for his cast win. They also complimented Jim on his good work. The weather had been bad in all the surrounding area and very few coons were scored on. Jim easily won the hunt and was overall high scoring hound of the hunt.

Jim had never been hunted with strange dogs before the young hunter began taking him along to try hounds, and hunting him in competition. Jim had a desire to beat any strange dog he was hunted with. He would usually tree a coon or two off to himself. In Jim's second hunt he completely dominated the cast with two shut-out coons and won this hunt too. There were some good hounds in the cast and the hunters once again complimented Jim's performance. He was making a name for himself.

The owner of Jim's sire and dam was present at the second hunt Jim won and also congratulated the young hunter on the win. He then asked if he could come hunt with Jim for a few nights. He had hunted with Jim when he was younger but Jim was now a two year old and turning the crank. A three night hunt was arranged for the following week. He was going to bring Jim's sire and dam to see how Jim compared.

After three nights of hunting Jim proved to be a lot like his sire in the woods. His dam was the best strike dog of the three and more open on track. All three were loud, stay-put tree dogs that stayed split to themselves a lot. At the end of the third night of hunting the young hunter was offered an outlandish price for Jim. Before the deal was completed, Jim's dam "Julie" was thrown in. All said and done Jim had a new owner and the young hunter had a pocket full of cash and owned Jim and Country's dam Julie.

The young hunter had not really wanted to sell Jim but he had Country and felt he was the better of the two. In fact, Country was the best young hound he had ever owned, or more the type hound he preferred - a completely balanced hound. He was a big good looking Redtick with a big mouth to match his size, and he was ready for the hunts. He also had the looks and breeding for a stud dog if he reproduced.

With several hunts approaching the young hunter hit the woods with Country, mostly alone, but occasionally took Julie along for a little competition. Country had been hunted as hard as Jim even though he was younger. He was a naturally straight hound that took very little correcting to break him from off game. Every time he was turned loose he wanted to tree a coon and please his handler. His kind was few and far between.

Three coons were treed and scored on Country's first hunt, and he had first strike and first tree on all three. One of the coons was a lay-up on which he totally shut the other hounds out. Country looked really good and proved to the young hunter what he already knew that he had a winner on his leash. Country was complimented by all of the hunters on the cast as he had truly looked exceptional. Back at the clubhouse at deadline, Country had the winning score and had his first place win in his first hunt.

Because of other obligations the young hunter could not attend the weekend hunts for a short period of time, so Country was not competition hunted for several months. In the meantime the young hunter purchased a top reproducing female and bred her to Country. He wanted to see what type pups Country would produce. The female was heavy with pups and would soon be whelping.

When the young hunter was again ready to attend the hunts he found a hunt within driving distance. He had never hunted out of the club where the hunt was being held. On arrival the young hunter was acquainted with only a few of the competitors participating in the hunt. The hounds were drawn out and Country drew a four dog cast. The hunters drove to a secluded mountainous area and prepared to cast the hounds. The surrounding terrain was really rough and the judge and guide said the coon were very scarce in that part of the county.

The judge was thorough and explained the rules of the hunt and gave a short summary on the lay of the land they were going to hunt. With this completed, the hounds were released. Ten minutes passed before Country struck with his loud bawl and was put on the scorecard for first; the other three hounds joined in and were scored accordingly. The track was not very good but it was worked into a running track. Country threw his one big bawl locate and was immediately called treed and put on the card and time started. The other three hounds quickly backed Country and were also put on the card. As the hunters walked toward the tree three of the four hounds left out running what seemed to be a sight race. Only Country stayed put, the tree was searched and a coon spotted and his points were plussed. The other handlers stated that Country was sure a pressure tree dog to have stayed hooked with the other hounds running from the tree as they had. Country was turned back in to the other hounds whose track had now broken down. He did not open on their track but found one of his own and struck in for fourth on an old trailing track. He was soon joined by the other three hounds and a tree was made with Country taking last tree.

On arrival at the tree it was found they were split with Country farther in and alone. The young hunter walked on to Country and sit down to wait. The remaining cast members arrived at Country's tree after searching their own tree in which no coon was seen. Country was moved up to first on his tree and one of the other handlers quickly found the coon. With only a couple minute remaining in the hunt the time was walked out and Country won the cast.

On the long walk back to the trucks while following an old road the hunters ran across a large pile of dead chickens. A little farther along the road there were a couple dead house dogs. It was commented on, wondering what had killed the animals, and nothing else was said until the hunters returned to the clubhouse.

Back at the club house there was one cast with 25 more plus points than Country had and the other cast did not have plus points. Country placed second and the young hunter was proud of him as he had done his best. While the young hunter and the guide of his cast were discussing their hunt with another club member it was mentioned where they had hunted. The club member then stated that there was poison out in that area, possibly to kill coyotes. He said that they were taking a risk with the hounds by hunting in that area. That said they all departed.

The young hunter made the long drive home, unloaded Country, placed him in his kennel and went inside for some much needed sleep. Within an hour he was awakened by Country's steady barking from the kennel, something he never did. The young hunter yelled from the doorway for him to be quiet and returned to bed. After sleeping for a few hours he arose and went outside to feed and water all the livestock.

Country did not come out of his house to greet the young hunter so he stepped into the kennel and discovered Country lying on his side barely breathing. It suddenly registered what was wrong with Country and the young hunter quickly carried him to the truck and rushed to the vet. The young hunter advised the vet that Country had probably gotten into poison of some sort but he didn't know what kind. The vet said the prognosis didn't look good and began working with Country. Later that day Country died as nothing could be done to save him.

The loss of Country really upset the young hunter and he decided that his competition hunting days were over, at least until he recovered from the loss of his beloved hound. As time passed, the young hunter realized that bad things sometimes happen, but life must go on. He knew he would one day competition hunt again. Besides, he had a nice litter of redtick pups sired by Country and he owned Julie the source of Country and Jim. Yes, he would be back; just   give   him   time.

A LITTLE BIT DIFFERENT
4

Once a coonhunter gets a taste of competition hunting and if he or she has a competitive personality they will always want to try their luck at the hunts. Like any person who has ever had the opportunity to competition hunt and enjoy it I was bitten by the bug following the first hunt. I did quite well my first couple years participating in the hunts, but then began the hunt for something called a competition dog. I eventually found what I was looking for, something with a little more power and a lot more go. The three hounds were cut from the road directly into the hollow and almost immediately had a track going at an extremely fast pace.

"You think those hounds are after a coon?" My hunting buddy James asked. I grinned and replied, "I don't know, but I do know they will have a coon in a tree at the end of the track."

James knew nothing about the two older hounds and had only been to the woods a couple times with the youngest of the three. All three hounds were English Redticks; two males and a female. The outstanding young male was called Nation's Tree Screaming Jimi, a pup sired by the great Dual Grand Nite Champion Hobbs' Tree Screaming Rock. The female was Grand Champion, Nite Champion Hobbs' Tree Screaming Judy- a top female sired by Grand Nite Champion Adamson's Butch, and also Jimi's dam. The other male was Nite Champion Tree Screaming J .B., a single registered hound, and a coon treeing fool.

Neither J.B. or Judy had a bawl in them, they ran track with loud, clear chop mouths and ran every track to catch. They were two of the great track dogs of their time. Both hounds went hunting in a hard run, never looking back, with only one thing on their mind - that was to get struck and treed. They were outstanding blow-down, chop mouthed tree dogs that would not pull and almost always had a coon that could be seen in the trees they made.

Jimi, like the older hounds would also go hunting in a hard run and get under a coon. He would be taken off a tree somewhere every time released. He sparingly bawled and chopped on track and treed with a loud, ringing chop. Jimi was a very accurate hound for his age, he preferred to get alone if possible and he would split tree and stay hooked.

Jimi was purchased from my old friend Leonard Hobbs of Tennessee as a weaning pup. He was an extraordinary pup at a very young age; a classy and powerful tree dog. He received his name the second night in the woods when he split from the other hounds, fell treed deep in the country with a screaming chop and stayed put with a coon in the tree. A friend along on this hunt stated, "That young hound sounds almost good as Jimi Hendrix did when playing a screaming solo." Jimi was given his name that night and it stuck.

Jimi's sire Rock was one of the great hounds of his time, also a screaming tree dog and a hound I would have liked to have owned. I hunted with Rock on occasion and was impressed with his ability, the main reason for purchasing a pup sired by him. Jimi progressed so well that his dam Judy and also Tree Screaming J.B. were later purchased from Leonard Hobbs. Leonard proclaimed Judy to be one of the best females he ever owned and said J.B. was the best pressure tree dog he had ever seen.

Judy, Jimi and J.B. were good hounds, but they were a different type hound from what I usually hunted. Jimi hunted with his head in the air and said very little on the ground, he was a broke, coon treeing hound at a young age. J.B. and Judy were outstanding strike, track and tree dogs that quickly got struck, but not always on a coon track. Regardless, they would end up treed and have a coon most of the time. Whatever they ran they always ran it to catch and when they crossed a coon track they would promptly switch over and tree it. They were not pleasure hounds and were extremely hard to handle, yet they were action packed and a thrill to hunt.

J.B. and Judy were purchased with the sole intent of competition hunting them along with Jimi. My plans did not culminate and of the three hounds only Jimi was entered in a competition hunt; his only hunt, and a hunt that he would win. These three hounds, when hunted together, had no reverse or handle on them; and subsequently would cost me a divorce in the end.

I owned these hounds at a time before telemetry systems were popular or heavily used and I would not leave a hound in the woods unless it was absolutely unavoidable. Needless to say I didn't come home until after daylight most nights these hounds were hunted together. I would take them off a tree somewhere every time released and would, many times, release them again.

My wife at that time gave me a solid ultimatum, "Get rid of those dogs or I'm leaving." Well, I told her, "Goodbye" and kept on hunting. At that time I also owned several other hounds, some more suitable to my style of hunting; yet I enjoyed the thrill of the chase when hunting Jimi, J.B and Judy together. Jimi handled a little better when hunted alone or with my other hounds, but he did his own thing anyway.

The other hounds I owned were balanced, broke hounds that ran only coon. They bawled on track and could trail an old cold track and have a coon in the tree at the end of it. They were honest, dependable hounds and a pleasure to hunt, but not quite as action packed as Judy, J.B. and Jimi.

As James and I stood listening to the three hounds running the track for all they were worth they crossed the creek and came back in our direction. James commented, "If that is a coon it's going to have to climb and soon. Those hounds are putting the pressure on that critter, and it can't continue to run like that."

"I think it's probably a coon because Jimi is opening on it, and yes it's going to have to go somewhere and soon," I replied.

No sooner than the words were spoken all three hounds began to tree; each barking well over 120 barks per minute. "Now, that is what I call tree dogs. It can't get much better than that. I've got to say I had my doubts they were running tree game," James stated.

"They run every track in that manner, and as I said before, they will put a tree at the end of the track and have a coon," I smiled and replied. The hounds had crossed a small country road and treed on the side of the ridge, only a short distance from where we stood. We slowly walked to the tree, savoring the sound of the hard treeing hounds. All three were stretched high as possible on an extremely large pine; a sight for any admirer of tree dogs. They were leashed back and the tree thoroughly searched before eyes were spotted high in the tree. James swiftly and efficiently put the big boar coon out to the waiting hounds, which were allowed to wool it a little. The hounds were then led back to the vehicle and loaded into the box. Our plans were to move to another location more appropriate for the hunting style of the three hounds. The area had roads around the perimeter which would allow us easier access in reaching the hounds if they got out of pocket.

Following a ten minute drive we arrived at a spot suitable to our needs. An extremely large section of woods composed of rolling hills and hollows with creeks and streams flowing through them. If coons could not be treed in this area they would not be treed anywhere.

The hounds were released from the small isolated dirt road, where we had parked, directly onto a clear stream. All three left the road in a hard run, never looking back. An hour passed and we had yet to hear a bark from either hound - an unusual occurrence. We should have been able to hear the hounds a great distance if they were barking, so it was assumed they were not. A track of some sort should have been struck by this time, because the surrounding hollows were full of an assortment of game. We sat and waited minutes longer, but still not a sound.

Far in the distance headlights were approaching and we wondered who else might be back in the hill country at this time of night. The slow moving vehicle pulled to a stop behind our truck and we immediately noted it was another coonhunter. The older hunter climbed from his vehicle and greeted us in a friendly manner, asking if we had treed anything. We showed him the large coon treed earlier, and advised him we had released the hounds into the hollow over an hour before and had not heard a bark. He said he had heard a single dog treed much farther over the road - a screaming tree dog. He also stated that he had heard a couple fox dogs running hard and coming in our direction. As the hunter continued to talk Judy and J.B. topped the ridge giving much more mouth than needed. The old hunter exclaimed, "Boy's, here come those fox dogs now! Pushing that fox like they are doing it will either hole up or they'll catch it, and right quick like."

The hounds ran within a few hundred yards of where we stood and without a locate of any kind began to tree in their blow-down style. The hard treeing hounds quickly brought a smile to my face as I stated, "Well, there's J.B. and Judy."

The old hunter replied, "I thought they were fox dogs. I didn't know a coon dog could run a track like that. Mind if I walk to the tree with you? I'd like to take a gaze at those hounds." James and I replied, "Let's go see what they have up the tree."

The hounds were treed on a large oak. They were leashed back, the tree shined, and a coon swiftly spotted and given to the two hounds. The old hunter said, "That's an old ridge runner and he sure put up a race. Those two hounds brought him through the country and put him up that tree slick as a whistle." "J.B and Judy run every track they start in the same manner, and they'll end up on a tree somewhere," I responded. "Yeah, that's a fact from what I've seen so far," stated James.

"Y'all still have a dog missing so that was probably him I heard treed back down the road. I imagine you should go to him before he trees out. It won't take long, hard as he was treeing," said the old hunter. "We'll drive that way and walk in to get him. We're going to make one more drop after we retrieve Jimi and you are welcome to come along if you want," said James to the old-timer.

"Being as you asked, reckon I'll tag along because I'd like to see those two hounds run another track in that fashion. Don't know if my pot licker "Spud" can keep up or not. Ain't often you see hounds can move a coon track that way, right proper like. Well, guess we better move on down the road to that other hard treeing maniac before he gives out," replied the smiling old hunter.

We hurriedly drove in the direction the old hunter had heard the treeing hound. As we came to a stop at the forks of the road Jimi was heard treeing loud and hard- he hadn't treed out and was nowhere near that point.

"We can drive right to him, I think," declared James. Sure enough, only a short drive farther we drove within a few hundred feet of the treeing hound. As we walked in to the tree the old hunter stated, "Now days hounds run tracks and tree a little different than they used to. That young hound is a treeing machine. He is treeing as hard now as he was when I first heard him."

Proceeding on to the tree and leashing Jimi back we noticed he was treed on a gnarled old apple tree in an abandoned orchard. The coon was easily spotted and given to the hard treeing young hound before we returned to the vehicles. Both James and the old hunter said they had treed many coons in the orchard over the years.

"Those coons sure like to hang around that orchard. I believe we could cut the hounds loose along the other side and tree another coon or two," stated the smiling old hunter.

With all in agreement to release the hounds into the hollow on the other side of the orchard we began removing the hounds from the boxes. "Ole Spud will tree you a coon or two, has a big mouth, and he is right easy to handle for an old timer like me," the old man stated as he removed an extremely large Blue Gascon Hound from the box.

Walking only a short distance from the vehicles the hounds were cut into the hollow. Judy, J.B. and Jimi left the leash as if shot from a gun. Spud sauntered off in the opposite direction, paying little attention to the other hounds actions. In only a matter of minutes Spud opened with a loud, booming and drawn out bawl and was quickly joined by Jimi. In the meantime J.B. and Judy fired up a track of their own and rapidly took it through the country.

Spud and Jimi worked their track back in the direction of the orchard before Spud came on a tree with one of the longest locating bawls ever heard. Not to be out done Jimi rapidly picked a tree of his own and began treeing with his screaming chop. Spud settled into a solid heavy chop occasionally throwing in a bawl or two.

The old hunter said, "That varmint has traveled far as it is going to. We can go to them now. I'm sure that screaming tree dog is not going to move but I don't know about Spud, never has before, but you just can't tell."

J.B and Judy ran their track out of hearing as we walked to the other treed hounds. Spud was in the apple orchard and had a small coon up his tree. He was leashed and led from the tree as the old hunter said he didn't need a coon put out to him.

Jimi was at the edge of the orchard only a couple hundred feet from where Spud was treed. He was leashed back and the large tree shined. Nothing was seen on the outside other than several holes where a coon could have been. Both Jimi and Spud were led back to the trucks and loaded up. Our next goal was to locate J.B. and Judy.

We drove in the general direction in which they had departed, stopping to listen at the top of the highest ridge. From that point, high on the ridge we clearly heard the hounds running at an extremely fast pace.

Both James and the old hunter uttered, "Those hounds are moving that animal like they are tied to it. If it can climb a tree it's going to have to do just that, and real quick like." Whether or not it was a coon the two were originally running they did an exceptional job of moving the track, and true to form they were soon treed. "Those hounds never even gave a change up before they began treeing. They were running full out one second and treed the next. And a couple of tree dogs they are," stated the still smiling old hunter.

"Yeah they are about as good a pair of tree dogs as you will ever hear. Let's walk in and get them and we'll still have time to make another drop," responded James.

The hounds were treed up a small leaning tree and the first thing that came to mind was they had run a fox up the tree. The hounds were leashed back and upon shining the small tree it was found to grow into a much larger one. More shining of the larger tree resulted in an extremely large coon being found hiding in a fork up near the top. The coon was left to run again because the hounds didn't need another coon. Back at the vehicles it was decided for our next drop we should move to a nearby hollow, said by the old hunter to be full of hard running coon.

All four hounds were released from the small dirt road directly onto the creek bank and struck as they left the leash. They swiftly run the track up the hollow and out of hearing. The old hunter, pointing at the creek and no longer smiling stated, "That there is Little Pine Log Creek and the direction those hounds took the track is rough and almost inaccessible. We need to drive to the top of the ridge and see if we can hear them from there." Once at the top of the ridge the hounds were heard far in the distance - treed solid. "I think we should try driving a little farther to see if we can get closer. If not, it is going to be a long walk in to them from here," declared the old hunter.

The hounds seemed to be even farther away after moving a short distance down and off the ridge. It appeared we would be walking in from the top of the ridge and the location where they were first heard. It was going to be a long and hard walk any way looked at. We slowly began the walk into the hollow and could no longer hear the hounds after walking only a scant distance. "Well, I guess they quit treeing. I don't reckon there is any use in going farther. Might as well go back to the trucks and see what they do," said James.

Topping the ridge the hounds were once again heard treeing loud and hard; they had not moved or quit treeing. "I don't know why we can't hear them when we walk closer," voiced the old hunter.

Wanting to save my fellow hunters from further walking I volunteered to walk back into the hollow toward the treed hounds to again see if they could be heard from the closer location. With a compass reading on the location of the treeing hounds I began the walk toward them. As I came near the spot where we had walked the first time and could no longer hear the treeing hounds the same thing happened. Nothing was heard but the quietness of the night. Walking even farther still not a sound was heard from the treeing hounds. Back up the ridge I walked, to the spot where James and the old hunter stood. The hounds were still treeing as hard as before.

"I couldn't hear them when I walked closer and I even went a ways farther than we did the first time. Nothing but the sounds of the night down in that hollow," I advised my companions.

"The hounds have not shut up since you departed so that started us to thinking. We both believe they are over near Yarborough Mill and the sound is carrying up the ridge. Once off in the hollow they can't be heard even though it is closer to them. Let's drive toward Yarborough Mill and see if we are correct," replied James.

Following a lengthy drive to the vicinity of the mill the hounds were, in fact, heard loud and clear- still treed. They were treeing just as hard, if not harder, than when first treed. The old hunter said, "Those hounds have not even begun to tire, but I think old Spud is about treed out. Guess we better try to get in there to them."

Following some very careful maneuvering we were able to cross the creek, making it to the tree in due time. All four hounds were stretched high on the side of an extremely large and vine covered hardwood. They were leashed back and the tree shined without luck, at first, of finding anything. Suddenly the old hunter yelled, "Here the big rascal is. He's trying to hide in that clump of tangled vines."

"Do y'all want to put the coon out to the hounds?" James asked. "Guess we should leave it to run again. Those hounds don't need all the coons they tree to keep them treeing," replied the old hunter. "That's for sure," I stated. "Let's get on out of here. It's almost daylight and the missus is going to start wondering where I'm at, as I don't usually hunt all night. Alone anyways," said the again smiling old hunter.

Daylight began peeking from the distant ridges as we loaded the hounds into the boxes and said our goodbyes. "Yep, I have to say, those hounds can flat run a track and tree a coon, but they are a little bit different than what I'm used to hunting. Don't know if I could still handle that much dog power. If I was only a little younger it would sure be a challenge though," said the still smiling old hunter as he drove away.

"Well, I reckon we better head for the house too, unless you want to turn those hounds loose one more time," said James. "I've had enough for now, but we'll try it again tonight," I answered. "I'd be surprised if every track those hounds started tonight was a coon, but as you said, they ended up on a tree with a coon that could be seen. It is going to be a chore to hunt those hounds in this rough and mountainous terrain. I think they just might wear a good coon hunter or two down. As the old hunter said they are just a little bit different," James surmised as we drove toward home. We had put another successful night behind us.

PREPARATION PAYS OFF

5

The three English hounds, two Redticks and the other a Bluetick worked a bad track further into the rough country as two hunters stood listening to the superb track work. The hounds had already put four coon up and would tree several more before the eastern sky begin to lighten. The two hunters had come to the area a week prior to the N.K.C. World Championship, with intentions of allowing the hounds to become acclimated to the terrain and also obtain a little fine tuning. Our ambitions were to place the hounds in the top twenty of the big hunt. One of the Redtick hounds had placed the previous year and was capable of placing or winning again. The other two hounds had been competition hunted only sparingly, even though both were Nite Champions.

The blue colored hound was a top coonhound anywhere hunted, a completely balanced, accurate tree dog that was absolutely broke from off game. His owner and I thought he had potential to win the whole hunt - he was a good hound. The white hound with big blue ticks weighed 65 pounds, run track with a loud bawl and treed with a solid chop, he had a good nose and could tree any kind of coon. The hounds registered name was Nite Champion Salacoa Valley Rudy; he was a single registered hound and a pleasure coon hunters dream.

One of the Redtick hounds was only a country coondog; not very flashy or fancy. He was a medium sized, open ticked hound that could tree coon easily when he wanted too. He sometimes didn't want to perform to perfection, but he would end up placing well in the hunt, maybe by luck of the draw. His registered name was Dual Nite Champion Hopsing II, but called Two, I owned Two along with his sire Dual Grand Champion Fuller's Hopsing. Two run track with a chop, squall and bawl and treed with a solid chop. Two was not in the same class as his sire or some of the other hounds we owned; we really thought the entry fee would be wasted on him. He was being hunted only because of an injury to another hound we had planned

to hunt. Two was the only other hound we had along and because of this he would get to prove his worth.

The other Redtick hound was U.K.C. Grand Nite Champion, N.K.C. Nite Champion, A.C.H.A. Nite Champion DeGraves Ace, one of the winningest hounds of his time. Ace had placed third in the N.K.C. World Championship the previous year and he would place in the top twenty again that year. Ace was a good hound in thick coon, he didn't hunt very deep but treed coon behind other dogs and absolutely stayed put when he treed. Ace was an accurate tree dog and solid broke from off game, he run track with a bawl and treed with a chop. He was sired by Dual Grand Champion Penny's

Kentucky Kojak. Ace was a freak that could tree coon behind, in front of, and all around other dogs, while seemingly doing nothing in a hurry.

The hunt was to be held in Carmi, Illinois; a good location for a large hunt. There was good hunting and an ample coon population in the area. The hunt was sponsored by an excellent coon club with good judges and guides.

Rudy's owner Ronnie Tinsley and I had been hunting in the area for almost a week. We drove from Georgia to Golconda, Illinois and the home of Bob Williams, to hunt a few nights and accustom the hounds to the area. Actually the terrain wasn't much different from our terrain in North Georgia, maybe not as mountainous, but consisting of rolling hills. Bob had arranged for us to camp in a small cabin at the edge of the Shawnee National Forest, where we could hunt out the back door, if we so desired. Bob proclaimed the area was too rough to hunt but Ronnie and I hunted it every night, following our early hunts with Bob. The area had lots of rock cliffs and holes for coon to tree in, yet we treed our share and more up trees and on the outside; there were lots of coon there.

We had already treed four coons while hunting with Bob earlier in the night, but decided to turn the hounds loose again when we arrived back at the cabin. Rudy had struck an old bad track almost instantly after being released into the woods, Two and Ace joined in and they were trailing the track deeper into the rough country. Proclaimed rough by Bob, that is. Ronnie and I stood listening to the hounds work the track; as they swiftly got it up and running. Ace fell out of the race, located a tree and started to chop hard and steady. Rudy and Two continued on into the country and picked a tree of their own, both were treeing hard and steady. Ronnie and I stood on the edge of a clearing listening to the treeing hounds; both with a big smile on our face. We slowly walked to Ace first and spotted a coon in a small mulberry. Ace was given a little praise and cut back in toward the other hounds; he didn't cover them, but struck another track going in the opposite direction. We weren't concerned where he ran the track; we had all night to hunt. We listened to Ace trail the track out of hearing as we walked to Rudy and Two.

Rudy and Two were treed on a hardwood growing alongside the creek, both were leashed and the tree shined. A coon was swiftly found sitting high in the tree. The hounds were given a little petting and we then walked from the tree in the direction Ace had trailed his track. Rudy and Two were released in the general direction Ace had been going, it was assumed they would strike another track or go to Ace.

Topping a small ridge Ace was heard trailing further in the country, momentarily he was joined by the other hounds, and a tree quickly made. We walked to the hounds and found them treed on a hollow den tree, leashed the hounds back and shined the tree without luck of seeing anything. All three hounds were then led a short distance from the tree and released to hunt further into the country.

Rudy was the hardest hunter of the three; he quickly went deep and struck a cold track. Two joined in and Ace was also soon heard working the track. The hounds worked the track deeper into the country before it began to warm up; it was moving at a good pace, rapidly turning into a running track. All three hounds were running the track to catch; they took the track almost out of hearing before turning and coming back in our direction. As we stood in a field along the edge of the timber we witnessed the coon attempt to cut across the field, sense our presence, and turn back into the timber.

The hounds were hot on his trail; only inches separating the three, and feet separating them from their prey. The coon knew what time it was and swiftly took refuge in the nearest tree, less than 100 yards from where Ronnie and I stood. We listened to the sound of the treeing hounds echo off the surrounding hills for several minutes before walking in their direction. "That coon was almost dog food, lucky he found a tree," stated a smiling Ronnie.

We proceeded to the tree and found all three hounds shuffling for position on a tree not much bigger than your arm. Neither hound had an ill hair on them, so there was no growling or bristling, they quickly settled on and around the tree. Ace had both feet wrapped around the small tree, standing straight up and treeing with a hard chop. Rudy was at the base of the tree letting us know the coon was up there with a loud, steady chop. Two was several feet back and treeing with a good chop, paying little attention to the other hounds. We spotted the large coon not more than ten feet up the very small tree, had a good laugh, leashed the hounds and walked away. All three hounds had done a great job on that coon; in fact they were operating to perfection. Maybe they would all perform to the same level in the hunt.

The sun would soon be rising in the eastern sky, but we had plenty of time to tree another coon. The hounds were released onto a small stream that ran into the creek near our camp; we sent them in that direction. We slowly walked along hoping to tree one more track before calling it a night. In only a matter of minutes Rudy once again had a track going, old and cold at best, but we would hear the hounds work the track and put a tree on it. Rudy bawled long and loud, several times before Two and Ace joined in. All three hounds worked the old feed track along the stream, in the direction of the creek, as we followed behind them. They trailed onto the creek, up the hillside, and crossed the dirt drive of the cabin where we were camping. They never ran the track as it was too cold, but a tree was put on the end of it; with the bonus being the tree was only a few hundred yards from our camp.

We walked to the tree, and as expected it was a large den. With the sun peeking over the ridges and the sky fully lighted, looking the tree over was easy. Nothing was seen up the tree but it was a legitimate den and probably had a coon on the inside. We didn't see a coon at the end of the track but heard some good track work by three bawl mouthed hounds; all three had done well on the track. It was time to get a little rest and prepare for one more night of hunting before the event started. We leashed the hounds, walked to our camp, fed and watered the hounds, then retired for a little much needed rest.

Around noon we were awakened by Bob wanting us to come to his home for lunch. We informed him of our hunting all night and that we had done quite well in the rough country behind the cabin. He only laughed and said, "Y'all are tougher than I am to hunt that rough stuff. The only coons I treed were in den trees or rock cliffs the few times I hunted in there, and that was enough for me." Ronnie and I only smiled to ourselves, thinking that Bob should see some of the rough stuff we hunted in the mountains of North Georgia.

After lunch we lounged around the remainder of the day, sleeping the evening away, awoke and drove to Bob's for our nightly hunt, as darkness settled in. Bob wanted to make only one turnout as he thought, we, along with the hounds needed to be rested for the big hunt. In the end he was correct as one of the hounds would give out; maybe because of the heat, or from being hunted too hard prior to the hunt. We turned the hounds loose in a good area near Dixon Springs, where they swiftly struck and treed a coon; making it appear easy. Rudy seemed to be performing best of the three hounds; he was the one our hopes were on to win or place in the hunt.

Ronnie and I returned to the cabin early in the night, unable to sleep, and failing to follow Bob's advice, we once again released the hounds into the rough country behind the cabin. Releasing the hounds again was possibly a bad mistake for both men and hounds. Up until that point our hunts behind the cabin had been decent ones, but that was about to change. The hounds struck a track in record time, quickly taking it deep into the country and out of hearing range. Ronnie and I walked and walked some more as there were no roads in the area to get closer to the hounds; probably one of the reasons Bob did not hunt there. After a long and hard walk we were able to hear the hounds deep in the country - they were treed. The humidity was very high and the temperature terribly hot, we needed to get to the hounds soon as possible. Our walk to them began, through some rough, rocky and hilly terrain. Following a time consuming, tiring walk we arrived at the tree, a large den with no game seen on the outside. All three hounds were hot and tired, also Ace seemed to be severely over heated, more so than the other two hounds. We leashed the hounds and begin the long walk back to the cabin; wishing we had adhered to Bob's advice. We had experienced the rough country he had spoken of, and it was truly hard on the hounds. Finally arriving back at the cabin the hounds were fed and given fresh water. We then retired to get a little much needed rest.

Bright and early the next morning Bob awoke us to prepare for our short trip to Carmi and the hunt. He wanted to arrive early to visit with everyone and purchase a few hunting supplies. Upon seeing the hounds he knew we had hunted most of the night and also knew all three hounds were still exhausted from treeing the long period of time it had taken us to get to the tree. We advised him that we now knew what he meant about the rough country and treeing coon in den trees. We also advised him that the hunt, along with the heat had taken its toll on the hounds and we hoped it wouldn't affect their performance in the hunt. Our supplies along with the hounds were loaded and we drove the short distance to Carmi, to meet with friends and set up camp.

After several nights of hunting and the competition eliminated down to the top twenty we had a couple hounds remaining in the hunt. The hound our hopes were on had been eliminated from the competition. Rudy did not make the top twenty, but Ace and Two were solidly in and would hunt the next night.

The final night of the hunt, Ace was eliminated in the early round; he was totally exhausted, possibly from our over hunting him, or overheating on the last tree the hounds had made in the rough country. He really didn't perform to perfection from the beginning of the hunt and finally ran out of steam; he would place 19th overall in the event. Two came in with a cast win and advanced on to the final four. Two placed 4th overall in the final cast; he was also exhausted and in need of rest. Our preparation for the hunt had paid off as two out of three hounds in the top twenty was not bad. We hadn't won the overall hunt but we had placed two hounds and that accomplishment was satisfactory. Ace would be hunted in several more competition hunts while in my kennel, winning or placing in his share before being sold back to his original owner Mike DeGraves of Wisconsin. Ace won or placed in many large hunts but he wasn't the type hound that I really liked, he didn't hunt as hard as I liked. He possessed tree power and was an accurate stay put tree dog that didn't move once treed; regardless of circumstances. I once saw him treed with a dog latched onto his shoulder, teeth sunk deep, and Ace never missed a bark; treeing as if nothing was happening. Mike kept Ace until the end.

Hopsing II was never entered in another competition hunt while I owned him. He made Dual Nite Champion while in my kennel and placed in the N.K.C. World Hunt proving that an average hound can, and does, win in the hunts. Hopsing II was colored like his sire and favored him in looks, but the comparison ended there. Two was sold to Jimmy Pierce of North Carolina who resold him to someone that promoted him. He had other hounds to compete with while in my kennel and didn't receive very much promotion as I owned other hounds I liked better.

Rudy was owned by Ronnie until the end, he was a completely balanced hound that any real coon hunter would have been proud to have owned. We had hopes of Rudy winning or placing in the hunt but luck wasn't with him. Shortly thereafter he placed in one of the larger money hunts of the time, advancing to the final four with me handling him; proving that he could win against top competition. He was an all around good coonhound; consistent night after night.

Coon treeing hounds such as Rudy were hard to come by, because their owners didn't sell them.

Maybe good hounds with the bloodlines of these hounds of the past can still be found today in the kennels of some dedicated breeders. · Remember that preparation can and will pay off in the end.

A GOOD HUNT

6

The cold night air was shattered by the loud, coarse bawl of a Hound high on the mountainside. The hound was Grand Champion, Grand Nite Champion Fuller's Hopsing, an English Redtick and a grand old hound. My hunting buddy Howard and I were slowly moving along the creek bank, at the base of the rolling mountain ridges where the hounds had been released some 20 minutes earlier. It was a cold January night and we were walking to just stay warm. Three hounds had been released up the swift running creek in hope that they would swiftly strike a coon track and remain on the flatland at the base of the mountain. We were hunting Hopsing and a nice young son of his, Grand Champion, Nite Champion Carter's Cooning King and Grand Nite Champion, ACHA Nite Champion,

NKC Nite Champion DeGraves Ace. All three were English Redticks, and hounds that could tree coons in the cold winter months without worries of them chasing off game, as this area was loaded with deer and fox.

Howard casually stated, "I sure hope ol' Hoppy comes down this way because it's going to be a hard climb if he trees up on the mountainside." Hopsing's track was improving by the minute; but we had not heard Ace or King and assumed they had hunted into a swampy area further down the creek. This assumption proved true as both opened together, on a separate track, directly in front of us.

We momentarily stopped walking and stood at the fields' edge enjoying the hound music as Hopsing smoked his track down a hollow, coming off of the mountain, almost back at the point where we had parked our vehicle. Howard and I both enjoyed listening to Hopsing run a track; he was a great track dog with a beautiful coarse bawl mouth. He ran every track to catch and if this animal he was now running did not go somewhere quick that was exactly what he was going to do. He was running straight toward the field where we stood and appeared to be looking at the coon, which thought about trying to cross the field and make a run for the creek. Having second thoughts the coon immediately turned and started back up the mountain; it ran only 100 yards before being forced to either fight or take refuge. The coon chose to climb.

Hopsing located with one roaring locate and turned it over to 120 plus barks per minute letting us know to, "Come look at this one." In the meantime Ace and King began to get their track up and moving at a pace that would soon take them out of hearing range. We quickly walked to Hopsing's tree; and found him glued to the side of a large oak, belly rubbing and slobbers slinging. Howard spotted the coon in less than 30 seconds and said he was about to put it out. The coon looked to be extremely large and I held Hopsing back because I did not want him getting chewed up by a big, mad coon. The coon hit the ground dead, and Hopsing was allowed to get a taste of it. The big ringtail weighed over 20 lbs. and was exceptionally large for our area of the country; it along with Hopsing would be dropped off at the truck before we began the walk toward Ace and King. We then began walking in the direction of our vehicle to better hear how Ace and King were progressing with their track.

Back at the vehicle we faintly heard Ace and King, almost out of hearing, but still at the base of the mountain. They were on the creek in an area where we could get much closer by driving to them. Saving us a long walk we drove in the direction of the trailing hounds, stopping at intervals to listen. They had crossed the road at the point where the creek flowed underneath and were now following it across pasture land, running hard in the sparse timber along the creek bank.

"At least we won't have to climb that mountain if they tree down here," Howard said. I thought, "Yeah, this has been pretty easy tonight."

We sat on the tailgate savoring the sound of the two hounds running the track for all they were worth. Both hounds had nice bawl mouths and were a pleasure to hear working a track, but we were now waiting on the big locates and the hard loud chops that should soon be coming. The two moved on through the country forcing us to drive further to stay within hearing range .Driving closer and stopping at a side road both hounds were found to be treed - chopping loud and hard. They were only a short distance from the road and we slowly walked to the tree; a big hollow oak with many holes in it. As I leashed the hounds, I looked up into the hollow at the bottom of the tree but it extended only a short distance before coming to an end. "Here he is on the outside and he is trying to get over in another tree," Howard yelled as he quickly put the coon out. This was another big ol' boar coon and made it 2 for 2 and the night was still early.

We were a good distance from home in an area only hunted in the winter months, because of the snakes and extremely rough going in the summer months. We had already taken one coon more than usual, yet we wanted to make one more turnout before calling it a night. It was decided our last drop would be made nearer our home in some rolling ridge country; another coon would not be taken. We didn't take coon from that area because it was used to hunt young dogs and occasionally listen to a good coon race.

Arriving at the area we drove along a power line until reaching a small stream where the hounds were released. They struck a good track almost instantly, Hopsing opened first followed by King and Ace joining in. We sat on the tailgate listening to the three hounds running the track to catch before going over a ridge and out of hearing range. Driving closer we found the hounds treed together on a large pine.

All three were treeing straight up on the tree, no growling, climbing or head slinging and they were shelling it out over 100 barks per minute. Best of all they had another coon up the tree. After a little praise the hounds were led back to the truck, loaded into the box and we headed for home, another good hunt behind us.

I thought to myself, I was lucky to own these hounds as they gave no aggravation, and treed coons when I turned them loose, they also came home with me when I was ready to call it a night.

Old Hopsing was a pleasure to hunt; he was a good looking hound with an extremely loud mouth, a completely balanced hound that was an accurate stay-put tree dog. Another plus was him being a reproducer of top hounds, including World Champion Fuller's Red Rooster and many more. He was a single registered hound and was not used as he should have been or he could have improved some things within the breed, such as nose, track power and tree power with accuracy. He had a couple of faults, but the good traits far outweighed the bad. Hopsing is buried out by the barn in the North Georgia clay alongside several other "good ones."

Ace was a nice hound too, but he did not have the hunt that I liked in a dog. Ace won and placed in many hunts and would absolutely stay treed, he was good about having a coon when he treed and gave no problems on off game. He was poison in kitten coon or in the summer time. He would tree the whole litter of kittens then the ol' sow. At times it seemed he was sauntering around behind other dogs and bam, he would tree and have a coon. Ace spent his last days with his original owner Mike DeGraves in Green Bay, Wisconsin.

King was sired by Hopsing and a female named Salacoa Valley Missy that I owned and bred to Hopsing a couple more times with good results. King was a good looking Redtick with a big bawl mouth, a big locate, and a solid chop mouthed tree dog, he was very accurate and a pleasure to hunt. He was a completely balanced hound that would go hunting every time released, get struck on a coon, and get treed to stay with a coon that could be seen up the tree. King was killed on the highway before he could make his mark on the English world. He is buried alongside his sire.

RUNNIN' BUSTHEAD

7

Many nights when wanting to tree a couple coons and come home early we hunted an area only a few miles from home. We could run and tree a coon there at any time. In fact, the same coon could be struck and treed on any given night. The coon would come to be called, "Busthead", toward the end of his great runs. Ole Busthead had been run and treed many times but he always managed to make it home to a big safe den, until one cold winter night.

My younger Brother and I ran and treed Busthead numerous times over a two year period, always in the same tree. He had only briefly been seen once before as he peered from a hollow high up in the tree - until he was finally treed on the outside. We had tagged the name "Busthead" on the coon the week prior to him finally being treed up a tree other than his den. Even if he had been treed on the outside in earlier times he would not have been taken as he was somewhat of a novelty. When hunting the area he was always struck at the same location regardless of where the hounds were released. They would immediately go to that certain spot and the race would be on.

The week before treeing and seeing Busthead, he was struck at precisely the same area. As the dogs ran the track my Brother and I crossed the pasture following a clear all season stream into the wooded area where Busthead was always struck. Walking along the small stream we began to smell a strong, sweet odor. Upon arriving at the origin of the stream, an artesian spring, we discovered the source of the smell. Embedded in the bank of the spring was a copper moonshine still - sometimes called a groundhog. Covering the top of the groundhog was a piece of plywood with a small opening at one edge. Further inspection of the still revealed that it was filled with fermenting corn, the source of the smell, and food for the coon. The coons wet footprints remained on the plywood where it had been standing to reach into the opening for the fermenting corn. Bringing a cupped handful of the fermenting liquid from the still, then smelling and tasting the brew my Brother stated, "If that coon is drinking that bust head he is sure to have a headache." Thus the coon "Busthead" received his name.

Busthead would run long and hard giving us several years of quality enjoyment running and treeing him. The first time Busthead was treed we were hunting Grand Champion, Grand Nite Champion Thompson's Rip, a big blue English Hound, a beautiful English Redtick that would be known as Dual Nite Champion Chigger Hill Golden Sonny and a young started blue English Hound that would be known as Nite Champion Nation's Blue Lightning. Busthead was struck at the head of the stream same as he would be for the next couple years. Rip was first to open with a long loud bawl, followed by Sonny with several chops, then the pup Lightning with a loud

clear horn bawl. The coon quickly and directly ran straight to his den. Sonny was first to locate the tree, followed by Rip and Lightning. After listening to the treeing hounds for several minutes we began walking to them.

On the walk to the tree my Brother said he had never heard a dog tree hard as Sonny was treeing; this was his first night in the woods with him. Walking in to the tree he would get to see one of the classiest most powerful tree dogs of that era stretched high on the side of the big den. Sonny was covered with slobber, letting the world know what time it was. Standing tall and proud beside Sonny was the big blue hound "Rip" treeing with a loud steady chop. Little Lightning was sitting at the base of the tree looking straight up and treeing with a short bawl and chop. The first time Busthead was treed fairly easy, but each proceeding time he would run longer and harder with his trail always ending at the same big den. As time progressed the hounds that treed Busthead would change other than Lightning, he would be along every time I can recall treeing that coon - the first and the last time.

The night Busthead was named we were hunting Grand Nite Champion Rock 'N' Roll Rowdy, Grand Champion, Nite Champion Carter's Cooning King and Nite Champion Nation's Blue Lightning. Ole Busthead made his usual run that night, crossing the creek numerous times, hitting the cutover timber and swamp, taking to the ridges and finally going home to his big den. We stated that night that we were going to see the coon the next time it was treed. This statement became a fact the following week.

Our plan to tree and see Busthead was put into effect on the next hunt that was made in the area. It was decided that my Brother would walk to the big den, sit down and wait. I would drive around and send the dogs toward the spring from the other side. We were going to hunt Rowdy, King and Lightning again. Lightning always seemed to be the one that struck Busthead. He had developed into a top honest strike dog and one of the best track dogs in the business, much of this development due to running Busthead.

We drove close as possible to Busthead's big den, and my Brother began the walk to the den while I drove around to the creek bridge. Stopping at the bridge I released the dogs across the field in the direction of the spring where Busthead was always struck. The dogs did not want to cooperate with the plan as they turned in the direction of the creek and immediately fell treed. Rowdy threw his head up as he came off the leash, ran to the creek bank and began to tree. He was quickly backed by King and Lightning. I spotted the coon walking in to the tree, leashed the dogs, gave them a little praise and led them back in the direction I wanted them to go; releasing them across the field toward the moonshine still.

Things went as planned after the dogs were released and Lightning soon opened with his loud horn bawl in the area Busthead was always struck. King soon joined the chase with a loud bawl, followed by Rowdy with a chop and bawl. Busthead wasted no time leaving the area; he headed for the creek, crossed back and forth several times then hit the swamp trying to make his getaway. The hounds would occasionally make a lose in the swampy area, but would quickly line the track out.

Busthead was making the hounds work to put him up a tree; he was not going to run straight to his den on this night. Finally he came out of the swamp with the hounds in hot pursuit, he briefly ran into the cutover, having second thoughts he changed directions. The three hounds were running to catch and very well could have caught him in the rough stuff with very few trees to climb. He then headed for the ridges and his big den. He ran up and down the ridges for fifteen minutes before running straight for his den. After five more minutes of hard running Rowdy located the tree followed by Lightning and King. I began walking to the tree thinking that Busthead had once again made it to his den; or the general area anyway.

Walking in to the tree I seen my Brother shining the tree and realized it was not the big den but a tree very near it. As I looked up I could see the outline of the coon in my Brother's light-beam. Ole Busthead was finally treed on the outside where we could get a good look at him. Rowdy and King were standing on the tree side by side treeing over 1 00 barks per minute. Lightning sat at the base of the tree, chopping and bawling. After leashing the dogs back we stood observing the coon which had evaded us for a couple years. The dark colored coon appeared to be of average size. We looked at Busthead for several minutes feeling content that we had accomplished what we had set out to do. Walking away from the tree leading Rowdy, King and Lightning, my Brother made a comment that I would later think about every time I hunted the three hounds. He said, "You know, if I could combine the good traits from these three dogs there would be no better coondog to be found."

Slowly walking back to the truck my Brother explained that as he sat at the base of Busthead's den and heard the hounds running in that direction that he had picked up a small stick. If not for having the stick in hand Busthead would once again have gotten into his den. He said Busthead had attempted to run into the hole at the base of the tree but he had swung the stick diverting the coon in the other direction. With the dogs very close upon him he was forced to climb the next tree he came to.

Busthead was left to run and tree again even though this would be the last time we treed him or hunted the area. This would also be one of the last hunts my Brother and I would hunt together because he was killed in an automobile accident only months after the hunt. He was a tough coon hunter who enjoyed hunting a good hound.

Dual Nite Champion Chigger Hill Golden Sonny was the first hound we owned that treed Busthead. Sonny was finished to Dual Nite Champion while in my kennel; he was one of the great tree dogs of his era. Too much tree dog, in fact he would put a tree on the end of every track he opened on, and absolutely could not be pulled. Sonny can be found in the pedigrees of many hounds being promoted today; he reproduced tree dogs. Sonny was sold to an English promoter, and later resold to and promoted by a dedicated English man from Kentucky, who still promotes his bloodline today.

Grand Nite Champion Rock 'N' Roll Rowdy was the last hound we owned that treed Busthead. Rowdy was a Nite Champion when purchased and was Granded out by 12 year old (at the time) Dustin Thomas. I acquired Rowdy from Eugene Boyd who had also owned his sire Grand Nite Champion Boyd's Rock. I saw Eugene at a large hunt in Indiana; he greeted me as always with a big smile and an, "I have a coondog for you Bubba." Needless to say Rowdy went home with me. Rowdy was a good honest broke hound, he was an accurate stay-put loud and classy tree dog. It was said by a few that Rowdy was mean, but I trained many pups with him. He would back up a couple steps with a mean dog then put on the brakes; I would want nothing less. Rowdy can be found in the pedigree of many hounds today, most through his famous daughter Grand Nite Champion Blue Magic Gold. Rowdy lived to a nice old age at my kennel.

Nite Champion Nation's Blue Lightning was along on every trip that Busthead was ran and treed. I trained Lightning from a pup and made him Nite Champion in three hunts, he was never again hunted in a competition hunt. Lightning was Boyd's Little Joe bred, he was an ugly hound, but looks never treed a coon. Lightning was one of the best coon striking dogs I've ever seen and a great track driving hound that took his tracks to the correct tree. He treed with a loud chop and bawls and stayed put. Lightning stayed at my kennel until he was an old hound before being sold to a pleasure coon hunter to enjoy.

Grand Champion, Nite Champion Carter's Cooning King came to my kennel from Tom Carter of Indiana. King also treed old Busthead many times; and he, like his great sire Grand Champion, Grand Nite Champion Fuller's Hopsing, would have spent his life at my kennel. King was an absolute pleasure to hunt, he was broke from off game, had a loud bawl mouth on track and a hard chop on the tree. King was a classy tree dog that would not pull, he was also very accurate. King was killed on the road while at the home of Steve Dorrough; he had gotten off his tie-out chain and was hit by a car in front of Steve's home. The good ones do not always live a long life.

THE WHOLE FAMILY PLUS THREE
8

The sow coon and her three kittens were foraging the waters edge in search of food. The sow was attempting to teach the kittens the ways of the wild, in preparation for being able to survive on their own. Little did she know that she and her young kittens would endure a learning experience on this murky night and live through the incident.

The sow and her kittens lived in an area that had previously been posted land with "No Hunting Allowed" until only recently. With a new owner, who was a hunter and outdoorsman, this large tract of land could now be hunted by houndsmen with hounds. The owner who owned no hounds of his own would allow his friends to hunt their hounds on any small game, but his favorite was coon, and he would often accompany them to listen to the hounds run and tree.

Late one summer evening the owner was surveying a large beaver pond that had engulfed many acres of his prime timber when he observed the old sow and her kittens. The animals appeared to be prowling the water's edge in search of food and did not notice him. Thinking about some good hound music, the owner quickly returned to his truck and drove home where he phoned Bill Gray, a hunter with a top hound that he very much enjoyed listening to while he run and treed a coon. He advised Bill of seeing the coons and asked if he would like to come over for a little hunt.

Bill and I had a hunt planned for this night, so upon hearing about the coons the location we would be hunting was changed. Bill phoned to inform me of the change of plans and said he would be over to pick me up, as the hunting tract was nearer to my home.

Bill owned one of the top English hounds of his time; he was a coon dog in any man's woods. I spent many nights in the woods with this grand old hound that had earned my respect and helped to train a couple of up-and- coming young hounds I was hunting. The old hounds name was Grand Nite Champion, ACHA Nite Champion Racf's Rcd Rusty. Bill did not hunt Rusty in competition, but only enjoyed him for the coon dog he was.

My old friend John Raef, a coon hunter who knows a coon dog, had owned and hunted Rusty in the hunts and made him a Champion. He had also placed him in the A.C.H.A. World Championship. Rusty was a medium sized dark rust colored Redtick that would go hunting and was a top, honest strike dog that did not pick his tracks but took them as they came, hot or cold. He ran track with one of the best loud, coarse bawls ever heard on a hound and was an outstanding, loud, accurate stay-put pressure tree dog. Bill would only bc bringing Rusty along on this hunt.

When Bill arrived, I loaded Grand Nite Champion, ACHA Nite Champion, NKC Nite Champion DeGraves Ace and Grand Nite Champion, ACHA Nite Champion Jewell's Tapp, both English Redticks and good hounds in their own right. I chose these two as they were easy to handle and did not hunt out of the country; both were old seasoned, broke hounds. I usually only hunted a couple of good young hounds I was finishing out when I hunted with Bill and Rusty. The young hounds were left at home on this night in favor of age and experience.

I'd owned Ace for a couple of years and hunted him in a few hunts, doing quite well with him. He was better where the coons were thick but all in all he was a good hound. Ace had been hunted two years in the NKC World Championship and placed in the top twenty both times with a 3rd one year and a 19th the following year. Ace had also placed in the top twenty of the ACHA World Championship. Ace didn't hunt real deep but treed a lot of lay-ups, and treed coons behind other hounds, and would absolutely stay treed. He ran track with a good clear bawl mouth and treed with a solid chop and was an accurate pressure tree dog. He would put a tree on the end of his tracks with a coon that could be seen in a large percentage of them.

Old Tapp had not been in my kennel very long but was also a good broke and very sensible hound that handled well. I first saw Tapp at English Days in Clay City, Indiana a few years earlier; he was on the lead of Eugene Boyd of Boyd's Little Joe fame. I think Eugene had sold him and was going to hunt him for the new owner, whom I later purchased him from. Tapp was a medium sized short coupled Redtick hound with a good head and ears and dark eyes. He was noticeable because part of his tail was missing. He was old stock breeding from around the southern Indiana, Kentucky area and had several famous ancestors and littermates.

Tapp was a hound that did not hunt out of the country and he also took his tracks as he came to them, hot or cold. When he opened he was after a coon and when he treed you could take your time getting to the tree and you would see a real live raccoon in the tree. Tapp ran track with a clear loud chop mouth but would occasionally bawl on a bad track; he gave an excessive amount of mouth on track, really more than I liked. When he went on a tree he was a great stay-put pressure tree dog with a loud clear ringing chop of 100 plus barks per minute- a tree dog without a mean hair on him. He was the same hound every night - consistent night after night.

While traveling to the hunting area, Bill and I discussed the layout of the area we would be hunting; it was a very large tract of land with old growth pine and hardwood timber. We had hunted this area a few times before and it was home to an abundant coon population. There was a large creek running through the center of the tract, several large stocked lakes and the big beaver pond where the coons had been seen. The terrain was mostly rolling hills and ridges with some flat land and plenty of access roads and trails. We were lucky to be allowed to hunt this area.

We drove directly to the beaver pond and met with the landowner who was already there and prepared for the hunt. He quickly pointed out where he had seen the coons, along the edge of the beaver pond. The owner asked to handle one of the hounds and we gave him a lead and told him to handle Tapp, which brought a big smile to his face. The hounds were released from the dirt road we were parked on, down the creek and into the beaver pond. Ace and Tapp hunted in the direction we pointed them but Rusty swam the creek and went up the other side in the opposite direction. The hounds quickly had tracks going in two different directions, with Rusty going one way and Ace and Tapp the other. The sow coon and her kittens had been roaming the beaver pond looking for food and had ranged a great distance from their safe den. The kittens had been playing on every tree and old snag they came upon, learning the ways of the wild. The kittens had never heard the sound of a hound let alone been run by one, and the old sow had probably never been run or trailed by a hound.

Rusty had found coon scent first and let us know with a loud coarse bawl and was beginning to pick up the pace on his track. Neither Ace nor Tapp opened where the land owner had seen the coons but went around the beaver pond before they struck and began steadily moving. Our only problem was Rusty trailing in one direction and Ace and Tapp going in the other. We decided to wait on the road and go to whichever treed first.

Rusty located with a big bawl and treed solid. The landowner said we could drive right to him. After listening to Ace and Tapp a few more minutes, we drove to Rusty who was treed alongside the road in a large pine. The coon was spotted from the road and Rusty retrieved and loaded into the dog box before returning to the beaver pond, where he was released towards the trailing Ace and Tapp. Just as Rusty was released Ace located a tree and turned it over to a solid chop. Seconds later, Tapp fell treed on a separate tree that Rusty honored by quickly falling treed with him.

We proceeded to Ace first, finding him stretched high on a small, leafy tree not missing a bark; he had one of the kitten coons up the tree. Following a little praise, he was led to Tapp and Rusty's tree. They were also on a small tree on the edge of the beaver pond; another of the kitten coons was up this tree. After more praise all three hounds were led a short distance from the tree and cut back into the beaver pond.

Ace opened once on the ground and fell treed, shutting Rusty and Tapp out on track and tree. As we walked to Ace he was covered by Rusty and Tapp. All hounds were leashed back and another kitten coon spotted in this tree. With all hounds on the leash we decided to move to another area, but as we were walking away from the tree, all three struck from the lead. We did the only thing a coon hunter could do- we cut them loose on what we assumed was the old sow coon.

We heard some good track work on this track with all three hounds running this coon for all they were worth. The old sow ran up and down the ridges, crossed the creek several times and came back to the beaver pond. She was finally run so hard that she was forced to tree in what was sure to be her den. This big tree was within 100 feet of where the land owner had first seen the sow and kittens at the edge of the beaver pond.

On arrival at the tree, we saw it was a huge old oak den with a large hole about halfway up the tree. The tree was shined looking for the coon, but nothing was seen on the outside. Bill blew the squaller a couple times and the coon ran out of the hole and into the top of the tree. With this coon seen we led the hounds back to the truck and loaded up.

The land owner stated that we had treed the whole family that he saw earlier- plus one. He then asked if we wanted to make one more turnout. Well, coon hunters always want to make one more turnout. We drove to one of the large lakes and cut the hounds loose for one more race, we hoped. Rusty would be the first to find coon scent on this turnout, joined by Tapp, on the other side of the lake. After a couple minutes, Ace was heard near the spillway of the lake, on a separate track. All three hounds were working the track and moving in the same general direction when the track suddenly became a running track and went over the ridge and out of hearing.

We walked back to the trucks and followed the land owner around to the other side of the ridge. All three hounds were treed when we stopped to listen; they appeared to be together. When we walked into the tree the hounds were found to be split about 100 feet apart, Rusty and Tapp were on one tree and Ace on another. Both trees had coons in them. Upon seeing the coons the hounds were led back to the truck and loaded up - another successful night behind us.

The landowner advised us how much he enjoyed the hunt and invited us to return for another hunt whenever we wanted. He said he would like to go along if we didn't mind. He liked to hear and see some good dog-work. With this we shook hands, thanked him and departed for home.

On the drive home, Bill and I talked about how much we liked a hard going dog. These hounds were living proof that a hound doesn't have to hunt three counties over to tree coons. Also, they were proof that a hound that is enjoyed on a pleasure hunt can win in competition and that you do not have to walk to a bunch of empty trees as a coondog trees coons not trees.

GOOD FORTUNE TIMES

TWO

9

Our chosen hunting grounds would be in the vicinity of the Shawnee National Forest in Southern Illinois, an area with rolling hills, big woods, creeks and scattered fields. The locality was home to an abundant coon population, many that would run and not go up the first tree they came to. It was an ideal setting for an enjoyable night of coon hunting. We would hear some good track work and see two hounds tree coons in style on this night; and a bonus would also be received. The two hounds that would be hunted were Grand Champion, Nite Champion Paxton Abernathy (Abner), an outstanding English Redtick, and a top young blue English Hound that would come to be known as Dual Nite Champion Nation's Hardwood JoJo.

This would be our first night in the woods with JoJo. He had been picked up earlier in the day at the home of Jack Cowgill in Taylorville, Illinois. Jack, one of the original promoters of the English breed owned JoJo and chose not to promote him because he was not out of his bloodlines. Jack advised me that he owned one of the top young English hounds in the country; a hound that needed to be in the hands of someone who would campaign him. Terms concerning the purchase of JoJo were negotiated by phone for several weeks before a deal was finalized - he would now be moving to Georgia.

JoJo was a 55 pound, tight made, dark blue hound with rich tan trim, dark intelligent eyes, and a good head and ears. He was sired by the great reproducing hound ACHA World Champion, Grand Nite Champion Hayes Hardtime Speck. Jack proclaimed JoJo to have one of the loudest mouths ever heard on a hound. Accompanying his loud mouth was an impressive one bark locating bawl that commanded appreciation. A locate that anyone would stand up and take notice of when they heard him locate an old hard running coon or a lay-up.

I drove to the home of Bob and Donna Williams in Golconda, Illinois on a Friday, taking Abner along for a night of pleasure hunting with Bob and Mike Seets. The following morning Bob and I made the trip to Jack's home to get JoJo, returning to Bob's late in the evening. Our plans were to hunt JoJo and Abner that night. Abner had been hunted hard all winter; we knew the type hound he was and enjoyed hunting him- he was an absolute pleasure to hunt. JoJo would have to prove his worth.

Abner came from Mike DeGraves of Green Bay, Wisconsin. Mike had attempted to run him on bear but he preferred coon and because of this I was able to negotiate a deal for him. Abner was a hard hunter, and a top first strike dog that knew where to strike a coon. He ran track with a loud bawl mouth, located with a distinctive bawl and treed with a hard loud chop and stayed put with a coon that could be seen. Abner was a stylish tree dog that treed up on the tree and didn't have a mean hair on him. He was also one of the best looking Redtick hounds ever sired by Dual Grand Champion Penny's Kentucky Kojak; another great reproducer of that era.

As darkness settled in the hounds were loaded and we proceeded to the section of timber Bob had selected for the first drop. We were about to discover what type hound JoJo was - and it wouldn't take long. Both hounds were cut across a low lying field towards a large woods consisting of very hilly terrain with small streams running through the bottom land. They immediately split up; one went right the other left. Within minutes Abner was struck, opening four or five times on a good track. JoJo didn't cover him but responded with one roaring locate and began to tree with a loud, coarse chop that would drown out most hounds. Bob and I slowly walked to JoJo as Abner worked his track farther into the country.

On arrival at JoJo's tree we witnessed a tree dog that would make anyone proud, and yes, he had a coon. JoJo had his toenails dug in and slobber was foaming down his neck and sides as he treed like few hounds do. A little praise was given him and he was led from the tree, allowing us to listen for Abner.

A tree had been put on the end of Abner's track by this time and we began the walk to him. JoJo remained on the leash. On arrival at Abner 's tree he was found stretched high on a big hardwood letting us know he had the groceries with a loud clear chop of 100 plus barks per minute. Yes, he also had the coon. With both hounds on the leashes we headed back to the truck and another drop.

Following a ten minute drive we arrived at another of Bob's choice hunting spots, a big section of woods with a large creek running through it, that the hounds were released directly onto. Both hounds went hunting and quickly had a track going; together this time. Abner was first to open with a big clear bawl and was soon joined by JoJo with a roaring bawl. The track was not very good but the two hounds worked together to get it moving and rapidly put a tree on the end of it. JoJo was first to locate, immediately followed by Abner.

Following a lengthy walk we arrived at the tree; a big hollow hardwood. The hounds were leashed back and the tree shined but nothing was found on the outside. The hounds were led a short distance and released once again. Abner swiftly struck another track and JoJo joined in on a running track that was run out of hearing. Driving to the other side of the section both hounds were found to be treed on the same tree, with another coon. It was unknown which hound first located the tree but they sure looked good standing side

by side and stretched high on the tree.

Several more drops were made with both hounds released together, and coons were treed on every one. Split tracks and split trees were made with the hounds swapping strikes and trees back and forth. We had hunted most of the night but now had both hounds in the box and decided to call it a night. It had been a very enjoyable hunt. As we drove along, Bob suddenly had a change of mind and said, "We should make one more drop and release only JoJo to see how he operates alone."

We pulled into an old deserted home place surrounded by big timber, pastureland and small ponds. JoJo was released towards one of the ponds and struck a track soon as he hit water's edge. He opened here and there with a booming bawl, drifted across a pasture, moving the track into the fence line on the other side, where he exploded on a tree.

Eyes were seen in the tree as we crossed the pasture to JoJo. Once at the tree, a cedar, the eyes were no longer visible. JoJo was leashed back and the tree thoroughly shined before Bob yelled, "Here it is, but it doesn't look right. I think it might be a possum." Only a small amount of white fur could be seen through the thick cedar limbs.

I then did a couple things I would never do today and should not have done at that time. I started to climb the tree for one, and after seeing the white coon I removed my coat and wrapped it around the animal, bringing it down alive. JoJo became almost unmanageable because of smelling the coon as Bob attempted to lead him back to the truck. After JoJo was loaded into the box and the coon secured in the tool box where he could not escape, we headed for Bob's home.

The coon was placed in a small cage and examined. He was white with reddish eyes and a faint yellowish tint where his mask and the rings around his tail should have been. He was not wild as a coon straight out of the wilderness should have been and we suspected that he could have been someone's pet that had escaped. Bob asked what I was going to do with the coon. After briefly thinking I replied, "I guess I'll take him home with me and try to raise a few white coons." Bob laughed and said, "Now that's an idea."

I departed for home around noon on Sunday following a short rest. Driving along I would occasionally catch myself smiling as I had a new hound that could possibly win big in the hunts, plus a white coon he had treed to boot. I had been blessed with good fortune times two. Abner remained at Bob's home for him and Mike Seets to hunt in a few of the local money hunts, where he proved to do exceptionally well, winning and placing in several.

Back home in Georgia I rested Sunday night and was awakened early Monday morning by my Dad; wanting to see the new hound I had brought home. I explained, in detail, the hunt with JoJo and showed him the albino coon while advising of my plans to attempt and breed a few white coons. He only smiled and shook his head after hearing my plans.

My Dad had not coon hunted in several years, but after hearing me describe how JoJo located and treed, he asked if I was hunting that night; if so, he wanted to accompany me. That evening he came over and said he had obtained permission for us to hunt a place that had not been hunted in many years.

As darkness settled in we loaded only JoJo and drove the short drive to a big farm on the river. A quick stop was made at the landowners home to inform him we were only going to tree the coons and not kill them as season was closed. He actually wanted us to thin the coons out before his corn came up.

Following the lengthy conversation we drove down a long field road ending at a large tract of old growth timber that backed up to the river. The section of woods was surrounded by fields where corn and soybeans were grown, and had drainage ditches running around its perimeter. The owner said it had not been hunted in over ten years unless someone had come in from the river. It looked ideal.

JoJo was released and swiftly struck and treed a coon. He was released three more times in the section of woods and he struck and treed a track every time turned loose. Out of the four trees made coons were seen in three of them and the fourth could have had a coon, but was so big and brushy we were unable to find it. My Dad was impressed with JoJo's mouth, his big locate and treeing style. He decided he might start hunting again. I was well satisfied with JoJo and eager to put him in the hunts. All in all our entire hunt was a successful one, I now knew that JoJo worked exceptionally well alone and needed no help of any kind. My Dad had also seen a tree dog that impressed and would influence him to occasionally hunt again.

JoJo was quickly made Champion in a couple different registries and then campaigned by Bob Williams and Mike Seets in a few of the money hunts in which he excelled. As summer advanced and the weather became hotter, I saw I had a big problem with JoJo. He was such a tremendous tree dog that he would sometimes overheat in extremely hot weather. If you did not get to the tree quick enough and he treed for too long a period, he would sometimes have a seizure causing him to fall out and have to be carried from the woods. In cooler or even moderate weather he was fine, but many of the big hunts are conducted during the warmer months. Because of this it pretty much ended JoJo's hot weather competition hunting. It was a bad break but he was still enjoyed in the woods in cooler weather with absolutely no problems.

My albino coon breeding never came to be as the white coon's cage was accidentally left unlatched. He along with a white sow I had purchased from a breeder in Iowa escaped. Hopefully they both survived and produced some albinos in the wild. I never heard of anyone catching a white coon around my home so maybe they made it.

JoJo and Abner were both good hounds that would have satisfied any coon hunter. JoJo was a tight mouthed hound but an outstanding locator and accurate stay-put pressure tree dog that did everything quick. Abner was a balanced first and first type hound that could do it all and stay put with the coon at the end of his tracks. JoJo was later sold but Abner spent the remainder of his life at my home. Abner and JoJo are now long gone as is my Dad, Bob Williams, and Jack Cowgill, men who enjoyed hearing a great locating tree dog. Hopefully they are listening to a good tree dog somewhere today.

SPECK—
A TREE DOG
10

Speck was used on a variety of game and called a combination dog by his owner. He wasn't a registered dog, but what was considered a Heinz 57 breed. His breeding consisted of hound, bird dog and several other breeds of dog blood coursing through his veins. He was a 55 pound dog with a big, wide, flat head that was black in color; he had short ears and dark intelligent eyes. His body was white and heavily ticked, with a little heavier coat of hair than most, and a slight flag tail. He wasn't much to look at, but he had good feet and legs and could carry the mail on a track of any kind and put game at the end of his tracks.

Speck was raised way back in the hills where the terrain was rough and the game scarce. Speck's original owner was a Baptist preacher who had raised him from a small pup with the intent of hunting him on squirrel only. In his younger years Speck kept squirrel on the table, until he acquired the taste for other tree game and began treeing this game. Even when hunted only in the daytime, Speck treed bobcats, coons and possums. After he began to run and tree the other game his hunting style began to change, and he ranged wider and wider.

The old Preacher liked Speck a lot, but wanted only a squirrel dog, and a close ranging one at that. Speck was nearing three years old and had never been hunted at night; only in the daytime. He was slowly starting to tree more and more of the other tree game; and with this there was much more walking involved for the old Preacher. Following much thought, the Preacher decided to sell Speck.

On a trip to visit relatives in a distant town, the Preacher stopped at a barber shop for a haircut. While sitting in the barber chair getting his hair cut, the Preacher told the Barber about Speck and said he would like to sell him to a good hunter. The Barber was a hunter too and was always in the market for a tree dog. After a little horse trading, Speck had a new owner.

The Barber cut hair five days a week and hunted five or six nights a week plus the two days he was off work. He hunted anything that would leave a trail for a dog. He owned beagles to run rabbits, Redbones and Black and Tans to run tree game with, and Birddogs to hunt birds. Speck joined this mixed pack of dogs but would soon become the favorite of his new owner.

The Barber had a large family including several sons but only one was interested in any kind of hunting. He often hunted alone, with his son, or a young hunter from the area, mainly to put food on the table and a little extra cash in the pocket. He would occasionally finish a young dog and sell it for a profit to help support his family. He hunted hard but never neglected his family.

After allowing Speck a couple days to become familiar with his new owner and surroundings, and hunting season in full swing, he was taken out on an early morning squirrel hunt. Speck quickly treed four or five squirrels without barking on the ground; he just set treed with a high pitched, loud ringing chop and had the squirrel. When released to hunt further, he was next heard not barking treed but trailing on the ground with a short, sharp chop and beginning to move the track deeper into the country.

The Barber listened with interest as Speck worked the track from an old cold trail into a moving track before he let out one loud squall locate and began to tree with the loud ringing chop. On arrival at the tree, the Barber saw a large nest in the tree and nothing else. He shot into the nest and heard a "plunk" and knew he had hit something so he shot into it again. This time a large boar coon rolled from the nest and to the ground - dead. With a load of game in his game bag the Barber leashed Speck and headed for the house -well pleased with Speck's first hunt.

As nightfall fell, the Barber stepped out his back door and observed the dark sky and cool night air. Prepared for a hunt, he slowly walked to his dog kennel and released Speck and two of his Redbone Hounds. He then headed across a pine thicket in the direction of a nearby swamp. All three dogs went hunting, paying little attention to the barking dogs still chained or kenneled. The Barber walked in the direction the dogs had gone; suddenly Speck located and treed without receiving help from the Redbones.

The Barber hoped Speck had not treed on a cold squirrel tree. He did not want to walk to a lot of trees where he couldn't find game of some sort. He continued on to the tree and shined his light up a small pine, spotting a possum almost immediately. Speck was given the possum and released to hunt further, as the barber walked on in the direction of the swamp. Speck treed two more possums before reaching the pasture bordering the swamp, and still not a sound from the two Redbones. This was not unusual as the Redbones had been broken off possums and were hunted on coon only.

Shortly after reaching the swamps edge "Jill" the Redbone female opened with a loud bawl mouth soon followed by the equally loud bawl of "Jack" her litter mate. Speck had been hunted alone all of his life and knew nothing about covering another dog. Upon hearing Jack and Jill he went to investigate and soon joined in on the track with his high pitched chop mouth. The three dogs worked the track in and around the swampy area, brought it out onto dry land and Speck nailed a tree. His loud squall locate and high pitched chops were followed by the big bawl locates and heavy loud chops of the two Redbones.

The Barber took his time walking to the tree, savoring the melodious sound of the three dogs hammering away. The tree was a big hardwood with many large limbs. After a couple of squalls from the coon squaller, the coon looked at the low flicker of the light and was quickly dispatched by the Barber. The coon was put into the game bag along with the possums; a good catch already.

The Barber pointed the dogs back in the direction he had come and started to circle back toward his home. In only a few minutes the dogs were again struck and trailing an old feed track. He noticed how Speck could be heard above the loud bawl mouths of the two Redbones and how he could trail the track well as the hounds. While standing there thinking about the deal he had gotten on Speck, he realized that all three dogs were treed again. As he walked in to the tree he spotted eyes in the low flicker of his light. He saw three sets of coon eyes in the tree and decided to leave all three. He only took one coon per tree and figured one of these was the sow coon. To avoid   accidentally taking her, he left them all.

With his game bag full anyway, and with three dogs to lead, he had his hands full. He had meat for the table and fur that would be skinned and sold to buy dog food. He was very happy with Speck's performance his first night in the woods. The Barber thought that, "Speck would fill the freezer, and the fur shed." He then wondered what other game Speck would run. He decided to try and run him with his beagles, on rabbits, the next day. Maybe he would be a complete combination dog.

The next day, bright and early, the Barber started out on a rabbit hunt with his pack of beagles and Speck. A rabbit was soon jumped and the beagles ran in the fields and thickets but not a sound was heard from Speck on the rabbit track. Then, the Barber heard Speck's familiar high pitched chop, he was treeing hard, at the end of the field on the fence row. After walking to Speck, he saw a squirrel in the tree, which he put out to him. Into the game bag the squirrel went and Speck onto the lead. "Well, he won't run a rabbit and prefers tree game," thought the Barber as he loaded Speck into the box. Later in the day, with a load of rabbits and a squirrel, he headed for home to rest and prepare for a hunt that night.

Shortly after dark, the Barber loaded Speck and Black Jack, a young Black and Tan he was finishing out, and drove a short distance to a good hunting spot. Black Jack was not yet fully broke; he would run an occasional deer and still tree anything that climbed. On the first drop both dogs went hunting, with the Barber walking in the general direction they had gone. Black Jack opened deep on a good track and was covered by Speck who took the track away from him and slammed a tree. Both dogs were on the tree when the Barber arrived and he put a big boar coon down to them.

After another short drive the two dogs were released into a bottom land directly on the creek. A split track was quickly started with Speck going one direction and Black Jack another. Black Jack treed first and on arrival at his tree it was found to be a den with no game seen. In the meantime, Speck had finished his track and had another coon at the end of it. Hunting back toward the truck, two more trees were made; both dogs were on them and possums seen in both. The Barber once again had his game bag almost full, but decided on one more drop. A couple of miles further down the road both dogs were released into an area called the "Frog Pond". On this turnout Black Jack struck before the Barber had time to leave the truck. The track was red hot but Speck did not open and soon came sneaking back to the Barber before crossing to the other side of the "Frog Pond". Speck then fell treed without barking on the ground, he was very close to the truck. He had another possum in the tree, which the Barber took; he then walked back to the truck with Speck on the lead. He thought to himself, "Speck will not run a deer but he is a little heavy on the possums -he will have to be corrected." With that thought in mind he began to drive, looking and listening for Black Jack. He had seen enough for the night.

Speck was hunted hard the remainder of the hunting season and improved with every trip to the woods. The Barber very easily broke Speck from possums and he gave no problems with fast game. He was still hunted on squirrel in the daytime and coon at night; he would occasionally tree a bobcat but was not encouraged to do so. Speck quickly made a name for himself as a track-driving tree dog that had the game at the end of the trail.

The Barber hunted with the young hunter from the area all summer, finishing Black Jack and polishing Speck. They hunted almost every night and watched Speck develop into a top coondog that would make the hard to please very proud. The young hunter owned two top coonhounds, and at the beginning of the coon season, Speck would give them a run for their money. He stayed split to himself a lot, and he would have game that could be seen at the end of his tracks. The Barber was well satisfied with him and began to sell off his other dogs; Speck was soon the only tree dog remaining.

As the season progressed, the Barber sold the beagles and the bird dogs. He was still hunting with the young hunter one or two nights a week; his hunting had slowed way down. Many nights he did not feel well and he would ask the young hunter to take Speck along if he was hunting that night. He didn't want Speck to remain in the kennel unhunted during the coon season.

With the end of the season fast approaching, the Barber asked the young hunter to come talk with him. The Barber asked him if he would be interested in buying Speck for a reasonable price. He explained that his hunting career was at an end. He went on to say that he had been diagnosed with a terminal illness and had only a short time to live. He said he wanted Speck to go to someone who would treat him well and appreciate him. With all said and done, the young hunter departed with Speck in his dog box and a sad, heavy heart.

The young hunter hunted Speck and his other dogs hard the remainder of the season and treed many coons. He phoned or visited the Barber weekly to check on his health and advise of Speck's progress. The Barber was pleased that his young friend was interested in his well being and advising him of Speck's progress. He told the young hunter that he knew he did not need Speck but if he sold him to make sure that the person who got him would take good care of him. This was one of the last times the young hunter would speak with the Barber before he passed away.

After the Barber was gone, the young hunter would often think of him while hunting Speck. The Barber had not been an old man but followed the customs of a man many years his senior. He was an old time hunter who possessed the traditions of the old timers whom he started hunting with. He still hunted with a carbide light until the end, even though they were years out of date. He felt he could find more coons with the flickering light. He was a real hunter, outdoorsman and dog man; he would be missed.

The young hunter hunted hard that summer, starting young hounds and getting ready for the upcoming season. Speck operated like a fine tuned machine by this time and could load a hunter down with squirrels and coons. About a week into the coon season the young hunter received a call from a gentleman from the hills wanting to take a hunt with Speck. A time was set for the hunt and the man arrived early that evening.

Following introductions and small talk, the young hunter took the man on a short squirrel hunt with Speck. Speck quickly treed several squirrels and was loaded back into the box. The man wanted to see Speck tree coons, and wanted to see him go alone. A little after dark the young hunter and the old man hit the woods with only Speck.

Speck did what came natural to him - he treed three single coons that were seen; about as fast as they could walk to him. Once back at the truck the old gentleman smiled and said to the young hunter, "Speck sounds and operates just like his sire did." With this he explained that he had owned Speck when he was born and had given him to the old Preacher, as a pup. He had owned his sire which was bird dog and hound, and his dam that was cur and some other stuff; both were tree dogs.

Speck's sire, also named Speck, had recently passed away and his dam, Nell, had been gone for several years. The gentleman then proclaimed he would like to purchase Speck if at all possible. The young hunter said he didn't really want to sell Speck, but that he didn't need him with all the other dogs he owned. Out of the blue the gentleman made a cash offer for Speck that couldn't be refused.

The young hunter knew Speck would be appreciated and well taken care of when he removed his collar and replaced it with the old gentleman's. He also knew that the Barber would have approved of this, knowing that Speck had made a full circle and was now going back home for good.

HUNTIN' COHUTTA

11

Nestled in the mountains of North Georgia is the Cohutta Wildlife Management area; some of the best hunting to be found, that is, if one doesn't mind hunting the mountains. I grew up coon hunting the mountains and feel there is no better hunting - period. Climbing the steep ridges is sometimes rough and there may not be the amount of game found in other areas, or possibly the game is only spread out farther because of the vast amount of wooded terrain. The clean fresh air along with the outdoor smells, hardwoods, evergreens and clear mountain streams invigorates ones body; this is country that anyone would savor. The Cohutta WMA is open for coon hunting only several nights per year, and when younger I tried to hunt it at every given opportunity.

On this particular hunt my Dad would be accompanying me; he had at one time been a hard hunter, but at the time only occasionally hunted with me. He was a devoted Plott man, but he really liked JoJo, one of the young English Hounds I owned and would go along just to hear him run and tree a coon. He said JoJo was probably the most powerful tree dog he had ever heard, and every time he located a tree it would make the hair on his neck stand up. My Dad had taken me on my first coon hunt when I was barely old enough to walk, and as I grew older he made certain I had a top hound that I could tree plenty of coons with. He also instilled within my mind a firm belief that you can feed a good hound as easily as a worthless one; it cost the same to feed either.

On this hunt we would be hunting all English Hounds, three males and a female. All four hounds would go hunting, get struck and treed and have game in the tree, they would also stay put once treed. As darkness approached my Dad arrived and I loaded Dual Nite Champion Nation's Hardwood JoJo, Champion, Nite Champion Dutch Hollow Duke, Grand Champion, Nite Champion Paxton Abernathy and Nite Champion Nation's Tree Screaming Sheba. We had a good little drive to the place we planned to hunt and as we drove I thought about the hounds we were going to hunt.

Jojo was a two year old dark blue English Hound that would go hunting and quickly get treed and stay put. He had one of the loudest mouths ever heard on a hound and was an exceptionally fast, accurate one bark locator and a tree dog like hunters dream about. JoJo ran no off game and was a pleasure to hunt, he ran track with a booming bawl and treed with a hard, heavy chop. His was sired by ACHA World Champion, Grand Nite Champion Hayes Hardtime Speck. I purchased JoJo from Jack Cowgill of Illinois, and the only reason I was able to own him was because he was not from Jack's breeding. Jojo was finished to Dual Nite Champion after he came to my kennel. He was also campaigned in some of the money hunts of the time and did a lot of winning with Mike Seets handling him.

Duke was a one year old Redtick that was good as they get at his age. He hunted hard and would get by himself and get treed every chance he had. Duke ran track with a loud high pitched chop that could be heard with the loudest of hounds, he located with one squall bawl and immediately turned it over to a never ending chop. Duke was an accurate stay put tree dog that would absolutely stay treed; no matter what. Duke was sired by one of the overlooked studs of the time, a hound called Nite Champion Christophersons Roper, which was sired by Grand Nite Champion Boyd's Little Joe. I believe Roper was only lightly bred but he sure sired some good hounds and could have helped the breed if he had been heavily used. I bought Duke from Steve Dorrough of Clifton Park, New York, he was a Show Champion and I finished him to Nite Champion.

Abernathy called "Abner" was a completely balanced hound, a top strike dog, a track dog and a loud, classy stay put accurate tree dog. Abner was Redtick in color and one of the best looking Redtick hounds to ever breathe coon scent. He was a hound that went hunting well, ran track the right way with a big bawl, had an outstanding locate and was a hard, loud chop mouthed tree dog that could tree any kind of coon. Abner was sired by Dual Grand Champion Penny's Kentucky Kojak; one of the many good hounds out of Kojak in that era. I acquired Abner from Mike DeGraves of Wisconsin who had attempted to hunt him on bear, but with poor results. Abner was a top coon hound but not much of a bear dog even though he would still occasionally run one; the only thing he ran other than coon, and something I preferred he leave alone. I made no attempt to finish Abner to Grand Nite but he was hunted in some of the money hunts, handled by Mike Seets and I, and he did his share of winning and more.

Sheba was a small Redtick hound that went hunting in a run, quickly got struck and could really move a track in the right direction and put the correct tree on the end of it. Coming on the tree she gave a screaming locate and was a blow down tree dog that would not pull. Sheba ran track with a loud, high pitched chop, squall and bawl and treed with a rapid chop; putting on a show at the tree. She was another of the good hounds sired by Dual Grand Champion Penny's Kentucky Kojak. I bought her with intentions to raise a litter of pups; she came out of Michigan from Jim Baumbach, the Walker man and owner of the great Dual Grand Champion Baumbach's Pulpwood.

As we arrived at our first drop I thought, "If we didn't tree coons on this night they couldn't be treed." We were hunting as much dog power as anyone. Driving to the end of a narrow lane routed alongside a clear mountain stream we prepared to release the hounds up the hollow into what looked to be prime coon country. I had hunted JoJo hard in the mountainous terrain of the surrounding area and he was accustomed to it and knew where to look for a coon track. Duke had also received much hunting in the mountains of my area and upstate New York, so he also knew how to hunt the mountainous terrain and where to strike a coon. I had not hunted Abner in the mountains but was sure he had been hunted in much more mountainous terrain where he came from, so he should also do well. Sheba had probably not seen mountains like she was about to be subjected to, so how she would perform was a question to soon be answered.

All four hounds were released onto the mountain stream and immediately split up. JoJo shot up the stream, Duke crossed the lane following a trail up the side of the mountain, Sheba and Abner entered a hollow running parallel to the road we had driven in on. I had hoped that the hounds would stay together and quickly get a track going but they were too independent for that.

A lot of walking would be involved if each hound struck a track of their own, and as luck would have it they soon were going in three directions. Oh well, sometimes hunting the mountains is tough.

JoJo was first to strike, opening only two or three times before his big coarse locate was heard, followed by the loud heavy chops; he was going no further. As we walked in the direction of JoJo's tree Duke was heard high on the side of the mountain working a track. At precisely the same time Abner and Sheba opened far in the distance and they were moving. Proceeding on to JoJo's tree, only a short walk up the stream, he was leashed and a large hardwood shined, the coon spotted and quickly given to him. The coon was a large mountain coon that JoJo had practically ambushed, but many of his coon were treed in the same manner; he did everything fast and efficient. Walking from the tree with JoJo on the leash not another hound was heard, they had all gotten out of hearing range. Our next task was walking back to the vehicle to check the tracker and find their locations.

Duke was found not to be a great distance away; he had crossed into another hollow and was treed solid. Sheba and Abner 's location was another story as the tracker was receiving a signal from neither, they had traveled a long distance or crossed the mountain; in time we would discover which. Duke was high on the mountain and only slightly over a ridge in another hollow, he was treed on a large white pine; a variety of tree that many coons are treed up in the mountains. Sometimes the white pines are extremely large and the coon hard to find if it does not look at the light. This was not the case this time as the coon looked at the light almost immediately and was swiftly given to, and dispatched by Duke. Another large dark colored mountain coon with prime fur, two trees and two coons the night was starting out really well. Now back to the vehicle to attempt to locate Sheba and Abner.

Still unable to receive a signal from either on the tracker we drove in the direction they had departed, stopping at intervals to check for a signal. A weak signal was finally received from the two hounds and we drove toward their general direction. It is sometimes hard to get very close to the hounds if they are deep in the mountains because usually there is only a road or two running through the area. We were still unable to hear the hounds but the signal continuously became better the farther we drove.

Several miles up the road we came upon a group of young people gathered around a large blazing fire alongside the creek. Stopping at the area to check the tracker once again and receiving a really strong signal but still unable to hear the hounds, we then asked the group if they had seen the hounds. The group began talking all at the same time, stating that "yes" they had saw two dogs probably an hour before, and they had also seen a small bear they were chasing.

Pointing in the direction the hounds were going one of the youngsters said he lived nearby and knew the area well, stating that the dogs were in a deep hollow at the back of his family's property and happily volunteered to show us an easy route to them. The youngster crawled in the vehicle and pointed us in the direction we needed to go. "Go through the gate up ahead and we can drive into the hollow where the dogs were going," stated the young man.

As we slowed to make the turn into the gated area both Sheba and Abner were heard loud and clear - treed. We proceeded to within 100 yards of the treed hounds, and walked in to the tree. Both hounds were leashed back from a large bushy cedar and the small bear spotted sitting midway up the tree.

The young man quickly pointed to Sheba and said, "That dog was nipping at the bear's heels when he came by us, the other one was not too close up on the bear. We thought they were going to catch it but were glad they ran it away from us. I've never seen dogs run bear before but it's pretty cool. We have a lot of bear around here."

"Well, we aren't bear hunting and are not supposed to tree them, so we need to get the hounds and get out of here," my Dad and I responded. I briefly scolded both hounds as I didn't want either to run bear because I only coon hunted and that is the only game I wanted my dogs to run. As we arrived back at the vehicle the young man asked what game we were hunting and upon showing him the coons we had already caught he inquired if maybe he could tag along and see a coon treed. We had no problem with the request, and he promptly stated he knew a place where there were plenty of coons. A few miles farther along the mountainous road we came to another gated area where the young man opened the gate for us to drive to a small field of unharvested corn. The young man stated that his father planted the field yearly for the wildlife; it was never harvested and the wildlife was abundant around the field. Coming to a stop on the back side of the field all four hounds were released along the timberline, all went hunting and soon had a track going. Abner was first to open with a loud bawl joined by the chops and squalls of Sheba, the shrill chops of Duke and the thundering bawl of JoJo. Duke and JoJo peeled off up the mountainside and rapidly ended their track when JoJo stole the tree away from Duke before he could get his one squall bawl locate out of his mouth. That's how JoJo operated most of the time; tight and right, not what I really liked but hard to dislike. Abner and Sheba ended their track at almost the same time and my Dad stated that if they didn't pull to JoJo and Duke he would be surprised. JoJo was surely loud and my Dad partial to him but he wasn't going to pull neither Abner nor Sheba as they were hooked to stay. The young man had a big smile on his face just from hearing the treeing hounds but the smile was nowhere near what it would be after seeing a couple coons up the trees.

We climbed the mountain to JoJo and Duke first, leashed them and shined the tree spotting another large coon lying in a fork high in the tree. Both hounds had already had a coon out to them so the coon was left to run again. With both JoJo and Duke remaining on the leash we walked along the mountainside to Abner and Sheba's tree. On arrival at a large oak they were leashed back along with JoJo and Duke, the tree shined and two coons spotted. The smiling young man asked if we were going to take the coons; with Abner and Sheba not having had a coon I replied, "We'll take one of them. Do you want to put it out to them?" The young man replied, "Yes, I want to put the coon out." He stood back and put the coon out with a single shot. I think it was at that moment a future coon hunter came to be.

As we returned to the vehicle the happy young man asked why I wanted to take only one coon from the tree and I explained that was how I had been taught. Leave some for seed and you will always have coons to tree; the dogs don't know how many coons are in the tree anyway so one is enough. I was glad to hear the young man asking questions; something that I probably asked my mentors more of than was needed, but questions properly answered allows one to learn.

It was decided, by my Dad, that we would make one more drop before calling it a night as he did not like to hunt all night. I think the young man and I were just getting started but I had to honor Pops request. Instead of moving to a new area we cut the hounds back in the direction of the corn field. In only minutes we had another red hot track going and the hounds were taking it straight up the mountain.

Abner had once again gotten the strike followed by Sheba, Duke and JoJo. The hounds took the track high up the mountain before dropping into another hollow out of hearing, and our long climb began. Following the lengthy climb to the top of a ridge partway up the mountain we were able to hear the echo of the treeing hounds and proceeded in their direction. Walking in to the tree was a sight to behold as we found all four hounds stretched high on the side of a large hardwood. All four were leashed back, the tree shined and another large coon spotted. All hounds were given a little praise and led from the tree; the coon was left to run again, we had taken enough for the night.

Back at the truck tired from the hard climb and also ready to call it a night I told my Dad and the young man that climbs like we had just made was the reason I hunted an accurate tree dog. Even though we didn't take the coon we knew it was there and was satisfied to leave it for another night. Hunting the mountains one does not have to walk to many empty trees before they are ready to get rid of the slick treeing dogs and get something more accurate. You can also know that I have walked to a few of this kind in some rough mountainous areas and will never do so again. Walking to empty trees in rough terrain will make a person despise a slick treeing dog for life. The old timers didn't walk to a lot of empty trees and there is no sense in doing so in this day and time.

Our night of hunting completed and ready to head for home I gave the young man my contact information in case he wanted to hunt again and dropped him at his house. That night made a coon hunter of the young man as he is still hunting today, and the amazing thing was that only the next day the young man phoned asking to go hunting again. The sport needs young people such as that to keep it alive; give a young person the opportunity to experience the great sport and sound of the hounds if ever given the chance, you'll be glad you did.

The young man hunted many nights with me in the following years and he was thankful for the opportunity to hunt with good hounds just as I had been so many years before. My Dad and I would still occasionally hunt until I sold JoJo; following that he just didn't care much for it.

Duke and JoJo were sold at the same time; both were good hounds that treed all the coons one could ask to tree. Both were accurate and treed the tracks they struck and stayed put once treed, they were good hounds but I was looking for something a little more balanced and a little bit better. Both hounds were no aggravation of any sort, and maybe they were good as I was going to find, but I never stopped looking for that hound with just a little bit extra. JoJo and Duke were replaced with one of the most powerful, completely balanced young Bluetick hounds of the time; probably the only reason I sold them.

Both Abner and Sheba stayed at my home until the end maybe by fate as Sheba was killed by a bulldog while at a friend's home, a waste of a great female and a sad loss. Abner did not live a long life but he was a good hound and the kind I liked to hunt. Both Sheba and Abner were only two of the many good hounds out of Penny's Kentucky Kojak at the time. The magazines were full of Kojak sired hounds being promoted at that time. I owned and hunted with many good hounds from Kojak and felt that Abner was good as any of them. Past owners of Kojak also said Abner was one of the better hounds sired by him but they also stated that Kojak's Talking Tom was possibly the best of the bunch. I never had the opportunity to hunt with Tom but I later owned several good hounds sired by him and know he reproduced some good hounds. If I would have been given the opportunity to hunt with Tom and he'd proven good as everyone surmised, I would have tried to own him if he could have been bought. Good hounds of the past are now only a distant dream, but more will eventually follow.

I hunted the mountains hard in my younger years and will again hunt them in the future, only at a slower pace. I always tried to hunt my hounds in an assortment of different terrain so as to have them accustomed to different type territory. I competition hunted a lot at that time and a top hound accustomed to mountains, swamps, cutover, river bottoms, patch woods, flatland, fences and rough terrain, etc., of all types will perform anywhere cut loose. Try a variety of terrain it'll help improve the dogs' ability and performance. The extra work can and will pay off in the end.

TIMES ARE CHANGIN'

12

The two hunters' one old and experienced, the other young, watchful, and willing to learn, slowly walked along the old railroad bed. The eldest hunter was leading a small blue speckled female, a product from years of old mountain breeding. The little females name was "Sue" and she would tree anything that went up a tree. Sue put meat on the table and hides in the shed for the old hunter.

The young hunter had on his leash a short coupled, blanket backed, red headed Treeing Walker female which he called "Belle." Ole Belle was the first registered hound the young hunter had owned; she was sired by a famous hound named "House's Chief". Belle's preferred game was coon, but she would tree anything that climbed, occasionally running a fox until she crossed a coon track and switched over onto the track and treed.

The two hunters favored hunting the mountains over the flatland, but with heavy snow and ice predicted to fall that night, and deer season open, they instead chose the flatland near the foot of the mountain. They hunted the area periodically and always had good luck there. It was a large, heavily wooded tract of land with roads on two sides, a pulpwood yard on one side and the old railroad bed they were now walking ran along the other side. There wasn't a creek or stream running through the woods, but it was swampy lowland and contained several ponds as a source of water. The night was cold and wintry with the temperature rapidly decreasing. It was a good night to tree a heap of game.

As the hunters approached the location where they would turn the two dogs loose, the older hunter looked skyward as he pivoted in a full observing circle. "Don't seem to be able to find the Little Dipper, or any stars as far as that goes," said he.

"I have my compass and I'll get a reading," replied the young hunter as he removed the device from his pocket. His father had taught him that the compass, when used correctly, could save a lot of walking because the stars are not always visible to guide you from the woods. "Well, I've been huntin' for many a moon and never had any use for one; always used the stars for direction," countered the elder hunter. With that said and a compass reading taken by the younger of the two, the dogs were released into the woods.

"Sure would rather have hunted the mountain but with deer season open didn't want to take the chance of losing a dog. Those deer hunters might shoot an old dog, especially if they thought it might be runnin' the deer off," said the old hunter.

As the hunters walked sluggishly along in the direction Sue and Belle had gone the snow began to lightly fall. The silence of the night was suddenly broken by the sound of the two dogs in the distance. Neither of the dogs had opened on track but they were treed when they barked. "I guess they have an ole grinner up a bush," stated the older hunter. "Yeah, let's go get it," replied the other.

The snow was getting heavier by the minute as the hunters approached the treed dogs. As the two hunters walked into the tree they begin to shine and both were surprised at what they saw, not a possum or a coon, but a medium sized bobcat. The cat was pacing back and forth on a narrow limb, peering nervously downward. The older hunter raised the rifle and put the cat out before it had a chance to jump and run. The cat was already dead before Sue and Belle grabbed it, in fact it was dead before it hit the ground.

"Never seen a cat treed that easy in all my years, dogs must have slipped up on it," said the old hunter. The hunters retrieved the bobcat from the dogs and placed it in the game bag. The dogs were then sent deeper into the big woods.

The frozen ground was quickly becoming blanketed by a carpet of fluffy white. Sue and Belle had been hunting for a quarter hour before Belle struck with a loud, clear bawl followed by Sue's high pitched chops and squalls. They were working the track in a low swampy area the snow had yet to cover. The track began to warm up and Sue began to bark sparingly, she suddenly let loose a couple of high pitched squalls and started to tree with a series of triple chops. Belle came on the tree before the first set of chops could leave Sue's mouth; she located with a wobbling bawl, choking down to a steady chop. The hunters began walking toward the treed dogs as another dog came on the tree with them. The dog located with an impressive bugle voice and turned it over to a booming chop.

As the hunters walked in to the tree they saw a dark blue hound of medium size standing straight up on the tree alongside Sue and Belle. The hunters did not recognize the hound or the owners name which the collar revealed. They both assumed there was another hunter in the woods. The tree was shined and a coon was spotted. After waiting an appropriate period of time for the other hunter to arrive, it was determined that the Blue hound must be lost, and a hunter would not be coming to retrieve him. The hunters put the coon out to the dogs, and after allowing them to get a taste it was placed into the game bag. The dogs were then released to hunt deeper into the woods.

Sue and Belle went hunting soon as released; the Blue hound had disappeared after the coon was taken from the dogs. The snow had now accumulated to a depth of several inches, and was falling in a flurry. There would be a knee deep snow by morning if it didn't soon cease. As the hunters stood viewing the falling snow with pleasure their thoughts were distracted by the piercing squalls of Sue locating a tree. Belle soon backed Sue and the hunters walked in the direction of the treed dogs. As they walked along they heard the Blue hound trailing farther in with a splendid carrying mouth. The hunters shined Sue and Belle's tree as they approached; spotted a possum low in the tree and let them have it. The possum was placed in the game bag with their other game and the dogs released to hunt again.

The Blue hound, still working his track, was soon joined by Sue and Belle. "My, My what a mouth that Blue hound has, and he is blessed with outstanding tracking ability to move that track as he's doing in these conditions," said the elder hunter. Sue and Belle were attempting to trail with the Blue hound but with great difficulty. The Blue hound soon let loose his impressive bugle locate and started treeing. He was half-heartedly backed by the other two dogs. The hunters shined the tree as they were walking in, quickly spotting the eyes of a coon peering from high above. "We'll leave this one as our dogs didn't tree it and they aren't doing much of a job backing this fine Blue hound," said the elder hunter to his apprentice.

With the snow still steadily falling the hunters decided to turn the dogs loose once more and hunt in the direction of their vehicle. Sue and Belle promptly went hunting; the Blue hound had already disappeared into the night. The Blue hound soon struck another track and quickly put a tree on the end of it. He received very little help from Sue and Belle on this track too, but both females readily backed the Blue hound on the tree, seemingly more sure of it being in this tree than the last. The two hunters continued on to the tree, shined and spotted another coon. Sue and Belle were leashed, the older hunter then removed a piece of paper from his pocket, chipped a piece of bark from a tree and used it to write the name and phone number which was on the Blue hound's collar.

"We aren't taking this coon either because our dogs didn't tree it, but I'll own that Blue hound if he can be bought," stated the elder of the two as they walked from the tree leading their dogs. The Blue hound came off the tree and disappeared into the night; back in the direction he had come.

The hunters had become turned around because of the snow; with everything white it all looked the same. The younger of the two removed the compass from his pocket, pointed the direction they needed to go, and their walk began. They came out onto the railroad bed at almost the exact point where they entered the woods.

"You can read that compass fairly well," stated the elder hunter to the younger.

As the two hunters loaded their dogs into the dog box they heard the loud bugle locate of the Blue hound once again; he then began to tree loud and steady. The last thing they heard as they climbed into their vehicle was the steady chop of the Blue hound, deep in the section of woods.

Two weeks passed before the two hunters got together for another hunt. The elder came by to pick the younger up, as he was loading Belle into the dog box he saw not Sue in the box but the Blue hound that had come to them while hunting in the Flatwoods.

"That hounds name is "Jim" and I've been hunting him every night, alone, just the two of us. He's a good one, won't run anything but a coon," the old hunter stated.

They drove toward the mountain where a hunt had been arranged with another hunter who lived on the mountain. The other hunter whose name was "Frank" owned two young hounds and asked to take them along. Frank grabbed his rifle, his two hounds and walked from the yard, the other two hunters followed along leading Jim and Belle.

"Turn them dogs up this creek," said Frank as they came to a stream running off the mountain.

Jim quickly struck a track and was joined by Belle and the two young hounds. The dogs run the track up the stream, high up on the mountainside before crossing into another hollow, out of hearing. The hunters climbed the ridge getting within earshot of the dogs once again. As they topped the ridge Jim's impressive locate was heard, on the next ridge over, followed by the wobbling bawl locate of Belle. Jim and Belle were chopping hard before the young hounds settled in on the tree. The three hunters proceeded on to the tree, spotted a coon, and Frank put it out before the hunters had time to leash their dogs.

The old hunter then leashed Jim and the younger did the same with Belle, Frank made no effort to leash his two hounds. Suddenly one of the young hounds grabbed the coon and run off down the mountain with it, the other young hound followed in hot pursuit.

"That coon wasn't much size anyway, maybe we'll tree another one," Frank said.

Keeping their opinions to themselves the other two hunters released Jim and Belle back into the hollow. Jim quickly struck another track and Belle joined in to help. The track was cold and had to be worked into a good running track; which was soon done. The two young hounds had not been seen since they ran off with the coon. Unexpectedly the two young hounds topped the ridge running a red hot track; they were coming up the ridge where the hunters were standing. Almost instantaneously a large buck deer ran passed the hunters with the young hounds close on his heels. The young hounds then crossed the mountain and went out of hearing range. Not a word was spoken between the hunters, until Jim and Belle were heard locating another tree; far in the distance.

"Well boy's my hounds won't be back tonight and I've about had enough," Frank said as he walked away; back in the direction of his home, taking the rifle with him.

The two hunters looked to one another and both decided that would be their first and last hunt with Frank. The younger hunter then took a compass reading of the treeing Jim and Belle, and they walked toward the treed hounds. When the hunters finally arrived at the tree, it was a large tree with a hollow three feet above the ground. Upon further examination a coon was seen sitting a few feet up inside the hole. Jim and Belle were leashed back from the tree while the old hunter cut a flexible tree branch with a fork on one end. He then sat down and began to twist the coon from the hole using the forked branch. The coon was pulled from the hole, but the young hunter was a little too slow releasing the hounds and the coon run about fifty feet before being treed again. "Well we tried, we'll never be able to get him now, let's get out of here," said the old hunter.

Following a long walk back to Frank's home, where their vehicle was parked the two hunters loaded their hounds and began the drive home. On the drive home the old hunter told the story of his acquiring "Jim" whose registered name was "PR Snake Creek Blue Jim". After the hunt where the Blue hound came to the hunters in the Flatwoods the old hunter had been unable to sleep that night, for thinking about the Blue hound. Early the following morning he had phoned the number off the hound's collar to inquire about the hound. The owner, who lived on the other side of the Flatwoods asserted the hound to be a top coonhound, that run coon only. He no longer coon hunted but occasionally turned the hound loose to hunt on his own. He went on to say "Yes" he would sell the hound and give a two week trial on him. He had raised the hound from a pup and treed many coons with him; he should please any coonhunter. The old hunter told Jim's owner he would be over to get the Blue hound soon as possible.

The old hunter fought the snow covered roads and soon had the Blue hound in his possession. After acquiring the hound he had hunted him every night, even on the frozen snow, and the hound had shown coon at the end of his tracks. On the evening the two hunters were to hunt with Frank the old hunter had phoned Jim's previous owner to inform him he would be keeping Jim. The old hunter was accustomed to hunting dogs that treed any and all game, but after hunting Jim his customs would soon be transformed.

The day following their hunt at Frank's, the young hunter received a phone call from his elder friend, to say he had lost his wallet the night before. He thought it had been lost while at the tree where he twisted the coon from the hole. After much discussion the two hunters agreed to return to the mountain and try locating the tree. The hunters parked at Frank's and walked to the ridge where the first coon had been treed. The younger of the two removed his compass from his pocket, took a reading, and pointed, "That direction," he said.

The hunters then proceeded to walk within a few feet of the tree with the hole, and found the wallet, at the base of the tree. They then looked to the tree the coon had run to after being twisted from the hole and discovered the coon still lying on a limb high in the tree.

"Glad we didn't take that coon. Don't reckon I would have found my wallet if you hadn't taken that compass reading, think I'll buy me one. Used to be happy with my dogs treeing coon, possum or whatever, now since getting Jim, all I want them to tree is coon. I guess you are never too old to learn. My how times are changin'," the old hunter smiled and said.

OLE TWO TOES

13

The grizzled old boar coon stood and stretched his weary bones. He had been sleeping on a flat limb near the top of his big den, soaking up a few rays of sun on a cool winter day. He was battle scarred and missing part of his left front foot and most of one ear, but all in all over the years life had been good to him. He had lived his whole life within a five mile radius of his home. After being captured in a steel trap he had lost part of his foot in the act of freeing himself, but he learned from this incident. He had been run by hounds many, many times and savored the thoughts of causing the hounds to hang up on empty trees or entirely losing them from his trail in the rough old swamp that surrounded his home.

When he was young and uneducated, he had been caught on the ground by a couple of young hounds and still carried the scars as a reminder of this episode. Following a fierce fight he narrowly escaped with his life, but just barely, and it had taken weeks for his body to heal. He had learned from this experience too, and he knew if the hounds had been old and seasoned he would not be alive today to think back on it.

During the old coon's life he had lived through hard winters when food was scarce, and he had to scrounge for edibles just to survive. He had also seen good times when the food was abundant and he had corn, fish, nuts, berries and plenty of other things. He was prone to get fat and lazy during these good times. This year was one of the good years and he was fat and out of shape.

Ole Two Toes proceeded to stretch and prepare for his nightly excursions. At dusky dark he came down from his big den and began making his nightly rounds, letting his mind roam to the good times of the past. He thought of his offspring scattered throughout the swamp, but it seemed he never ran across any of them in his part of the swampy domain.

He came upon an old rotten log and dug under it looking for bugs and snails. He soon grew bored with the log and decided to move on. He came upon a large dozer pile at the swamps edge, where trees, stumps and brush had been pushed into a tangled mess.

The old coon crawled into the dozer pile and began looking around for anything of interest, climbing every limb and vine he found in the process. He soon grew tired of the dozer pile and moved into a nearby corn field on the outskirts of the big swamp. He traveled from row to row looking for bits and pieces of corn left from the harvest; found several ears and ate what he wanted.

The dry corn caused a powerful thirst so Two Toes headed for the creek that fed the swamp. He drank until satisfied, looked around and noticed a light far up the creek that aroused his curiosity. He had never explored that far before and decided to investigate, traveling further from his home than he ever had.

The further he traveled the thinner the cover and the smaller the trees became. The light was much further than he had thought, but he eventually came to a clearing containing a small campsite. The old coon stopped at the clearings edge, and looking into the campsite noticed the light that had attracted his attention was a small camp fire. Sitting near the fire was a lone man, heating coffee and preparing tasty smelling food of some sort. As the old coon observed with interest the stillness of the night was suddenly broken by the loud, loud bawl of a big blue hound tied off to the side of the camp. The bawl was followed by several more before the man yelled, "Shut up Mack, you'll get turned loose soon enough."

The old coon decided he had seen enough and turned to start back to his swamp. He traveled back to the corn field, waddled up and down the rows, then climbed up and over the dozer pile into the swamp. He searched the water's edge for crawfish and minnows to munch on. The trip to investigate the light had used up much of his energy; he was now hungry again. He ate as he went, taking a morsel of this and that as he continued his nightly rounds.

The old coon's gnarled ears suddenly perked up as he heard the loud bawl of the big blue hound he had seen at the campsite. He knew from hearing hounds in the past that the hound was now trailing a track, not just barking on the chain. Thinking nothing of it, he went on about his business, wandering farther from his home with every step.

The big blue hound had smelled the old coon when he came investigating the campfire, he had bawled a few times to let his master know he had caught scent of game, with the hope of being released onto the trail. The blue hound patiently waited as his master ate and drank coffee, and proceeded to put on his boots. The man placed the hard hat with the bright light mounted to it upon his head and walked over to the big blue hound and leashed him. He was led to the edge of the clearing and released onto the creek bank, where he immediately smelled the old coon and gave mouth accordingly, signaling his master he had smelled the scent of coon. The big hound drifted down the creek opening with his loud bawl mouth and soon came to the corn field to find the old coon had been everywhere in the field. He quickly sorted the track out and trailed to the dozer pile. He had a little trouble determining the correct direction, but soon came out on the other side and into the swamp.

The old coon had stopped to listen to the big bawl mouthed hound and now knew that the hound was in his swamp. It did not take long for him to decide that the track the hound was trailing was his own. He was still a good distance ahead of the hound, but was also a good stroll from his big, safe den. He knew the swamp well and thought he would hang this hound up on an empty tree or lose him in the moving water of the swamp.

The coon cut across the swamp in the direction of his home and began to climb on every tree he came to. He swam from tree to tree like he had so many times before, knowing that the big bawl mouthed hound would soon hang up on one of the trees. He might even lose the track entirely in the moving water of the swamp.

Two Toes had been careless by traveling so far from his home, and going even further after hearing the big hound trailing his track. He was now thinking about his mistake as he moved as fast as possible back toward his home. Most of the other hounds that had trailed him in the past had either hung up on an empty tree or lost the trail out in the swamp. If they were lucky and actually treed him, he was always safe in his den.

As the coon listened to this hound he realized he was different from the others who had trailed him. This hound had begun to pick up speed and was no longer trailing but was now running to catch. He had not hung up on any of the trees the old coon had crawled up on, nor had he lost the trail in the deep water. He had trailed the track up, drifted, got it up and running, and was now going to run this old coon and force him to tree or fight. Two Toes now saw that he was going to have to run to survive as all of his tricks had failed. He started toward his home as fast as his old legs would carry him. He had to make it to his big safe den, or he was afraid he would not live to run another night.

The coon's old legs just would not move fast enough to let him get away from the big blue hound. The hound was a hundred yards behind him, and then a hundred feet, then only a few feet was separating the hound and his prey. The old coon in his younger days would have turned and fought, but was now forced to climb the nearest tree, which was not much more than a bush.

The big blue hound hit the tree with a roaring locate and began to chop hard as he could, letting his master know that another one had reached the end of the line. The longer the hound treed the harder and louder he barked thought the old coon who was now looking down at the big blue hound and knowing that his time was near its end. After what seemed an eternity the owner of the hound arrived at the tree. He reached down and petted the hound then leashed him back from the tree. The hunter shined his light into the small tree and spotted the old coon; he raised his rifle to give Mack the coon, but suddenly had a change of mind.

The hunter was close enough to see the mangled front foot, the gnarled ears, and the old battle scars. He could see that the once black mask was now gray and even the rings around the tail were gray. The hunter had just listened to one of the best coon races he had ever heard, surely the best he had heard Mack run. After seeing the old coon and knowing that this animal had survived many wars he just couldn't bring himself to kill the old timer. He reached down and retrieved Mack's lead and said, "Ole Buddy, you did a good job on this one but we will get him another time." The hunter walked away leading the big blue hound knowing he had done the right thing.

MISTY

14

Misty was well on her way to being a top hound when she moved from Illinois to Georgia. She was very young and already a dependable night after night coon treeing hound. Misty was a 50 pound, beautiful blue English female that was sired by Dual Grand Champion Fuller's Hopsing and her dam was Grand Champion Oney's Widowmaker. She inherited many of her sire's traits, including a big, coarse bawl mouth, a cold nose, outstanding striking ability, plus track and tree power. I couldn't say what traits came from her mother as I never had the opportunity to hunt with her, but I will say Misty was tough as leather and had a stubborn streak that came from somewhere. I spent many nights following Misty and became chilled more than one cold winter night waiting for her to finish an old bad track. She was cold nosed, much colder than most people like, but she would put a tree on the end of her tracks with a coon in the tree.

One evening as I prepared for a hunt the phone rang and upon answering I heard the voice of my old friend and English breeder Jack Cowgill. Jack said after much thought he had decided to sell Misty. I had known about her for quite a while but Jack didn't want to sell her. He was now going to allow me first option to purchase her. Jack was having some health problems at the time and said if I wanted Misty he would also give me four other reproducing females as he was cutting back on hounds.

Misty's sire, Dual Grand Champion Fuller's Hopsing, a hound that I really enjoyed in the woods had also been purchased from Jack. He said Misty had a big, coarse bawl mouth same as Hopsing and when hunted together it was hard to distinguish between the two. She was also colored like Hopsing only where he was redtick she was bluetick. Misty had never been bred so Jack didn't know what type pups she would produce, but he said she was well worth his asking price if only coon hunted. I advised Jack that I would inform him the following day if I wanted to purchase her or not.

As I loaded the hounds I thought to myself why I had not told Jack, "Yes, I wanted the little female." I then returned to the house and phoned him, letting him know I would drive up to get Misty in a few days. After all I would be getting Misty and four other females that were proven reproducers when bred to old Hopsing, for only the price of Misty. One or two good litters of pups from one of the other proven reproducing females would pay for her. Old Hopsing had sired UKC World Champion Fuller's Red Rooster and many other good hounds, pups from him were sold fast as I could raise them; I just didn't raise very many.

A few days later a friend and I traveled to Illinois to pick Misty up. It was winter and very cold with a chance of heavy snow moving into Illinois, we were attempting to beat the winter storm. After visiting with Jack for a few hours the snow began to fall and we promptly loaded the dogs and hit the highway toward home. Going back to Georgia along with Misty, were four other females Jack had given me. There were two older Redtick female littermates, a Redtick called Grand Champion Peach Tree Freckles and a good little Redtick female called Missy. Freckles and the Redtick female that would come to be named Salacoa Valley Missy along with Misty would produce some outstanding hounds and stay at my kennel until the end. They were the cheapest reproducing females I ever obtained. They would pay for this deal many times over.

As luck would have it we did not make it out of Illinois before a major storm front pushed through and closed most major highways. Stubborn as I was I didn't want to pull over and attempted to drive on at a very slow pace. Following hours of being stranded in the slow moving traffic we finally were able to get off an exit and find a motel with vacancies. Two days later we arrived back in Georgia to a little decent weather, and very eager to hunt Misty.

Misty was given several days to become accustomed to her new surroundings and owners before being put in the woods. According to Jack she was fine tuned and ready to tree coons anywhere turned loose. The other females had not been hunted for quite a while so they would need some work, they would be hunted later. Our plans were to put Misty in the woods alone and then with her sire to see what we had. Those were the two hounds that would be hunted that night.

At that time there was a lot of very good hunting near my home. Located to the north was Cohutta, Grassy or Fort Mountains, some very good mountainous hunting. Traveling west we could hunt Johns Mountain, or go east to the Carter's Lake area. To the south only a few miles there were swamps and river bottoms. I preferred to hunt the mountains but my neighbor "Junior" who would be accompanying me on the hunt did not want to hunt the mountainous terrain. We settled on the swamps and river bottoms, an area with plenty of roads for easy access even if the dogs crossed the river.

The first drop was on a fence row that ran into a large swampy section adjoining the river. Misty was cut loose along the fence row, alone, and went hunting instantly. Only a few minutes passed before she opened two or three times with the same coarse bawl as her sire; she was at the edge of the swamp. She then threw a big coarse locate and began to chop, loud and steady. We listened to her tree for several minutes before beginning the walk to her. On arrival we found her standing at the base of a small tree, looking up and steadily barking. She was not as classy on the tree as her sire but she had what counted, and that was a big coon, which we let her have. Not a bad way to start the night with a new hound.

The next drop both Misty and Hopsing were released along a slough alongside the river. Hopsing was first to open, but only by half a bark before Misty joined in. The track was a good running track and sure enough it was hard to distinguish between the hounds at a distance. They ran the track up the river and around the bluff out of hearing. We drove closer and upon stopping found that both hounds were treed together. Misty was loud as Hopsing and true enough her track mouth sounded similar to his but her tree mouth was different. She treed around 80 heavy chops per minute where he treed at 120 barks or more per minute.

As we walked toward the tree, Junior who was an old coon hunter made the comment that Misty was a nice female if she continued doing as she had. The tree was a large tree with both Hopsing and Misty stretched high on its side. We would learn that Misty treed with her feet on the larger trees, on the smaller ones she would tree at the base and look up but never move. The hounds were leashed back and the tree shined, the coon quickly found high in the tree and put out to the hounds. The land owner who had given us permission to hunt wanted a couple coons or the coon would have been left to run again.

Walking from the tree with both hounds on the leash we decided to cut them loose into a swampy area running away from the river. Both went hunting soon as released and we continued to slowly walk back toward the truck. Hopsing soon struck a track in the distance, far from the river. Only minutes later Misty struck in the opposite direction. Hopsing's track was moving faster than Misty's so we followed him. He soon put a tree on the end of the track with a coon in it; which we left. In the meantime Misty had trailed out of hearing, and we swiftly began walking back toward the truck to drive around and attempt to find her.

We drove around the river bend, stopping at intervals to listen, faintly hearing her across the river and up a hollow on the other side. The hollow Misty was trailing in crossed the highway and I didn't want her crossing to the other side. We rapidly drove to the river bridge and crossed to the other side in an attempt to head Misty off before she reached the highway. Following the route in which the road ran it was at least an 8 mile drive to where the hollow crossed the highway. We drove to this point and stopped to listen. Misty was heard back in the direction of the river but farther in front of us; she was really moving the track. We drove in that direction and turned onto a side road that ran to the river. The next time we stopped Misty was treed solid, near the end of the road we were on.

Continuing to the end of the road to the home of a land owner friend, and stopping in his driveway we found that Misty was treed in his yard. My friend then walked up with his flashlight in hand, and stated he had checked Misty's collar and saw my name on it and knew I'd be along sooner or later. He also stated that she had a big coon up the tree. This was at a time before people began shooting dogs for coming onto their land. This landowner was not a hunter but became interested after seeing Misty treeing the coon. The coon was left to run again even though we were given the option to take it.

Misty steadily improved with age and experience - becoming a hound that would be enjoyed in the woods for many years. She was never entered in a competition hunt, even though she could have won. Misty was broke from off game and used to train young hounds, and for pleasure only. Many relaxing nights were spent by me, and numerous friends, listening to the soothing coarse bawls of Misty and her sire.

When it was decided that Misty would be bred our first choice was to breed her to Grand Nite Champion DeGraves Ace, a Redtick hound I owned. Ace was not an aggressive breeder and the attempts to breed her failed. After conferring with friend and English Breeder

Bob Williams, Misty was bred to her sire Hopsing. Bob said he would purchase the whole litter if she was bred to Hopsing. Misty raised a large litter of the worst colored pups I had ever seen; not a pup was colored like her or Hopsing. True to his word Bob bought the whole litter, ugly as they were.

I didn't keep track of the pups from the first litter as Bob had distributed them out to hunters and friends to start for him. He would later say that most went to pleasure coon hunters to enjoy their loud mouths, trailing ability and tree power. Bob then asked if I would breed Misty to Grand Nite Champion Jewell's Tapp, an older Redtick hound out of my kennel. He stated that he would also purchase that whole litter. The mating of Tapp and Misty was made but she did not take; the cross was never attempted again. Bob went on to say he would buy Misty's pups from whatever stud I decided to breed her to next time around. He liked Misty in the woods, stating that she had coondog sense and put that into her pups.

Misty was coon hunted hard for the next year and a half and was not bred. She was also hunted by friends and family who wanted to go tree a coon or two and come in early. She saw lots of hunting and treed a lot of coons. By this time her sire had passed away and I had sold Ace and Tapp. I had a top young Bluetick named "Scooter" that I thought about mating her with, but I would have had to single register the pups if they amounted to anything. She was finally bred to Grand Nite Champion Rock 'N' Roll Rowdy, a good Redtick hound that I owned.

The cross between Misty and Rowdy produced a nice litter of pups of which only five lived. Three of the five were sold to Bob Williams and the other two were kept by my hunting buddy and me.

140

All five made good coon treeing hounds, with the two we kept starting young and finishing out quickly. As far as I know none of the five were ever entered in a competition hunt, they were only pleasure hunted. At some point I had the opportunity to hunt with all five and they were loud mouthed, track driving, tree dogs. With this thought in mind and liking what we had seen from Misty's offspring she would be bred for the final time to the Bluetick "Scooter," a proven reproducer by this time. The pups from this cross were going to be kept by my hunting buddy and me. They would be single registered if they turned out.

At that time it had been over two years since Misty had whelped her last litter of pups. She was still being hunted by friends and family when they wanted to take a short hunt and tree a coon. After being bred to Scooter they continued to hunt her, hoping the exercise would be good for her. Within a few weeks of her whelping date Misty was taken out for what was to be a short hunt, she was lost and never again seen. She was thought to have drowned in the river. She had given years of pleasurable hunts and produced some good hounds. The arrival of the pups from Misty and Scooter was anticipated as I had hopes of a super hound from the cross. I enjoyed hunting Misty's sire 'Hopsing,' and the Bluetick 'Scooter' as much as any of the dogs I ever hunted with, and was hoping for something comparable to the two. I'll always wonder but never know how the pups would've turned out.

THE LAST NIGHT OF THE SEASON

15

The three blue hounds had been trailing the track for ten minutes before getting it up and running. The animal they were running was about to have to go somewhere, and real quick like. The hounds had been released into the large section of timber on a stream that fed a large fishing lake, and the track quickly struck where the spillway ran from the lake.

Our hunting party, on this night, consisted of Alan, a neighbor youngster, my old hunting buddy James, who I had not hunted with for several years, and me. The hounds being hunting were Grand Champion, Grand Nite Champion Davis' Blue Scooter, three years old at the time, Grand Champion, Grand Nite Champion Moyer 's Blue Chubbs, which was two years old and a son of Scooter, and Grand Champion, Grand Nite Champion Harris' Rose, a four year old female. They were all Blueticks, and hounds that could absolutely tree coons in the cold winter months when no leaves were on the trees.

We were enjoying the race but the hounds were going in the wrong direction and were almost out of hearing. The decision was made to drive around and try to avoid a long walk in rough cutover, hilly terrain. The hounds had gotten really deep and were sure to cross into the hollow on the opposite side of a small mountain they were about to top.

Following a drive of several miles to the other side of the mountain, and stopping to listen, all three hounds were heard treed solid. They were still deep in the country and a lengthy walk from our location. Proceeding to, and parking at, an old barn owned by a friend our walk to the treeing hounds began. Walking across a cattle filled pasture, following the shallow creek and soon coming to a standstill at the edge of a really rough looking beaver pond, which had not been there a few years earlier. It looked as if the next 100 yards into the tree was going to be very difficult to negotiate.

The creek had been damned up by the beavers making the area extremely hard to navigate. The only benefit being it was now coon territory. The hounds were either in the beaver pond or across on the other side, hopefully the water was not too deep. After a slow tedious walk we managed to arrive at the tree without getting wet.

As we approached the tree all three hounds were found to be on the same tree. Rose was stretched high as possible, shelling it out over 100 barks per minute. Chubbs was up on the tree alongside Rose treeing with his short, loud steady bawl. Scooter was a few feet back, standing in knee deep water letting us know the coon was up there with a loud chop and bawl.

The hounds were leashed back and the tree shined. An excited young Alan quickly spotted the coon, and asked to dispatch it. The coon turned out to be a large old boar coon with only a partial tail. This would be Alan's trophy for the night.

The beaver pond appeared to be such a cooney looking place, containing an abundance of big timber that the hounds were again cut loose on the ponds outer edge. We assumed we could maneuver around on the beaver decks if the hounds treed out in the pond. The hounds rapidly shot from the leashes and into the dark. Scooter was first to strike with a loud squall bawl followed by the loud clear bawl of Chubbs. Rose opened on a separate track directly behind where we stood. She was treed when she barked.

We walked in to Rose and spotted a coon lying in a fork halfway up the tree, leashed her, gave her a little praise, and walked away to listen for Scooter and Chubbs. Rose's coon was left to run again, as normally only one coon per night was taken. Some nights all were left because it had not been too many years in the past that the coon population was pretty thin in the area.

Scooter and Chubbs were working their track in the beaver pond. Rose was cut in to them and quickly joined in; all three hounds were now back together on one track. The track was not very good; it appeared the coon had been feeding in the water and on the beaver decks. The hounds struggled, but soon had it up and running, swiftly bringing it out of the beaver pond. The three hounds were really moving the track with Scooter and Chubbs giving plenty of mouth and Rose opening only occasionally, trying to get out front. It was going to be a very difficult accomplishment for her to achieve as both hounds could really run a track.

The coon was run hard for ten minutes before the hounds suddenly slammed a tree with it being hard to determine which one located first. Twenty minutes of hard walking and the tree was finally seen. A tree located on the side of the mountain back in the direction of where the hounds had first been released. All three were on the tree, a small hardwood in the middle of a rough patch of cutover timber. The hounds were covered with mud and upon shining the tree and spotting the coon we noted it was also covered in mud. The hounds were leashed and led from the tree, leaving the coon to run again.

Walking away from the tree and discussing the good time that we were having it was decided to cut the hounds loose one more time, back toward the beaver pond as it was in the direction of the truck anyway. This was almost a big mistake.

Forty five minutes passed as we slowly walked back to the beaver pond without hearing a bark. It was decided that the hounds had crossed back over the mountain and gotten out of hearing, or possibly crossed the beaver pond and followed the creek to the four-lane highway a few miles from where we had parked.

We walked back to the truck to check the tracker and determine the hounds' location. An hour and a half had passed since they were last released. The tracker showed the hounds to be in the direction of the beaver pond, but only deeper. They were not across the mountain as the tracker would be unable to receive a signal from there. As we were discussing our plans the hounds came into hearing, and they were running to catch, coming across the beaver pond then crossing the pasture, following the creek. The creek bank was treeless where it crossed the pasture and the hounds appeared to be running in the shallow creek as they crossed the cattle filled pasture. They were heading in the direction of the four-lane highway. Not a good thing.

James and I knew that the hounds were going to cross the highway if they didn't catch the animal first. We were even beginning to wonder if they could be after fast game because of the extremely fast pace it was moving. We quickly drove in the direction of the highway to try and head the hounds off. Stopping a couple hundred yards from the highway where the creek ran alongside the access road we were on before running under the four-lane in a large culvert. The hounds were almost upon us as Alan and I ran in toward the creek to try and catch the three hounds before they crossed the highway. Even though it was late there was still traffic on the highway and we didn't want to take a chance of the hounds being hit by a car.

Scooter was out front coming down the middle of the creek running with his head up and screaming. Chubbs was a few feet behind him, and Rose a few feet behind Chubbs. We managed to catch Rose, but Scooter and Chubbs crossed under the highway, in the big culvert.

Once on the other side there were some small trees along the creek bank and the coon made it only a short distance before he climbed. Alan and I walked back to the truck, loaded Rose into the box and drove to the other side of the highway. James smiling widely the whole time stated, "Now that's how a Blue Dog is supposed to run a coon."

We walked in to the tree and observed the coon which looked like a small bear cub sitting in a bush. Scooter and Chubbs were treeing hard and really wanted this coon and Alan wanted to climb the tree and knock it out, or even shoot it out. The old coon had run for his life and he deserved to live to run again, he was left in the tree for the next season. This was the last night of the coon season and we had seen coon at the end of every track. The last track could have been a disaster with the hounds crossing the highway, but all ended well.

James and I had coon hunted since I was Alan's age, he was an old time coon hunter that would hunt all night every night. Alan was an up and coming coon hunter, new to the sport. The companionship was the best as we had all enjoyed this night and left coons for seed. Remember to leave some for the next year.

BLUE POWER—YOUNG AND OLD

16

The big loud bawl of the ancient hound could be heard far in the distance, trailing a track that many dogs would never have given mouth on. The hounds name was Nite Champion Russell's Blue Smoker, possibly one of, if not the last living son of the great Smokey River Blue Diamond Jim. Smoker was around thirteen years old, but the old hound was still in good physical condition, being able to hunt nightly and at times treeing coons that other dogs never knew were in the woods; making it look easy. "That old hound still has a good mouth even at his age, and can really move a cold track," stated Philip.

Philip was a coonhunter who wanted to breed his good female to either Smoker or the other good young hound we were hunting that night. The other outstanding young hound was a two year old hound named Grand Nite Champion Coz' Sparetime Spanky, a hound sired by Dual Grand Champion Russ Treein' Blue Luke. Spanky was a top young hound that was virtually unknown to the coon hound world at that time, but he would make his mark as time passed. Spanky would win many, many major coonhound events which included the Purina outstanding Bluetick hound of the year for 1989 and 1990, numerous Breed Days and 5th place high scoring Bluetick in the 1990 A.K.C World Championship, and then rebound to win the A.K.C. World Championship in 1991. Spanky could very well be the winningest Bluetick hound in history, not to mention that he sired countless good hounds. Philip had come to see the two hounds in the woods and determine which he wanted to breed to. I was always happy to show my hounds in the woods, hunters then knew the type hound they were breeding to; no guesswork involved. Smoker and Spanky were cut loose into one of my favorite hunting spots, a swampy area atop some rolling hills. The two hounds had separated with Smoker getting deep and striking a cold feed track, but moving it at a steady pace. Spanky didn't hunt as deep as Smoker and did not cover him when he struck. He soon had a track of his own going, opening only occasionally with a distinguishing bawl mouth, moving the track a great distance in a short period of time before exploding with a screaming locate, immediately turning it over to a hard loud chop. As Spanky began to tree; Smoker trailing his track along the creek, went out of hearing range. We walked in to Spanky's tree to find him stretched high on the side of a large oak surrounded by knee deep water. I leashed Spanky to a small nearby bush, and we then began to shine the tree. A large coon was quickly found sprawled on a limb midway up the tree. Leaving the coon to run again we walked back to the truck to begin the task of locating Smoker. "That Spanky is one nice tree dog," commented Philip as we walked from the tree. "Yes he is, and best of all he is very accurate and does not move once treed," I replied.

Once back at the truck I checked the tracker and received a strong signal in the direction Smoker had been trailing. The tree switch was also registering we then began to drive in that direction. I knew exactly where we would find him and my calculations proved true as we stopped to listen. Smoker was treeing as hard as his old heart would allow, right in the midst of a swamp located on the grounds of the historic Barnsley Gardens; lying in ruins at the time, but now a National Landmark and tourist attraction. I have ran many coon into that swamp, in times long before Barnsley Gardens was renovated and opened to the public. If hunting in that general area, even now, you are subject to run a coon onto the grounds of the Historic site; seems the coon know where to run.

We parked on the road and hurriedly walked into the thigh deep water to retrieve the grand old Blue hound. On arrival at the tree we witnessed a sight to behold, stretched high on the side of a dead snag stood the half submerged dark blue hound. Smoker was a true straight up, belly rubbing, slobber mouthed tree dog that would make any houndsman take notice and appreciate a tree dog. Sure enough he had a coon sitting atop the snag. Smoker was also a very accurate hound that had the coon most of the time. Oh! What I would have given to have owned him when he was young; he would have been known by the entire coonhound world. With little time to admire this great tree dog I quickly leashed him and we withdrew from the area, walked back to the truck, loaded Smoker and drove to another nearby woods.

"Man, that Smoker is also a tree dog," Philip stated as we drove away. "It's going to be hard to decide which hound I breed to."

Following a drive of several miles both hounds were again cut into a good wooded section of mixed timber and small streams; a good place to tree a coon. Both hounds went hunting and only minutes passed before Spanky loaded up on a laid up coon, not barking on the ground but treed when he opened. Spanky was one of the all time great lay-up dogs of his era or any era. Smoker did not cover this tree either but treed a quick track of his own, opening twice on the ground before rolling up on the tree with a big bawl locate. "Philip is getting to see some good dog work I thought to myself," as we stood and relished the sound of the treeing hounds.

"Well, I see both dogs will hold tree pressure and they are both sure enough good tree dogs with good volume. You think they both have coon in their trees?" An animated Philip asked.

"I don't know for sure but I'd be willing to bet they do. We'll soon see. Which one do you want to go to first?" I inquired. "Doesn't matter to me as I don't think either one is going to move," replied Philip. Spanky's tree was the first shined as he was closest and had also made his tree first. He was putting on a show at the tree, as always, and he did have a small coon up a little tree. Following a small amount of praise Spanky was led from his tree and on to Smoker's. As we walked within sight of the tree Philip exclaimed, "There's eyes up there as I just seen them!"

I leashed Spanky back and gave Smoker a pet on the head before leashing him back too. Shining the tree we spotted two small coons sitting in the tree. I suppose we had gotten into a litter of coon and treed three of them. Having a good night and proud of both hounds we headed back to the truck leading the hounds. It was getting late but Philip wanted to make one more drop, hopefully to see the two hounds on a track and tree together. That was okay with me as we were having a great hunt and seeing some good dog work.

We decided to cut the hounds into the timber on the opposite side of the road, which prevented having to move to another location. There was also some good hunting in that tract of timber. Both hounds immediately went hunting in a hard run, Smoker swiftly struck a track and Spanky joined in- just what we were waiting for. The track was not very good but maybe we would get to hear the hounds work together and possibly end up on the same tree at the end of the trail.

Spanky could drift an old bad track and get away from other dogs at times, but old Smoker was coon smart and was having none of that. Both hounds drifted the track deep into the section of timber and Spanky was heard locating the tree first, but only by a fraction of a second. We listened to the hounds' tree for several minutes before beginning the long walk to them.

Approaching the tree we found Spanky treeing at the base of the tree and Smoker lying against the side of a large hollow oak. This was true Blue tree power at its best. Both hounds were leashed back before we began searching the tree. After a scant time we determined the coon was on the inside as nothing was seen on the outside. We then commenced the long walk back to the truck. Philip said he had seen enough, but was still undecided on which hound he would breed to. He resolved the dilemma by flipping a coin. In the end Spanky was the hound his female was bred to; probably the first female ever bred to him. The female delivered a sizable litter that lived only a few weeks before expiring to corona disease.

Old Smoker came to my kennel from the kennel of Tom Russell in Michigan. I kept him only a short period of time before selling him. Several people bred to him while I owned him and he still produced large litters. I wish I would have had semen collected and frozen from him as he produced some good hounds. I also wish I could have owned him as a young hound; if that would have been the case he would have been Granded and then some, and would never have departed my kennel. I bought Smoker from Tom Russell over the phone and on his word and he was exactly as Tom described him. Hounds such as Smoker were few and far between. Tom originally purchased Smoker from Warren Haslouer as a young hound.

Spanky was located for me by Russ Downing of Wisconsin. I originally purchased Spanky for Earl Lockard to hunt in the competition hunts; I asked Russ if he knew of a good young hound that was easy to call. Russ replied he knew of just the hound and Spanky was that hound. Spanky was only a Nite Champion when I purchased him, he was Granded out while in my kennel by Earl Lockard. Spanky won many hunts with Earl as his handler, one of his big wins was overall winner of the 1989 Treeing Walker Days, one of the largest hunts ever; and many more.

Spanky was also handled by Jerry Winn while in my kennel; Jerry did much winning with Spanky and also bred numerous females to him. Jerry handled Spanky to his 5th place win in the 1990 A.K.C. World Championship and also to the overall win in the 1991 A.K.C. World Championship. I bought Spanky on the word of Russ Downing and he was much better than Russ allowed; probably one of the best deals I ever received in a dog deal. Spanky's registration papers were signed over to Dave Dean in late 1995 knowing that Dave was the devoted Bluetick breeder that he is and hoping that Spanky could help do his part for a great breed of hound.

These two hounds were great Blue hounds of the past, Blue hounds that could compete against dogs of any breed and win their share and more.

A HUNT AT THE RED

BARN

17

As tradition continued a Christmas night coon hunt was planned by friends and family. We wanted to hunt an area where several coons could be treed. With this in mind I thought of the idea spot. My belief is the rougher the area is the more game that area is home to. Rough terrain defined as cutover, blow down, briars, thickets, rough mountains, beaver ponds, deep swamps, uncrossable creeks and rivers, etc., etc. The harder the walking and rougher the terrain it is probable there are coons in the area if food is available to support them.

We loaded three hounds that I enjoyed hunting, and headed to a favorite, lifelong hunting spot. All three hounds were balanced, cold nosed, loud mouthed, first strike and first tree type hounds. We were going to hunt Grand Champion, Grand Nite Champion Davis' Blue Scooter, Grand Champion, Grand Nite Champion Sugar Creek J.R. and a good son of J.R., Grand Nite Champion Raef's Big John- three coon dogs.

Scooter was a four year old Bluetick sired by the great reproducing hound, "Nite Champion Uchtman's Blue Rebel," with his dam being, "Nite Champion Stower's Blue Sadie Mae." Scooter's sire Rebel was a top reproducer of coon dogs and reproducers - a hound that should have been bred to more often. Rebel was owned by Wilbern Uchtman of Gainesville, Missouri. Scooter inherited the ability to reproduce coondogs and was himself a highly intelligent, top coondog at a young age. Scooter hunted hard and deep, taking his tracks as they came, hot or cold. He knew where to strike a coon and how to run a track, hot or cold. He ran track with a loud screaming squall bawl, coming on the tree with a good locate and treeing with a loud chop and bawl. On smaller trees he would tree back from the tree when other hounds were on it, but he stayed put regardless. Scooter was very accurate, he liked to stay split from other hounds, and would by-pass dogs hung up on an empty tree, putting the correct tree at the end of the track. He also possessed the ability to tree cold lay-ups without barking on the ground. Scooter was a hound with looks and ability.

J.R. was a good looking seven year old Blue English hound sired by the great English Redtick, "Grand Champion, Grand Nite Champion Pinehill True boy," and his dam was "Champion Little's

Copper Penny". Trueboy sired many good hounds, he was owned by Bobby Rachaels of Lincolnton, Georgia. J.R. also inherited the ability to reproduce top hounds, and was himself a top coondog. J.R. hunted hard, a top strike dog, not picking his tracks, but running them to catch, hot or cold, with a loud clear bawl. He came on the tree with an outstanding bawl locate turning it over to a never ending loud, hard chop. J.R. would not pull after he located a tree; he was a very accurate hound, good about having a coon that could be seen in most trees he made.

John was a four year old English Redtick sired by J.R., his dam was "Grand Nite Champion Raefs Freckles." He was a top coondog, with coondog ancestors. John went hunting hard; he did not look back and did not pick his tracks. He struck quick with a loud booming bawl mouth, and was an outstanding track dog that drifted a track. John was a one bark locator with a loud, long bawl locate, turning it over to a hard, loud ringing chop. John would not pull and had a coon the majority of the time he treed.

The area we planned to hunt was extremely rough; a deep river sized creek which was almost uncrossable surrounded the perimeter. Over the years a few large trees had been cut or had fallen across the creek, at different intervals, for crossing. Drainage ditches crossed fields where corn was grown, with the fields backing up to the creek. The creek banks and edges of the drainage ditches were a tangled mess of briars, underbrush and gnarly old trees. Across the creek the rough terrain really began, with old growth timber, rough rolling hills, thickets, overgrown swampy arcas, and cutover from years gone by.

I hunted this area for many years, treeing coon there when they couldn't be treed elsewhere. While hunting the area years earlier an old hunting buddy said, "You know we always tree coon here because it's so rough nobody else hunts it." He was speaking truth, even so, we enjoyed many nights of hunting in the area. The area received its name "Red Barn" due to a large red barn on the hillside overlooking the creek. Hunters used the "Red Barn" as an area to park, turning their dogs down a hollow toward the creek.

As our small group entered the field lane leading to the Red Barn, eyes were spotted across the field, at the edge of a drainage ditch, but the hounds did not strike from the box. We drove on to the Red Barn, released the hounds toward the creek and prepared for the hunt. As everyone finished readying themselves for the hunt the stillness of the night was suddenly broken by the high pitched squall bawl of Scooter, followed by a booming bawl from John. They were together across the creek and moving at a good pace. J.R. suddenly opened with a loud bawl, behind us, on the drainage ditch where we had seen the eyes. He was moving his track also.

John and Scooter quickly treed across the creek. J.R treed on our side, he had run his track along the drainage ditch onto the creek bank, coming treed on a willow tree a few feet from the foot log we would have to cross going to Scooter and John. We stopped at J.R.'s tree first, found the coon, leashed him and proceeded to the other tree, leaving the coon to run again. Scooter and John had what appeared to be a nice sized coon up a small tree. It was also left to run again. After walking a short distance from the tree the hounds were released into a tangled jungle of underbrush engulfed by standing water.

158

Our intent was to put a coon out to the hounds if we could make a tree with all three on it. It would eventually happen but later on in the night; a track and tree well worth the wait. As we stood and waited, Scooter once again struck with his screaming bawl- he was alone. John and J.R. momentarily struck a track of their own, far to the left. Our small group listened and contemplated the long hard walk we would encounter if the hounds remained split and treed their tracks. There would be no driving around to them, just hard walking- the old fashioned way.

We stood on a ridge top, enjoying the cool night and listening to some good track work. Both tracks had picked up speed, after twenty minutes Scooter located and treed. We slowly walked to him and found his coon on the outside. Some of the hunters wanted to give it to him, but we decided against it. Walking away from the tree leading Scooter, we heard John go on a tree with one loud, long locate and J.R. quickly backed him. Following a lengthy and rough walk we arrived at the tree, quickly spotting two coons sitting high in the tree. John and J.R. were given a little praise and led away from the tree. The coons were left to run again.

With all dogs on the leashes and two ridges over from the trucks, we decided to cut them back loose in the direction of the Red Barn. All three left the leash in a hard run, all going in the same general direction. Easing along the ridge reminiscing of past hunts our conversation was suddenly disrupted by a booming bawl from John. Four bawls later, J.R. joined with a loud bawl immediately followed by a squall bawl from Scooter. We had finally accomplished what we were waiting for; a track with all the hounds on it.

The three hounds were working in a large swampy blow down area. A tornado had touched down at some point in time, cutting a wide tangled path toward the creek and connecting fields. The hounds worked the track in the direction of the creek experiencing an occasional loss, but one or the other would pick it back up. At first the track was old and seemed hard for the hounds to work, but it quickly warmed up. As the hounds approached the creek, all working together, the track suddenly became a running track. The three hounds crossed the creek taking the track along one of the drainage ditches, crossed the country road, and ran over a ridge out of hearing.

Our small group continued on to the trucks where we checked the tracker, determining we could get closer. If the hounds remained across the road in their present position we could get much closer by driving. After a drive of several miles, and stopping to listen we heard all three hounds together, still running hard. They were on the creek heading back in the direction they had come from. All three were close together without a noticeable gap between them. It had been a while since a race of this caliber was heard.

Hurriedly we drove back around, stopping at the creek bridge. The three hounds had already crossed and were going back in the direction of the Red Barn. We then drove back to the Red Barn and stood on the hill listening to hound music that any houndsman would appreciate. The three hounds were across the creek in the rough stuff but moving swiftly. Old J.R. was running head to head with the other two, showing he could hold his own with the younger hounds. J.R. had been hit by a car when he was younger and had a pin in his hip. After this long hard race he was going to be sore and stiff the next day.

The hounds had been running hard for over an hour now, a lot of ground had been covered. The hunters were beginning to get anxious; thinking maybe off game was being run. As the three hounds crossed the ridges going almost out of hearing it was commented that maybe they were running a fox. The race suddenly changed direction coming straight back toward the creek and the Red Barn. As they neared the creek it was evident J.R. was leading the race. All three had shortened their bawls and were running extremely hard. They were in knee deep water, that being, could have caused the change in voice, or the fact they were only feet from their prey.

Our group had walked back to the creek bank, only a few hundred yards from the excellent race. Possibly the animal heard us, or maybe from exhaustion and fear of being caught on the ground it decided to climb a tree. J.R. did not locate but immediately began treeing, John was locating coming into the tree, as was Scooter. We stood and listened to the three letting the world know their track had come to an end. All were amazed that J .R. could move that fast, he had put his whole heart into the entire race.

We slowly threaded our way along the creek bank to the foot log, crossed to the other side and preceded to the tree. Walking into the tree we saw all three hounds stretched high upon an enormous oak tree. The tree was surrounded by knee deep water on all sides. The hounds were leashed and the tree shined. The coon was spotted on a large limb low in the tree. The hounds received a little praise and then their reward. One of the young hunters received the honor of

161

dispatching the coon to the deserving hounds. The coon was a large light colored boar coon, large for our area anyway.

As we prepared to leave the tree I noticed something that stuck in my mind for years. Embedded in the side of the tree was the head of a single bladed axe, containing a short portion of the handle. Years later while hunting "Nite Champions Calico Rock, Banging Blue Cat and Wild 'N' Blue Mr. Quick" at the Red Barn my eldest son and I would hear a race comparable to the Christmas hunt. The exciting race would end at the same large oak with the axe still embedded to the hilt. That coon was left to run again, leaving a memory to last forever.

Our little group of hunters worked our way back to the truck, some thinking maybe the dogs had ran off game eventually switching to the coon. Back at the trucks the coon was thoroughly looked over, he had already begun to stiffen, the doubtful hunters then decided it was indeed the coon the dogs had run. The coon was weighted at twenty one pounds and nine ounces containing absolutely no fat on his body. He was long legged and lean, what some old timers call a ridge runner. One of the hunters in our group would have him mounted as a reminder of the hunt.

Examining the coon we thought he was probably a coon that had been turned loose by the coon clubs. Most of the coons from our area were a darker color. At one time the coon population was thin in that part of the country. The local coon clubs would purchase several hundred coons yearly to be distributed among members who turned them loose at their chosen site. Many of the coons the clubs bought came from Florida or South Carolina; they were a lighter, yellowish colored coon. The importation of coon over the years resulted in the population growing to proportion. With coon conservation by hunters the coon population in that area is now sufficient to support hard hunting.

Scooter, J.R. and John were all well balanced hounds that treed coon year round without a lot of aggravation. Not only were they good hounds but they reproduced their likeness or better from several different bloodlines. They were not bred as much as they should have been, nor was their sires. They all lived a relatively short life and were gone before it was realized how well they would reproduce. Even though we owned several good offspring from them to carry on the bloodline, we wished more pups had been raised from them. And, or that we had even bred our good females to their sires.

At that time we were looking at the present not the future. But you live and learn.

A thought in closing: Some great reproducing hounds are not utilized because of their geographical locations or because they aren't or weren't promoted by their owners. Jealousy has also caused many people to ignore a great reproducer. Many times these hounds are long gone before it is realized they are great reproducers that could have helped their breed become better as a whole. Currently with modern technology and frozen semen this legacy can be preserved and handed down. There are numerous proven superior reproducers being promoted from every breed today, some that really stand out. There are no guarantees, but if you are planning to breed your good female, do a little research, make an extra effort, then breed to one of these reproducers. You will eventually be glad you did.

THE SOUND OF MUSIC

18

The nocturnal sounds of the night ascended up the hollow to the keen ears of the Old Man as darkness began to reign over the distant swamp. Countless weeks had passed since rainfall had blessed the region and the swamp contained the only water in the vicinity. Considering the dry conditions of the area the swamp became the only source of food and water for an assortment of wildlife. It also became the hunting grounds for creatures of all types including the Old Man and his grand hound "Music".

Actually the swamp had been a favorite hunting ground for the Old Man for over half a century. The terrain was rough and the area was seldom hunted by houndsmen. The swamp had always been home to numerous species of game regardless of the weather conditions, wet or dry. Raccoon were abundant in the swamp; this was the one and only game the Old Man pursued. The Old Man often came to the swamp alone, turned Music loose, and enjoyed the tranquility the surroundings conveyed upon him. He had never failed to tree coon there, nor had he ever been disturbed by other hunters.

On this cold January night the big Blue hound called Music had been released down a hollow which ended at the vast swamps outer edge. Music had immediately burrowed his great head several inches into the layer of dead leaves covering the ground, threw his big head back and let out a thundering long bawl. He then began to trail in the direction of the swamp, drifting and opening with his impressive bawl as he moved the track.

The Old Man sat on the tailgate pondering on hunts of the past, and the hounds he had hunted in the swamp. He thought that Music could possibly be the last hound he would ever hunt there, or close to it anyway. He listened as the big mouthed hound trailed a track that most hounds would never have given mouth on. He knew Music would put a tree on the end of the track and have a coon or a den. No reason to think otherwise; he had always done so before, he always finished what he started.

The big hound soon reached the outskirts of the swamp and the track began to warm up. He had worked hard to get the track to its present point. With the dry conditions it was almost impossible to trail a track on the dry brittle leaves, unless it was red hot. Music had now reached moist ground and the Old Man knew he could quickly put a tree on the end of the track. He swiftly took the track into the swamp, bawling here and there with his melodious bawl. He soon raised his large head into the air, threw an earth rattling locate and began to tree with a loud, heavy, hound chop. Music was letting the Old Man know come get this one, as it was going no further.

The Old Man got to his feet, retrieved his rifle from the truck, and began walking slowly in the direction of his treed hound. He thought that maybe he did have time to train another hound or two. He didn't want to let the bloodline he had invested so many years into and kept up to par just die away. Music was a hound that would have made his ancestors proud, a hound whose bloodline could be traced back to the first registered Blueticks, and even farther back. He had raised this line of hounds for many years; he needed to find a good female to raise one last litter from. With this thought on his mind he proceeded on to Music's tree.

Music was stretched high on the side of a large, leaning tree, surrounded by water. The Old Man shined the tree as he approached and spotted the coon sprawled on a limb, high in the tree. He then gave Music a little praise but did not leash him at the tree. He was going to let Music have the coon and feared if he was leashed when he put it out that the coon would either sink or escape. He then let Music have the coon, which he quickly dispatched.

The Old Man then leashed Music, picked up the coon and headed for higher ground. Upon reaching a flat, dry, patch of land at the edge of the swamp he once again cut Music loose, sending him around the perimeter. He sat down and begin to skin the coon; no sense in having to haul the heavy coon back to the truck.

As he completed the task of skinning the coon the Old Man heard the loud, rolling bawl of another hound, far in the distance, trailing in the direction of the big swamp. He was thinking "With these dry conditions, there is a hound that can trail with old Music." He stood in order to get a better perspective on the trailing hound; he enjoyed nothing more than to listen to a big mouthed hound trail an old bad track. In the meantime Music struck a track of his own and began to move it back into the swamp.

Only a few miles away at precisely the same time the Old Man was releasing Music into the swamp a Young Man was also preparing for a short hunt. The Youngster had come into the house shortly after dark and asked his father if he wanted to go hunting.

His rather replied, "Not tonight, I'm tired and it's too dry to have an enjoyable hunt." The Youngster told his father he was going to walk down to the creek and try to tree a coon or two. To which his father replied, "Don't turn a bunch of those dogs loose, just take ole Blue Gal, she will be able to trail in these dry conditions and you can get her caught up when you are ready to come in." With this the Youngster dressed for the hunt, gathered up his light, lead and rifle, and walked to the barn to get Blue Gal.

With Blue Gal on the lead and the other hounds barking to be released the Youngster walked down the hill and crossed the road toward the creek. Or should he say the creek bed as it was dry other than an occasional small pool of water here and there. He released Blue Gal into the dry creek bed and slowly walked along waiting for her to find a track. He knew if she barked it would be a coon because she ran no off game. The Youngster was confident Blue Gal would quickly strike a coon track, but this was not to be. He had not seen the blue female since releasing her, so he continued walking down the hollow following the creek bed. He soon heard Blue Gal strike far ahead of him, almost out of hearing range. He walked on in the direction he had last heard her, considerably picking up his pace. After walking hard for thirty minutes he came to the highway and discovered Blue Gal had crossed to the other side and was now moving the track. The Youngster crossed the highway and trudged on in the direction Blue Gal was trailing. He could hear another hound trailing further in - a hound with a thundering bawl voice. He soon heard Blue Gal get the track up and running and she soon threw a couple of big bawl locates and began to tree with a coarse solid chop. He picked up his pace and started in the direction Blue Gal was treed. The Youngster heard the other big mouthed hound locate with a long bawl and begin to tree with a loud, heavy chop. The hound was either with Blue Gal or really close. He now picked up his pace even more as he didn't know who owned the other hound or what their intentions might be.

The Old Man had sat and marveled at the tracking ability of the other hound that had trailed up the draw. The hound had trailed a great distance across some rough, dry country, came into the edge of the swamp, picked up speed and put a tree on the end of the track. The hound had a loud, clear, rolling bawl on track, a distinctive bawl locate and was a hard, loud, chop mouthed tree dog. As he listened to the dog tree, he heard Music, which had been trailing a track of his own, turn and go in the direction of the treed hound. Music continued to trail past the other hound a hundred yards or so, let out a long locate and begin to chop. The Old Man stood and listened to the two hounds tree; delighted at what he heard. He soon saw a lone light moving towards the treed hounds from the other direction. He began to walk towards the treed hounds too.

Both hunters arrived at their hounds trees almost simultaneously and yelled greetings to the other. The Old Man leashed Music at his tree and walked to the tree of the other hound. He was curious as to just what kind of hound this was. On arrival at the tree he was surprised to see a young man, really not much more than a child, petting a big, good looking Bluetick female. He said, "Young man you have a real tree dog there." The Youngster grinned and replied, "Sounds like you have one of your own treed right over there."

The Old Man asked the Youngster if he had seen anything up the tree and he replied, "No" he had not yet shined it. They both begin to shine the tree and the Old Man said "Here it is!" They saw a large coon sitting in a fork of the tree. The Old Man told the Youngster to put the coon out if he wanted; and he did with only one shot. He then leashed Blue Gal, put the coon in a burlap sack and said to the Old Man, "Let's go to your dog now."

The two hunters then walked to Music's tree and begin to shine a big, hollow den tree. After several minutes of shining the Old Man said, "Must be on the inside, I wasn't going to take it anyway." With this he grabbed Music's leash and the two hunters led their hounds away from the tree.

The two hunters then finally introduced themselves and began general conversation. The Old Man asked the Youngster where he lived and he pointed and said, "On that hill way over there."

The Old Man replied, "Why that's five miles over there. Did you walk all that way?" The Youngster smiled and said, "Yeah, it didn't seem that far." Following a little more talk the Old Man asked if the Youngster would like to turn Blue Gal loose with Music. Not wanting to miss the opportunity to tree another coon and hunt with another Blue dog the Youngster replied, "Yes!"

The two hunters cut the blue hounds back into the swamp and sat down to wait. A few minutes passed before Music let loose a roaring bawl immediately followed by the rolling bawl of Blue Gal. The two hounds worked as one and soon had the track moving at a good pace. Surprisingly, the coon did not stay in the swamp but run up the hillside and crossed the ridge, out of hearing. The hunters walked to the top of the ridge and heard both hounds treed solid on the same tree. They walked to the tree and saw the two blue hounds standing tall and proud on the side of a large hardwood. They leashed both hounds back and shined the tree, quickly finding the coon. The Old Man told the Youngster to put the coon out to the two hounds and he'd have two coons to take home with him. The coon hit the ground and the hounds wooled it a little. The Youngster then put the coon in his burlap sack with the other coon.

With both hounds on the lead the Old Man told the Youngster that with two coons and the rifle to carry along with leading Blue Gal that he pretty much had a load. He said he would drop him off at his home. They walked to the Old Man's truck, loaded their hounds and the Youngster placed the coons in the bed of the truck.

On the drive to the Youngsters home the Old Man inquired of the bloodline of Blue Gal and the Youngster answered, "She goes back to Mountain Music breeding." The Old Man smiled and said, "That's what I thought, so does Music." He proceeded to give the Youngster his contact information and advised he phone any night he wanted to go on a hunt. That was their first hunt, but would not be their last. The two big Blue hounds would be hunted together many nights and they would tree a truck load of coon and raise some good pups together before it was over.

A FAIR CHANCE

19

It was a hot summer night with the moon low in the sky and heat lightning illuminating the distant Southern sky. I had released a big, good looking Bluetick hound down the steep ridge and into the hollow some thirty minutes prior. I was now waiting to hear this hound strike a track.

I was standing in an old field road enjoying the night and recollecting a hunt of several years in the past, at this same spot. On that night I was hunting a couple of young hounds and listening to a good fox race until they switched over and treed a coon.

My train of thought was disturbed as the stillness of the night was broken by the melodious bawl of the big Blue hound. He was almost out of hearing range, far down the ridge near the creek. The hound was Grand Nite Champion, Grand Champion Moyer's Blue Chubbs, and this was the first night I had hunted him.

My hunting partner Jerrell Thomas had hunted Chubbs for over a week and told me he would not do "anything" and that I needed to send him back to Missouri as quick as possible.

Chubbs had been raised, trained and made Champion by Joe Moyer. He had never been hunted or handled by different people even though he was friendly with everyone. I had purchased Chubbs only the week before.

Joe had told me what Chubbs would do and I believed what he had said, as he stood behind what he sold. I assumed that Chubbs only needed to become accustomed to his new handlers and surroundings. I was going to hunt him all night that night, just him and I alone in the woods. Chubbs was approaching two years of age and was already Dual Grand so I knew he would have to do "something" at least to have earned the degree. I proceeded to walk in the direction he was trailing as the track began to improve. He was now moving along the creek bank, giving more mouth as he began to run the track. He suddenly located with a couple of big loud bawls and that was the end of it, not another bark.

Fifteen minutes passed and Chubbs came in, reared up on me wanting to play as if he had did something good. I leashed him and started toward the truck, thinking that maybe he had run the track into a hole on the creek bank. I was going to move to another area and try again.

I had some good hunting territories nearby where I could always strike a coon. There were four or five good turnouts within a few miles of each other. I slowly drove to this area with hopes that Chubbs would perform much better.

Stopping on a small creek bridge I released Chubbs down a clear, fast running shallow creek. He struck almost immediately with his big loud bawl and ran the track hard and fast almost out of hearing range before turning and coming back in the direction where he had been released. He was looking at whatever he was running and he was going to cross the road directly in front of me. Shining my light down the road I saw Mr. Coon cross with Chubbs only a few feet behind him, running to catch. The coon headed down the ridge toward an area of rock cliffs and rough terrain but didn't quite make it. Chubbs located with a couple of loud, long locates and began to tree with a short, steady bawl.

I let him tree for a while and then slowly walked to him. I leashed him, petted him a little and began looking the tree over, swiftly finding the coon. Chubbs was petted a little more before I headed for the truck to move to another area and another drop. Thinking, well he will do "something" as I had just heard him run the legs off a coon and put it up a tree. But, will he do it again? I was about to see.

Moving several miles down the road Chubbs was released onto a stream that ran alongside a couple chicken houses. I then patiently waited, but not for long. Chubbs soon struck, ran the track a few minutes opening here and there, located the tree and began to tree same as the first tree. I walked to him, leashed him, shined the tree and quickly found another coon. Feeling pretty good at this point I gave him a little petting and headed out to another drop.

Driving to the edge of a small fishing lake surrounded by willows, Chubbs was released onto the lakes perimeter. He does it again - strikes quickly, runs the track and rapidly trees at the tracks end. He stays put and has another coon up the tree. I'm now feeling much better about this good looking Bluetick Hound. I still wanted to see him tree one more before I phoned Jerrell to inform him of the night's results.

Driving back in the direction of my home and onto an old dirt road routed up the mountainside, Chubbs struck from the box. I stopped and cut him onto the track which he treed within 100 yards of the road and had another coon. Giving Chubbs a little more petting and then loading him into the box for the short drive home, I was confident he was now accustomed to his new owner and surroundings. It was 4:30 A.M. and I had seen four single coons and was sure he would tree more if released again.

On arrival at the house I placed Chubbs into the kennel, gave him feed and water then went inside to phone Jerrell. He answered and said, 'I figured you would have called way before now. What did I tell you?" I replied, "You're not going to believe it but he treed four single coons that I saw." Jerrell wanted to see this for himself, so, we planned a hunt for that night. I hoped that Chubbs would perform as he had the night before. I also wanted to hunt him with another dog to see how he operated with company.

As darkness approached I loaded Chubbs and Grand Nite Champion, Grand Champion Harris' Rose, a top Bluetick female that would tree coons where it was said there were no coons. Rose did not hunt out of the country, treed a lot of lay-ups and did not run off game. She would get treed and stay hooked with anything, as they didn't get too mean or aggressive for her.

Jerrell and I met and decided on a good hunting area on Salacoa Creek. Parking in a field near the creek Chubbs and Rose were cut loose in the direction of the creek. We sat on the tailgate to wait for the action to begin.

"At least he went hunting," Jerrell stated. About that time Chubbs opened on the creek straight ahead and was joined by Rose. They worked the track along the steep, rough bank and in the deep water of the river sized creek. They were having a hard time getting the track up and running because of the rough terrain. Finally, trailing toward the road we had come in on they began to move at a good pace. Rose suddenly exploded on a tree, but Chubbs continued on.

Looking over at Jerrell I noticed he had a big smile on his face as if to say, "I told you so." We walked to the tree as we listened to Chubbs run the track out of hearing range. Rose was treed up a small tree on the creek bank, at a difficult place to get near her. We shined the tree and could see it was slick, which was a rare occurrence for her. Rose was taken off the tree and sent in the direction Chubbs had gone. Chubbs was already out of hearing range, but following a quick check of the tracker and determining his location we drove nearer to him.

Stopping to listen we heard Chubbs treed solid and still alone, a good distance from our location. We could get much closer and drove farther stopping again to listen. As we came to a stop Rose came on the tree with Chubbs. Knowing we were close as possible to the hounds our walk to them began. As we approached the tree we found both hounds stretched high on the side of a large oak, covered with vines and leaves. Chubbs was treeing with a short loud bawl and Rose with hard, fast chops. The hounds were leashed back, the tree shined and the coon spotted.

"Well, Chubbs did a pretty good job on that one; now let's cut them loose again right off this tree," said Jerrell. And that's exactly what we did. Both hounds went hunting and split up, with Rose falling treed first after opening only a couple times. Chubbs did not cover her but started a separate track trailing away from us. We walked in to Rose leashed her, saw the coon and headed for the truck.

Chubbs was through the country but treed solid and in an area we could get much closer by driving. Moving closer and walking in to the tree we found that he did have another coon. Another good night of hunting was now behind us and we were the proud owners of a top young Blue hound. Jerrell said, "I would have sent him back and would not have believed he did what he has done tonight if I hadn't seen it. Maybe he was homesick or hadn't become adjusted to us or a new home when I hunted him."

From that night on Chubbs consistently treed coons anytime turned loose, regardless of his handler. He treed many coon for us and was used as a check dog and to try other hounds with. When he opened it was a coon and when he treed there was a coon in a very, very high percentage of his trees. He was too honest to be a great competition dog like his sire Dual Grand Champion Davis' Blue Scooter or his dam Nite Champion Gregory's Blue Scat. He couldn't take the stress of hauling long distances to many of the larger hunts. He was better where the coon were thin and the off game thick, but treed coons anywhere hunted. Chubbs also reproduced some good pups and young hounds. Joe and I raised several good hounds from him and there were others scattered around the country. He shows up in the pedigrees of many hounds today.

I owned his sire and dam, both of which died at a young age, several of his brothers and sisters and still owned Chubbs when he died back home at Joe Moyer's. This just goes to show you that sometimes you have to give a hound a "Fair Chance".

Hunting camp in South Carolina
Pictured are Bob Williams and Tommy King

Pictured are Bart Nation and Bill Gray at the home of Bob and Donna Williams in Golconda, IL, circa 1981 Photo are compliments of Donna Williams

Hounds owned by Jerrell Thomas. Mike Seets pictured

An ad from 1985

Dual Nite Champion Nation's Blue Buck (left) Dual Grand Champion Davis' Blue Scooter (middle) Dual Grand Champion Moyer's Blue Chubbs (right)

Dual Grand Champion, PKC Champion, NKC Nite Champion, AKC Nite Champion Posted Land Swamp Dancer, owner Bart Nation.

GRNT. CH. UCHTMANS
HAWK JR.
BART NATION

Champion, Grand Nite Champion Uchtman's Blue
Hawk Jr, owner Bart Nation.

Grand Nite Champion Coz' Sparetime Spanky. 1991 AKC World Champion.
Pictured here when he won the 1990 Georgia State Championship with
handler Jerry Winn. Spanky was owned by Bart Nation

Bart Nation and his mother

Joe Moyer, Wilbern Uchtman and Orb May

Nite Champion Nation's Wild 'n' Blue Mr Quick, A top young
hound out of the kennel of Mackie Manns

Grand Nite Champion Rock 'n' Roll Rowdy, owner Bart Nation

Grand Champion May's Blue Pretty. Picture courtesy of Joe Moyer

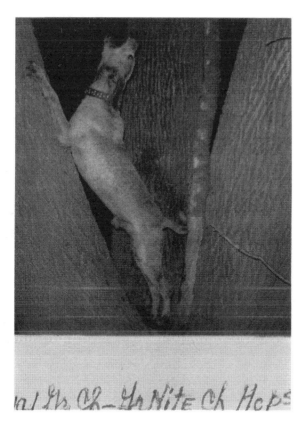

Grand Show Champion, Grand Nite Champion, ACHA Nite Champion, NKC Nite Champion, 1978 English World Champion Fuller's Hopsing. Sire of 1980 UKC World Champion Fuller's Red Rooster.

Misty, A Top English Female, heavy with pups from Rock n Roll Rowdy

189

This picture is the one I spoke of that is with Jerrell's pictures it has Dustin Thomas 12 year old with trophies he won the night he finished "Rock 'N' Roll Rowdy" to Grand Nite Champion. Also pictured are Bob Williams (center) and Jerrell Thomas (right)

Dustin Thomas, Bob Williams, Jerrell Thomas pictured with Grand Nite
Champion Rock 'N' Roll Rowdy

Grand Nite Champion, ACHA Nite Champion Nation's Dancin' Deamon

Dual Grand Champion, ACHA Nite Champion Gordon's Lucky Striker.
" A balanced hound with all the tools"

Grand Champion, Nite Champion Paxton Abernathy (Abner)
Owner, Gregory Bart Nation

Grand Nite Champion, Grand Show Champion, ACHA Nite Champion
Sugar Creek J.R.   Owner Gregory Bart Nation

Grand Champion, Grand Nite Champion, ACHA Nite Champion, AKC
Nite Champion Nation's Red Boy Banjo.

Grand Nite Champion, ACHA Nite Champion, NKC Nite Champion
DeGraves Ace, A stay-put Accurate tree dog.

Grand Nite Champion, ACHA Nite Champion Raef's Big John. Owner, Gregory Bart Nation

Grand Nite Champion, Nation's Blue Amos. Pictured with former owner Joe Moyer. Joe said Amos was the best all around hound he ever owned. He had a real nose on him. Picture courtesy of Joe Moyer.

HUNTIN' THE LOW COUNTRY
20

The State of South Carolina is home to some of the best coon hunting the south has to offer, with a large coon population and a variety of hunting terrain. The farther south, the flatter and swampier the land becomes. This area is called the "Low Country". Years back some friends and I began going to South Carolina almost monthly and hunting the rough swampland. As time passed my hunting buddy Jerrell and I purchased two adjoining tracts of land near Manning, S.C. to be used as a hunting camp. We did much hunting there, training and polishing the hounds prior to Hurricane Hugo hitting the area. For a while following Hugo some of the swampland was too rough for man or beast. The hunt we are about to take was made when the hunting was at its best. At the time Jerrell and I were promoting Grand Nite Champion Nation's Blue Amos, Grand Nite Champion, Grand Champion Davis' Blue Scooter and two good sons of Scooter, Dual Nite Champion

Nation's Blue Buck and Grand Nite Champion, Grand Champion Moyer 's Blue Chubbs - all Blueticks. Jerrell had been in South Carolina for a week or so, hunting the males getting them ready for the hunts. I traveled over from Georgia on a Friday bringing along four of our good females to polish up for the upcoming hunts. We hunted the females we raised pups from same as we did the males. I arrived at the hunting camp around noon bringing along Grand Cham- pion, Grand Nite Champion Harris' Rose, Grand Nite Champion Nation's Blue Zip, Nite Champion Gregory's Blue Scat and Grand Champion May's Blue Pretty, all four year old Bluetick females. Jerrell and I were going to hunt the females together and alone, putting a few coons out to them. We would be hunting only the females the next couple nights.

As darkness crept upon us we loaded the four females and drove a short distance to the Black River Swamp, one of our favorite hunting areas. On the first drop all four hounds were released from the road into the swamp and soon had tracks going in three directions. Zip was first to strike with her short, coarse bawl, she was deep in the swamp, alone and moving at a good pace. Pretty was next to strike with a high pitched screaming squall, she was to the right of Zip and giving lots of mouth on a good track. The next hound to open was Scat followed by Rose, together, straight in front of us and on a hot track. Rose and Scat made short work of their track with Rose exploding on a tree after only a few minutes. She was quickly covered by Scat and it sounded like a small war on their tree. Rose and Scat did not like each other and when hunted together one did her best to beat the other. Once treed together neither hound would sink teeth into the other, but it sounded as if there were four

197

or five dogs on the tree. Jerrell and I just grinned and said, "listen to that ", as we slowly walked to the tree. Rose was treeing well over 100 barks per minute while Scat was losing her breath trying to tree as hard as Rose. As we were making our way to the tree both Zip and Pretty put trees on their tracks and stayed put.

Rose and Scat were on a small vine covered tree with a coon sitting in the top. We quickly let them have the coon, leashed them and began the walk to Pretty's tree which was between our location and Zip's tree. Pretty was on a large dead snag surrounded by water. She was swimming around the tree letting us know she had Mr. Coon with a series of loud continuous squalls. We spotted the coon and let her have it, leashed her and began the walk to Zip. The walk to Zip was farther than anticipated, following some careful maneuvering we arrived at her tree. Zip was stretched high on the side of a large water oak, treeing with her steady coarse chop. She also had a coon which we let her have. With all dogs on the leashes we began the long journey back to the vehicle with intentions of moving to another area.

Following a short drive deeper into the swamp we prepared to release the hounds one at a time. Rose was Jerrell's favorite so naturally she was first to be released. She was cut off the leash from the road into prime coon hunting territory. Rose hunted the swamp with her head up, many times treeing lay-ups fast as you could walk to her. She wasted little time barking on the ground when hunted in the swamps. Rose threw her head up as she was cut from the leash, went 100 yards into the watery swamp, located and treed. We waded in to the tree which had two coons sitting in the top, leashed Rose and started back to the truck leaving both coons to run again. "Rose did that so quick she didn't have time to go hunting so let's turn her loose again," said Jerrell.

Rose was cut loose on the other side of the road this time, in an area not quite as swampy. She immediately went hunting and was not heard for 15 minutes until she actually opened on the ground. She opened here and there, drifted across a cutover area before going out of hearing range. After checking the tracker we drove around stopping occasionally to listen.

On the third stop we heard Rose on through the country as she located a tree and turned it over to her hard loud chops. Driving close as possible we walked in to the tree, leashed Rose and shined the tree. The tree was on dry land, only a hollow shell of a tree, full of holes. We did not see a coon in the tree but felt it could have been there. On the walk back to the truck we debated on which hound would be hunted next and where it would be turned loose.

Scat received the honors of being the next hound to show her coon treeing ability. We decided to move to higher ground and hunt a deer club nearby that contained roads and trails making it more accessible to reach a hard going hound. Scat hunted hard and would sometimes get out of pocket, with the abundant roads and trails we would be able to get near her where ever she went. She was cut into a large wooded section surrounded by roads on all four sides; the woods contained some swampy land but no deep water. Scat left the leash in a hard run and was soon struck on a good running track which she took across the section of woods, crossed the road and put a tree on it alongside the road. We drove around and spotted the coon in the tree from the truck, it couldn't get much easier than this. After a little praise Scat was loaded up and we moved to another section. It was time for Pretty to prove her ability. The woods where Pretty was released had some shallow water but nothing where she would have to swim. Pretty went hunting quickly and had a track going in only minutes. Jerrell and I sat on the tailgate listening to her run the track for all she was worth, finally putting a tree on the end of it. Pretty did a good job running the track and would have caught the coon on the ground had it not climbed. She was now screaming every breath with her high pitched screaming squall. We were close as we could get to her tree and after a good walk we arrived at another large water oak. Pretty was leashed back and the tree shined. A coon was spotted in a fork of the tree, a little praise was given to Pretty and we headed for the truck. All was going well so far.

Zip was the only hound that had not been turned loose alone, her time had arrived. She was released into an area at the edge of the swamp containing large timber and shallow, slowly moving water. Zip living up to her name zipped into the swamp as if shot from a gun. She had to hunt for a track which took close to 20 minutes before she struck; it was a cold trailing track at that, After another 20 minutes of struggling and drifting she had the track where she could do something with it. And that was, make it go somewhere and hopefully not to an old den tree. She ran the track for another 10 minutes before taking it out of the swamp into a large bare field where she let out a short coarse locating bawl and began to tree with a steady chop. There was only one tree in the field and she was treed on it. We were able to drive almost to the tree, look it over and see she had Mr. Ringtail sitting above her. Zip was given a little praise and loaded into the box, we were finished for the night -another easy drop completed.

As we drove along thinking it had been an easy night we saw a coon cross the road in front of us and the dogs struck from the box. With daylight still an hour or more away, we stopped and turned the hounds onto the red hot coon. All had been easy until this point, but this old coon was about to change that. The coon headed straight into the swamp running for his life with all four hounds scorching his track. He ran hard for 45 minutes before being forced to take refuge. Which hound treed him first would be hard to say as they were running one second and treeing hard the next. They didn't sound very deep in the swamp until we began the walk to them.

Over an hour passed before we arrived at the tree, it was daylight and we saw the coon right away. The hounds were leashed and given a little praise but the hard running coon was left to run again. With the sun high in the eastern sky Jerrell and I arrived back at the truck, wet and tired, but an enjoyable night behind us. That is what it is all about though.

Grand Champion, Grand Nite Champion Harris' Rose was a good looking top female and probably Jerrell's favorite as he finished her to Dual Grand. She was tight mouthed on some tracks but could run or trail a track if need be, she was also a lay-up specialist. Rose's breeding was out of Alabama, some local stuff tracing back to foundation Bluetick bloodlines. Rose was bred to Grand Nite Champion, Grand Champion Davis' Blue Scooter twice, the pups turned out well but raising them did not. The first litter contracted parvo, following an expensive vet bill, only two lived, a male and a female. The male named "Shorty" became a coondog but was never competition hunted. The female became known as Champion, Nite Champion Nation's Blue Jill, she was a good little tree dog but was never promoted hard. The second litter sired by Scooter only one pup lived, a male, he was doing well when he died from Blastomycosis, the same dreaded disease that killed Scooter.

Grand Nite Champion Nation's Blue Zip was a night after night coon dog; she was a fifty pound open ticked hound with one blue eye. Zip was old time Vaughn bred and showed a lot of their characteristics. Zip was bred to Grand Nite Champion, Grand Champion Davis' Blue Scooter one time and produced a litter of coon treeing dogs. The litter produced a couple of Nite Champions and the young Grand Nite Champion Rocket dog owned by Paul Rollins. Rocket was lost or stolen while hunting.

Grand Champion May's Blue Pretty was a beautiful dark blue female that could really run a track and put the correct tree on the end of it. Pretty was Texas Tree Banging Casey bred. She was bred to Grand Nite Champion, Grand Champion Davis' Blue Scooter one time and also produced a litter of good hounds. Grand Champion, Grand Nite Champion Sexton's Blue Jimmy is probably the best known hound out of the Scooter and Pretty cross. Jimmy was given to Joe Moyer by Jerrell and I as a weaning pup.

Nite Champion Gregory's Blue Scat was a hard hunting, coon treeing female that would get struck and treed with a coon that could be seen. Scat was Hammer bred, she was bred to Grand Nite Champion, Grand Champion Davis' Blue Scooter and produced reproducing coondogs. The dogs from the Scooter and Scat cross include Champion, Grand Nite Champion Russell's Blue Misty, Grand Nite Champion, Grand Champion Moyer 's Blue Chubbs, Dual Nite Champion Nation's Blue Buck, Nite Champion Charley Boy and Bonnie just to name a few. Scat died from sevin dust

202

poisoning before she could be bred again or finished to Grand Nite Champion.

Jerrell and I hunted the Black River, Pocatallego and Four Hole Swamps of South Carolina many nights. This is some of the best coon hunting to be found. I hope to one day hunt these areas again with females of the caliber described above.

THE ONE THAT GOT AWAY
21

Late one cool winter evening as I sat on the porch viewing the sunset and awaiting darkness to arrive my thoughts were disturbed by the ringing of the phone. "Hello. You don't know me but I'm a friend of a friend and new to your area, I'm also a coonhunter and would like to come over to visit and talk with you when possible," the voice on the phone explained. As our conversation continued I learned the hunter had recently relocated to our area from upstate New York and a friend from that area had recommended he contact me to hunt with some good hounds. The call ended something like this, "I'm going to hunt tonight and you're welcome to come over right now; look the dogs over and then we'll cut them loose sure as darkness falls. I don't mind showing any of my dogs in the woods, and always like to meet new coon hunters," I stated.

Directions were given and minutes later the newcomer appeared at my home prepared for a night of coon hunting in his new State. The man and his family had arrived in our area only a few days prior and he was anxious to get out and hit the woods, maybe see how our hunting compared to hunting in his home State. Introductions were made and we proceeded to the kennel to look over the hounds. The kennel was full of good hounds at that time, mostly Bluetick and English and I was proud to show any of them in the woods, male or female. The newcomer observed the dogs several times and returned to the kennel containing one of the finest young Bluetick Hounds to be found. Pointing to the hound he said, "I've seen your stud ads in the magazines on that dog, his name is Chubbs and I think he is one of the best looking Blue hounds I have ever saw. Do you think we can take him along with us tonight?" "Tell you what, we can hunt only Chubbs and a pup I'm working with, that way you can better see how he operates. I think you will like what you see, but you can be the judge of that," I replied.

The hound he wanted to hunt was Grand Nite Champion, Grand Show Champion Moyer's Blue Chubbs, a top young hound and the most broke hound I've ever hunted. When Chubbs opened it was a coon, he could trail with the best of them and put a tree on the end of the track with a coon that could be seen. Chubbs would go hunting good as any hound, ran a track with a loud bawl, drifting as it should be done and came on the tree with a big locate turning it

205

over to a short bawl and stayed put. Chubbs was also one of the most accurate tree dogs to be found; in other words load the rifle when you went to the tree. I also owned Chubbs sire and dam and several of his brothers and sisters. He was sired by Dual Grand Champion Davis' Blue Scooter and his dam was Nite Champion Gregory's Blue Scat, two top hounds that reproduced top hounds.

I also wanted to hunt a nice Redtick pup called Champion Nation's Red Striker; the pup was doing a great job for his age of 9 months, he needed only woods time and more hunting experience. Striker was sired by Grand Nite Champion Rock 'N' Roll Rowdy and his dam was Salacoa Valley Missy, two hounds I also owned; he was bred to be a tree dog, and that he was. Striker was a pup that ran loose around the house until he began to run and tree; he was then kenneled for his night hunt training to commence. He had treed several coons alone but only two or three were put out to him. Striker would go hunting hard, get struck with a bawl and chop, move a track in the right direction and come on the tree with a screaming locate turning it over to a loud ringing chop. He was a big, tough pup with the potential to make a top hound if his forward momentum continued.

As darkness drew near both Chubbs and Striker were loaded into the box for the drive to our hunting area. We were going to hunt an area of the Salacoa Creek bottoms, too rough an area for many to turn a dog loose; but I often hunted there. Driving to an isolated area where a small stream crossed the road before eventually running into the creek both hounds were released onto the stream which crossed a large field. The hounds were cut in the direction of the main creek; both left the lead in a hard run without looking back. I looked at my watch as the hounds left the lead and we stood waiting for a strike. Thirty minutes passed without a bark, thirty more rapidly flew by and still not a sound from either hound. The terrain was fairly flat where the hounds had been cut loose and we should have been able to hear them a great distance, so they were either not trailing or had really gotten deep and out of hearing range. I removed the tracker and took a reading of their location, finding they were deep in the section and the tree switches were going on and off - something very strange.

We could get much closer to the hounds by driving around, and that we did, stopping at the creek bridge to listen and clearly hearing both treed solid but fading in and out. The underbrush grew at such a thickness around the creek bridge that practically nobody hunted a dog in that area, it was almost inaccessible. Unable to determine which side of the creek the hounds were on we chose a side and slowly worked our way toward the treed hounds.

Finally coming into view of them and discovering we had made the wrong choice; they were across the very deep creek. That was not the only problem because they were treed under the creek bank in a horseshoe shaped hole; the reason we were unable to hear them from our first location and the reason for the on again off again tree switches. I prefer my dogs not tree in the ground, Striker knew no better but Chubbs had never before treed and stayed in the ground. Shining the light across the wide and deep creek I noticed the reason Chubbs had stayed at the hole, the big ragged looking coon was nervously peering from, and pacing the other end of the horseshoe, at- tempting to make his escape behind the hounds. Neither Chubbs nor Striker initially noticed the large coon emerge from the hole and bail into the creek, but upon seeing him they both immediately pounced upon him, a very bad mistake.

The coon was evidently a seasoned war veteran as he quickly retaliated against both hounds, causing Striker to retreat a couple of feet back only to swim and bay. The coon had swiftly put a whipping on both hounds but Chubbs refused to turn loose the coon and the fight continued as we stood helpless to do anything about it. The extremely large coon had crawled onto Chubbs head and was making an earnest effort to drown him and doing a right good job of it. I thought about jumping in and trying to get the coon off him but thought of the depth of the water and assumed the mad coon might possibly attack me. I then thought about trying to shoot the coon off the drowning dog but had second thoughts because of maybe hitting the dog. Striker would no longer make an attempt to grab the coon so any help from him would not be. I finally picked up several rocks and sticks from the creek bank and began throwing them at the coon, dislodging him from Chubbs head. The coon saw the culprit of the thrown objects and headed in my direction with damage on his mind. I quickly retreated up the creek bank out of harm's way allowing the coon to climb onto the bank where he shook himself off and turned to face off with the two hounds or any other danger. Chubbs unwilling to give up the fight crawled onto the bank in pursuit of the fiery animal, with a regrouped Striker closely following.

The fight resumed on the steep bank of the creek with neither dog nor coon able to gain footing. I noticed that Chubbs was bloated from all the water he had swallowed yet he refused to back up even a step, Striker had also regained his courage and joined the melee. I

208

stood observing the fight before thinking to look around for the rest of our hunting party who all stood dumbfounded not knowing what to do.

The fight continued up the thick brushy bank until the coon turned and departed with the hounds in hot pursuit. Both hounds were giving mouth on the track and the coon knew he was running for his life. He put up a race like very seldom heard and would occasionally lose the hounds, but they would then pick up his trail. The coon ran the rough underbrush and steep creek bank until finally being forced into taking refuge up a tree. The track broke down for only a few seconds and the next bark was Chubbs big bawl locate followed by the screaming locate of Striker.

I supposed the coon had made it home to a big and safe den, which proved to be correct. We walked to the tree and found Chubbs stretched high on one side and Striker high on the other of a big hollow hardwood alongside the creek. Shining the tree over with no results, then squalling a couple times the coon was seen glaring from a hole high in the tree. Even if the coon had been up on the outside of the tree he would not have been taken as he had definitely earned the right to live and run again. As we returned to the truck the newcomer advised that he had never seen the likes of what he had witnessed and that he now had something to tell the fellows back home. The newcomer did not stay in our area for long but moved back to his home State, and he did let the hunters of his area know what he had witnessed on that cold winter night. I received many calls from hunters living in that area wanting Chubbs bred pups, all because of the willingness to show him in the woods and word of mouth from a hunter who appreciated a good hound. We had used up a considerable amount of time with the coon and most everyone was ready to call it a night, so toward the house we drove. Following a little small talk and inviting everyone back for another hunt all departed for home - an exciting hunt behind them.

Following the departure of everyone I began to think about the damage the coon might have done to Striker and decided to take him a few miles down from the house and turn him loose alone to see how he performed. I don't like to get a pup chewed up by a coon as it is not good for them and can ruin or sidetrack many before they are started well. I hoped in Strikers case it had not harmed him as he was a big rugged pup and mentally mature for his age; possibly from running loose when younger. It is still not a good practice to get a pup or young hound chewed up by coons so I tried to avoid such.

Driving a couple miles from home I released Striker into a hollow toward a small lake. He went hunting in a run just as an older hound would have and soon had a track going. Opening with a couple chops and a big bawl he worked the track in the direction of the lake, what appeared to be a feed track, moving in one direction and eventually getting it up and moving. He worked around the lake and onto the side of the ridge before his screaming locate was heard and the hard loud chops began. I slowly walked to the tree, leashed him back, spotted a coon perched in a fork, gave him the coon and a small amount of praise and headed for home.

The whipping the coon put on Striker earlier in the night seemed luckily not to have affected him, and with the coon I'd just given him he was now going home with the best of thoughts in his head. He was taken home and returned to his kennel to think about the adventures of the night; he was going to make a good one if he continued to improve at the pace he was progressing.

THE GHOST
22

The big boar coon slowly crawled from his den but instead of going down the tree he lazily climbed toward the top. He crossed into an adjacent tree by way of a touching limb which ran from his den into the other. The big coon proceeded to climb even higher until he reached a large vine running from near the top into several adjoining trees. Climbing onto the large vine in a cunning maneuver he walked the vine three trees over to an old oak. The gigantic old oak grew at the end of the hollow, at the point where a stream fed into a large fishing lake. The old tree was used by the coon to exit and enter his den. He never climbed directly up or down the den, nor did his routine ever change.

The coon dropped to the ground from the old oak, moved into the shallow stream scantly looking for minnows or crawfish. Without luck of finding either he moved along the lake bank searching for frogs, with little effort, until he came to the dry, rock covered gully.

Up the gully he waddled, further into the hills to an easy meal. In times past, the big coon hunted for food but had recently discovered a place containing plenty of food; there for the taking. He followed the gully, actually a spillway from another lake located upon the crest of the hills. As he topped the hills, he cautiously moved around the tree lined shore of the lake, heading to his newly found food source. Sitting along the shore of the lake was a freshly constructed barn and big new home. Inside the yet completed barn lay the treats the coon had come to obtain.

The coon entered the barn, climbed into the loft by way of a support beam and followed the route of the utility lines. He dropped into a hole in the loft floor, following the wiring and water pipes onto a narrow ledge which supported them. The ledge was attached to the floor joist for the length of the barn and gave the coon access to a couple of sealed rooms along that side. The coon used the holes where the utility lines entered the feed and egg rooms to gain entry into his treasure chest. He first dropped from the ledge into the feed room and ate sweet feed, corn and dog food until satisfied, leaving the room in shambles as he departed. Advancing along the ledge, he then crawled into the egg room onto a nesting box. Following a brief disturbance from an old, mad hen he had his fill of eggs and slowly departed the way he came.

Upon exiting the barn, the coon scampered to the lake's edge, drank until satisfied and began his journey back down the rock filled gully. He climbed numerous trees and bushes as he went, looking for any mischief he might happen to find. For several weeks he had been visiting the barn nightly and leaving quite a mess on his departure. He left no sign of whom, or what had done the damage.

Little did he know that the angry owner, not knowing how something could be entering the secure feed and egg rooms had begun referring to him as "The Ghost." He also didn't know that time was short until the owner discovered the identity of the culprit.

The owner of the barn "Mr. Malone" was now in semi-retirement. He owned the property where he built his new home and barn and much of the surrounding land including the two large fishing lakes, timberland and pasture land. He previously lived down near the other lake, alongside the road, but it had been his dream as he neared retirement to build and move to the top of the hills. He had worked hard all his life and was now going to raise a few cattle, horses, mules and chickens, just to make ends meet. He was also going to do a little bird hunting and enjoy his golden years.

There was only one problem at Mr. Malone's new place. Something was raiding the feed and egg rooms in his new barn. He had no idea what could be causing such disarray with the doors to both rooms shut and latched. It seemed as if a ghost was passing through the walls of the closed rooms. He supposed something could be coming in from outside and somehow gaining entry into the rooms. The barn was still unfinished as it was lacking the installation of the outer doors. Mr. Malone was going to form and pour the concrete entry pads for the doors today and install the doors tomorrow. His problems with "The Ghost" or whatever should then be over.

Mr. Malone contemplated the deeds done by The Ghost the night before as he awaited the arrival of his two young farm hands. As morning approached noon, the two hands, Bobby and Kenny, arrived and began building the doorway entry forms. They figured to have the forms completed by mid-afternoon and have the concrete poured and finished by late evening. The job took longer than anticipated but they completed smoothing and finishing the concrete as dusk crept in. Mr. Malone stated to his two young helpers that they would install the doors the following day, and hopefully his problems with The Ghost would come to an end. With this, Bobby and Kenny departed for the night.

Shortly after dark, The Ghost exited his den in the usual manner, not pausing to look for food on the way, but going directly to the barn. There was no need in having to hunt for food when all he wanted or needed was in the barn. As he entered the barn, he noticed something different had been installed at his point of entry. Crossing the yet uncured concrete entering the barn, he left behind his footprints and also the identity of Mr. Malone's "ghost". He proceeded on and had his fill of feed and eggs, departing the way he had come, leaving less evidence of his departure in the now curing concrete.

Bright and early the following morning, Bobby and Kenny arrived to install the doors. Mr. Malone and the two walked to the barn to begin their work and discovered the coons large footprints embedded in the fresh concrete of the machinery entry way. Upon further inspection the feed and egg rooms were again found in shambles.

"Well, we now know The Ghost's identity," stated Mr. Malone. "We will have the doors installed today and that should keep the rogue out of the barn." Bobby and Kenny both replied, "Let us come over to catch that rascal and you will be rid of him for good." "We will see what happens after the doors are installed. If that doesn't work, you are welcome to come tree him with your dogs or whatever," said Mr. Malone. At day's end, all the doors were installed and the barn closed, "Sealed from the pesky ghost," thought Mr. Malone. Bobby and Kenny were glad to have completed the installation of the doors, but secretly hoped the coon would somehow still gain entry into the barn. They wanted to come run and tree the big footed rascal.

As darkness settled in, The Ghost descended from his den to begin making his nightly rounds. He was in no hurry to reach the barn as he knew there was an abundance of food there for the taking. When he finally made his way to the barn, he found it to be completely sealed, and began looking for an avenue to gain entry. After thoroughly searching he returned to the large machinery entry way, climbed up the door to where it attached to its sliding rail. In a clever move, he then inserted his head into the small space where the door connected to the rail and squeezed inside. It was a little more difficult than just walking in, but there was no stopping him as he could squeeze through the smallest openings.

The following morning Mr. Malone discovered his feed and egg rooms once again in total disorder. He was furious. He had no idea how The Ghost had gotten inside. He was indeed a ghost to be able to pass through the solid walls. He had no notion that the coon could squeeze through the small holes he was using for entry. He returned to his home and phoned Bobby and Kenny to ask them to bring their dogs over that night to try and catch the bandit. He told them to come early as he figured the coon made his rounds early because of the tracks he left in the wet concrete a couple nights prior.

If the coon had come later, the concrete would have been dry enough so that tracks would not have been left. Mr. Malone knew that Bobby and Kenny would tree the coon and his hide would soon be on the barn wall. If not, they would stay after him until they caught him.

Bobby and Kenny were delighted when Mr. Malone phoned to say the coon had again raided his barn and asked them to bring their dogs and catch the rascal. They owned two Redbone females that were making pretty fair coondogs. The two young hounds had been hunted hard with their Uncle Charlie's old dog "Big Boy," and needed no help to run and tree a coon on their own. Sure as darkness came, they would be happy to put "Mindy" and "Mandy" on the trail of the thieving old coon. The two young men arrived at Mr. Malone's around 9 PM and talked for an hour or so. "Well, The Ghost should have had plenty of time to have come and gone if he is coming tonight," said Mr. Malone.

Bobby and Kenny unloaded their hounds and walked in the direction of the barn with Mr. Malone following along. Both hounds struck on the lead as they approached the large machinery door and were released onto the track. The rogue coon must have just departed as the track was red hot. The hounds ran the critter from the barn to the lakes edge, then into the timber and down the rocky spillway towards the low lying lake.

Mindy and Mandy were giving it their all and running the bandit to catch. In short order, the loud, long bawl locate of Mandy was heard followed by Mindy's squalling locates. Then the hard loud chops began. "Treed solid! Let's go put an end to that rascal once and for all," Bobby stated to Mr. Malone and Kenny as they walked towards the treed hounds.

The Ghost had just finished filling his stomach and exited the barn when he caught scent of dog. He quickly ran towards the lake and into the timber when he realized the hounds were on his trail. He ran down the rocky spillway straight to the gigantic oak he used as a stepping stone to his den, up the oak he went, climbing through the trees and over into his den. He soon heard a loud bawl locate followed by the squall locate of another hound, and then came the hard, loud chops. The two hounds were on the oak; not his den. He was safe.

The two young hunters followed by Mr. Malone walked into the tree with anticipation of exterminating The Ghost once and for all. Mindy and Mandy had the varmint up a tree. The three saw the gigantic oak the two hounds were treed upon and begin to search the great tree looking for their prey. After ten minutes of shining Bobby said, "I think the crafty rascal has either crossed out or jumped into the lake or stream by way of the overhanging limbs. Mindy and Mandy don't miss many coons."

They shined a couple of the nearby trees without finding anything. It was finally determined that The Ghost must have jumped into the lake and escaped. "Just like a ghost to disappear," stated Mr. Malone. Bobby and Kenny retrieved their hounds and sent them on around the lake, in hopes of picking up the coon's trail, but to no avail.

The two hounds hunted the area working their way back into the hills where both struck with big bawl mouths and swiftly treed. The three men walked to the tree knowing this was not "The Ghost" the hounds had treed. Indeed, on arrival at a very small tree, they quickly spotted a half grown coon, which they took, and a conclusion was made that the coon was way too small to have left the footprints in the concrete that The Ghost had. Bobby and Kenny told Mr. Malone they would return the following night and Bobby would bring his tree climbers as they could have missed the coon in the large oak. It was agreed and they began the walk back to Mr. Malone's home.

The following night the two young hunters with their hounds showed up at Mr. Malone's to again try and rid him of The Ghost. The coon had made his rounds even earlier on this night for fear of the hounds again; and his premonitions proved true. He had only departed the barn a few minutes when the two hounds were on his trail. He gave them a run for the money though, hitting every large tree he could and running in and out of every hole along the rocky gully. He even swam the lake before running to and climbing the old oak in route to his den. All his tricks did not keep the two young hounds from treeing on the gigantic oak he used as a gateway to his den, but he had no worries; he was trees away in the safety of his den.

Bobby, Kenny and Mr. Malone immediately noted the tree was the same large oak the hounds treed on the night before. They shined for a few minutes without spotting a living thing when Bobby began strapping on the tree climbers. He had a reputation of being able to climb any tree there was with the climbers on. Up the tree he went using a safety strap as he climbed, higher and higher. Concluding a search of the whole tree and looking into the adjoining tree he yelled down that he couldn't find the tricky varmint. He then descended the tree. "Well, he escaped again, but I have an idea. We will get him tomorrow night," Bobby said as the three walked from the tree.

The next night Bobby and Kenny wanted to turn the hounds loose at the big oak and Mr. Malone agreed. The two hounds quickly struck the track and run it straight to the barn, where they briefly hung up at the large machinery door. Mandy soon picked up the trail where the coon had left the barn; Mindy joined in and the race back down the gully was on. The Ghost took the hounds for a good run before tiring and heading back to his den. Up the big oak and over into his den he went; safe again as usual. The two red hounds were stuck treeing on the large oak again, without a trace of coon to be found.

For the next two weeks, The Ghost continued to raid the barn and evade the hunters and hounds who were persistent in their pursuit of him. The Ghost would run hard, and at times, give the young hounds a tough time, but they always ended the trail at the gigantic oak- treed. After two weeks of unsuccessful attempts to catch the wily old coon, Bobby and Kenny grudgingly admitted that Mindy and Mandy couldn't tree the varmint. Bobby told Mr. Malone that he was going to ask his Uncle Charlie to come over and bring "Big Boy". He stated, "Big Boy can tree The Ghost if he can be treed. Big Boy does not miss. He is the most accurate dog I know of."

The next day Bobby and Kenny visited their Uncle Charlie and informed him of the ghost coon, explaining their problem. Charlie readily accepted the opportunity to put Big Boy on the coon's trail, and tree the hard to tree animal. They would all meet up at Mr. Malone's at 9 PM. As Bobby and Kenny drove away from their

Uncle Charlie's, both were smiling because they thought they would see The Ghost up a tree very soon. Big Boy would put him there.

Big Boy was half Redbone and half Pointer bird dog, 75 pounds of treeing machine. He treed by sight, sound and smell, was one of the best squirrel dogs to be found and a coondog deluxe. Big Boy followed a squirrel through the timber and treed on the tree it was in. He treed coon the same way. He hunted with his head up, sparingly giving mouth on track, until he threw his head back with a long, drawn out locate and begin to chop. He had his coon when he threw the big locate and that was it -period.

That night at the pre-arranged time the hunters met at Mr. Malone's. They all sat on the porch discussing the probability of catching the clever coon, and waiting to see what the weather did. A storm was rapidly approaching, but should quickly pass through the area. The thunder rumbled throughout the hills and lost itself in the distance as lightning illuminated the sky. A heavy rain soaked the area and withdrew quick as it had come. There was a solemn quietness after the storm as a blanket of blackness covered the night. The hunters surmised that this was the night they would tree and see The Ghost. Uncle Charlie, Bobby, Kenny and Mr. Malone walked towards the barn leading Big Boy, a fine specimen of a dog. He was about to demonstrate his coon treeing ability. It took but a few minutes before Big Boy had the track of The Ghost up and running. He ran track with a chop, barking only here and there. He struck the track at the barn, and proceeded to the lake and into the timber near the spillway. The rock covered gully was now gushing with water so The Ghost could not take to the holes in the rocks, but had to find other means of deceit. He quickly realized the dog on his trail did not bark much on track and moved a little faster than the hounds which had previously been running him. He ran up and over the ridges of the surrounding hills, finally taking to the lower lake. He swam to the other side and ran into a kudzu patch, but the big dog kept coming, barking only occasionally. He then swam the lake again and went back into the hills, trying to shake the dog from his trail.

It was soon evident to The Ghost that this dog was lightning fast and it was beyond a doubt he would soon have to climb or be caught. Back towards his den The Ghost ran; grateful to see the gigantic oak in the near distance. As he quickly scampered up the oak, he heard the loud, long locate of the big dog only feet behind him.

The hunters along with Mr. Malone stood on the hillside listening to Big Boy push The Ghost to the limit. They had just heard what they were waiting for the loud, long locating bawl at the end of the trail. But wait, something was not right as Big Boy did not start to chop following the big locate. Everything was silent.

"That smart rascal has fooled ole Big Boy," Uncle Charlie turned and declared. "Well, I think that was the big oak tree and he did not stay on it," replied Bobby.

Big Boy had been hot on the trail of The Ghost when he climbed the ancient oak. He threw a big locate but suddenly sensed the coon leaving the tree from above. He did not begin to tree but instead followed the coon as he would a squirrel. Several trees up the hollow the coon came to a stop and Big Boy once again threw his big locate and turned it over to a hard chop. His quarry was now treed to stay.

Following a brief silence the hunters heard Big Boy locate once again and begin to chop this time. "Big Boy has found the end of the road," stated a smiling Uncle Charlie. The men walked towards the treeing dog, bypassing the large oak and traveling almost 100 feet further up the hollow to another large tree. The big red dog with the white chest and white front feet was stretched high as he could reach on the tree.

The big tree was shined but the coon was not seen. Bobby then strapped on his tree climbers and using the safety strap started up the tree. He soon yelled back down, "Here's a hole and sitting down in it is the sly, old rascal we call The Ghost". He then climbed back to the ground.

A short conversation ensued after Bobby's descent from the tree. Bobby informed Mr. Malone that he could kill the coon if he so desired, but would rather catch it alive and relocate it to another area far from there. Mr. Malone stated that he originally wanted the thieving scoundrel killed, but after seeing the dogs run him for over two weeks, he could see relocating it. The coon through his cunning maneuvers had gained the respect of landowner and hunters alike. The Ghost would be allowed to live and run again.

As the others stayed at the tree, Bobby ran back to the barn and collected a piece of conduit, a length of rope, and a small cage. He then constructed a homemade catch pole of sorts from the items and headed back to the tree. With tree climbers strapped on and the catch pole in hand, up the tree he went and soon had "The Ghost" in captivity.

On examination of the coon, there was little difference between him and other coon his size. He was not extremely large, but had abnormally large feet. The cleverness possessed by the one called "The Ghost" had saved his life. He was transported and released into an isolated, coon filled hollow on the other side of the county. Mr. Malone's barn was never again raided and he and the hunters all were   satisfied.

MORE NOSE OR MORE BRAINS?

23

The day was very cold yet much warmer than the three previous days had been. An ice storm had ravaged the area for three days making roads impassable and travel impossible. The roads were now clear so following days of being cooped up inside I was going to turn a couple hounds loose, regardless of weather. As I sat contemplating which hounds would be hunted and where I would turn them loose, my thoughts were disturbed by the ringing of the phone. Upon answering the phone I heard the voice of Casey Woodward, a young hunter who sometimes hunted dogs for me. Casey asked if I was going to hunt that night and if so did I want to try a new place he had lined up. My response was, "Sure, I'll be over about dark. Make sure to dress for the cold weather as it is supposed to drop back into the single digits again." With that, we ended the call.

The temperature was only in the twenties at that time and the ground frozen solid so trailing would be tough. As the sun begin to set the temperature steadily dropped and I decided to hunt Grand Nite Champion Nation's Blue Amos and Grand Nite Champion Nation's Dancin' Deamon. It was going to take a hound with a good nose to tree coon on this rough night and Amos and Deamon both had the nose to do just that. They were balanced hounds that struck quickly and honestly, ran a track to catch, got treed quickly with a coon and stayed put. "We'll see just how good these two are tonight," I thought as I loaded the two hounds into the box for the drive to Casey's.

At the time of this hunt, Grand Nite Champion Nation's Blue Amos was four years old, a Bluetick sired by Grand Nite Champion Dabb's Blue Boy, a Diamond Jim bred hound. His dam was Nite Champion Davis' Blue Peggy, a Ranger II bred female. Amos was a big, dark blue, raw boned hound with good feet and legs, dark eyes and a good head and ears. Amos went hunting well, was a top strike dog that ran a track with a loud bawl and came on the tree with a good locate changing over to a hard chop on the tree. Amos did not move when treed and was exceptionally accurate. He missed very few coons. I'd owned Amos for about a year. Amos came from Joe Moyer of West Plains, Missouri. While one day speaking with Joe he stated, "I have a hound here that you'll like. He can take an old bad track out of those swamps and the rough stuff you hunt and leave dogs scattered behind him then put a tree on the end of it with a coon in it." I told Joe I had more dogs than I knew what to do with but if I could sell one, I'd buy him if I liked him. As Joe and I continued to talk, a deal was made. I would give Joe a broke, young

Bluetick male - the hound that came to be known as Grand Nite Champion Stoney Creek Blue Lite and pay the difference. Joe delivered Amos to Georgia and said if I didn't like him I knew where I got him; same as always. Amos passed the test and stayed in Georgia.

Amos had been in only one competition hunt when I acquired him and had a first place win. He was mostly pleasure coon hunted by my hunting partner Jerrell Thomas and me but did see some competition hunting, quickly finishing to Grand Nite. Amos also did a little winning in some of the larger hunts while being hunted by Randy Leonard. He could consistently tree coon and win in competition. Jerrell said Amos was one of the better track dogs that we had owned; and that was a credit to Amos as we had owned some good ones. Recently, while speaking with Joe Moyer, he stated Amos was the best "all around coon dog" that he ever sold me. That was saying a mouthful as I bought a lot of good hounds from Joe and he stood behind every one of them. Amos stayed at my kennel for many years until he was "lost" by his handlers. He was never recovered.

Grand Nite Champion Nation's Dancin' Deamon was a two year old Platte Valley bred English Redtick. He was sired by Nite Champion Willow Creek Golden Blaze and his dam was Haden's Kansas Sandy. Deamon was a 60 pound, cherry red hound with good feet and legs, a good head and ears and dark eyes. He went hunting well and was a phenomenal strike dog that struck coon tracks, not off game, dog tracks, or water. Yes, I said water, as I have seen a couple of the great striking competition hounds of the past open on water and continue to do so until they hit a track. Deamon didn't

227

babble nor did he bypass tracks, cold or hot, and he possessed one of the best squall bawl mouths ever put on a hound. He was loud. Deamon ran a track in one direction with his loud, squall bawl, had an outstanding locate and was a hard, loud, chop mouthed, stay put tree dog. He only improved the older he became. I had owned him one year at the time of this hunt.

Deamon came out of Penny's English Kennels. He was one and a half years old when I purchased him. He was at the home of my good friends, Rhonie and Marilyn Goggins, who lived at Marissa, Illinois at the time. Rhonie was doing what he does best and that was putting some finishing touches on Deamon and hunting him extra hard.

After conferring with Leroy Penny about Deamon, he and I met in Marissa at the home of Rhonie and Marilyn to let Deamon do his own talking. I was going to hunt a RQE in that area the following night and brought along the dog I had been hunting in the hunts to try Deamon with. It was August and terribly hot, dry and muggy when Deamon and my hound were cut loose. Neither hound looked very good that night but Deamon out-struck and out-trailed my older hound before a couple of trees were finally made. They didn't do anything wrong they just didn't look very good because of the heat.

Following the hunt, I inquired if Deamon had been competition hunted and found he hadn't. I told Leroy if he could persuade Rhonie to hunt Deamon in the RQE hunt the following night that I would buy him. Well, all came together and Rhonie hunted Deamon and qualified him with a 4th place win and he went back to Georgia. Deamon quickly made Grand Nite Champion with limited competition hunting and was only coon hunted afterwards. He was bred very little but can be found in the pedigrees of some of the good English Hounds being promoted today. While talking with Leroy awhile back about Deamon, he said, "I knew Deamon was special when I saw him take an old bad track that other dogs couldn't smell and run it in there a half mile and have a coon at the end of it." Deamon stayed at my home for three years before being sold to Kerry Rooks. As I drove toward Casey's, I thought to myself that it was going to be hard to tree a coon with all the ice and frozen ground. If we treed coon on this cold night, the dogs were going to put forth some extra effort. I didn't know the area or type of terrain we would be hunting but would soon find it to be superb coon country.

Casey was looking out the window as I pulled into the drive. He exited the house before I came to a stop. He loaded his hunting gear and said he would be right back and walked behind the house. He returned leading a good looking Redtick hound that he called "Tick." He stated that Tick was a good dog as he loaded him into the box. We drove further up the mountain towards the new hunting territory, ten miles or so, where the mountain began to flatten out. The area contained miles and miles of hardwood timber with rolling ridges and hollows. It sure looked good.

We drove along a ridge top with deep hollows on both sides, stopping at a point where another hollow intersected the one on the left This was some rough terrain and it seemed even colder at that elevation on the mountain. There were icicles hanging from the trees and everything seemed frozen solid. As we removed the hounds from the box, both Amos and Deamon threw their heads into the air to the left as if they smelled game. This was a trait of both hounds as

229

they came out of the box, if there was a coon in the area they would have it going in short order.

All three dogs were released into the intersecting hollows to the left. Amos and Deamon left immediately and Tick stopped to wet the bushes. In less than one minute, Amos opened with a loud bawl followed by the extremely loud squall bawl of Deamon. The track was fresh and the two hounds were joined by Tick with a high pitched squall. The hounds ran the track up one hollow and back along the top of the adjacent ridge before crossing out of hearing range. We drove further along the ridge and stopped to listen. All three dogs were treed solid, across the hollow, on the side of the other ridge. Only twenty minutes had passed since the track was struck; it was going to take much longer to walk to the treed hounds. The walk down the ridge was easy with the exception of several patches of slick, frozen areas. The climb up the· other side was a little harder, having to deal with the slick ground, but we arrived at the tree in due time.

All three hounds were stretched high on the side of an ancient oak, which was not much more than a shell. There were holes at the bottom and on the large lower limbs, and no telling how many up higher that we couldn't see. We shined the outside and looked up into the hole from the bottom but saw nothing. The track had been hot and it had run straight to a den. The night was not starting out very well. As we walked from the tree, Casey said we were lucky to have made a tree because of the cold temperature. The temperature was now in the low teens and still dropping.

Topping the ridge and walking towards the truck, we decided to cut the hounds into the hollow on the other side of the road. We cut all three into the hollow, back in the direction we had cut them loose the first time. Ten minutes or so passed before we heard Deamon open, far up the hollow. We drove back to where we had made the first drop and stopped to listen. Deamon was trailing at a steady pace but was still alone. Following several minutes of listening to Deamon's loud squalling bawls, he was joined by Amos. The two hounds worked the track, drifting and bawling here and there, moving on down the hollow. Once again we drove along the ridge top in the direction they were trailing, and stopped to listen. The track was still cold but both hounds were doing a good job on it. Tick had not opened as of yet.

"You think that's a coon? I haven't heard Tick say a word," Casey commented. "I don't know what it is," I replied. "I guess we'll soon see."

No sooner than the words left my mouth, we heard the roaring locate and hard chops as Deamon came to the end of the line. He was immediately backed by Amos, but Tick never opened his mouth. "Must be a possum or something," Casey said as we walked toward the tree. The dogs were treed at the end of the hollow where the terrain began to level out. There was a lot of small streams and water, mostly frozen solid, in the area where the dogs were treed. Walking in to the tree we saw that it was another large hardwood and the first thing I thought was "den tree." Surprisingly, the tree seemed to have no holes and we soon spotted a large coon perched in a fork, high in the tree. Tick was at the tree but was not treeing. He acted as if he couldn't smell the coon. Casey leashed Tick back from the tree and put the coon out to Amos and Deamon. He said if Tick wasn't treeing on it, he didn't need to get hold of it. The coon was a large dark colored mountain coon which Deamon and Amos quickly dealt with.

As we walked from the tree, Casey asked, "Why do you think Tick wouldn't tree on that tree?" I didn't want to hurt his feelings, so I replied, "I don't know." We were admiring the cooney looking woods when Casey said, "Let's turn them loose again."

In only a couple minutes, Deamon opened once again with a roaring squall bawl and was soon joined by Amos. The track was another cold track and the two worked it for twenty minutes or so before Deamon threw another big locate followed by the loud, bawl locate of Amos even before he could begin to chop. Both hounds were chopping loud and hard but Tick was not on this tree either. We slowly walked toward the tree giving Tick time to get there.

The tree was another big hardwood that had Deamon and Amos stretched high on its side. Tick was rearing up on the tree attempting to smell the coon but never opened his mouth. He tried to find a track, coming to or leaving the tree, but again never opened his mouth. We shined the tree and spotted a large hole halfway up the tree. I squalled a couple times and Casey yelled, "Here he is! It just ran out of the hole."

I looked at the coon and started to walk away, leading Deamon and Amos. They didn't need another coon. Casey followed leading Tick and shaking his head in disbelief. We loaded the hounds and started the drive out of the area. Casey hadn't said very much since we departed the last tree. I asked if he was ready to call it a night as the wind had picked up a little. "Turn in that side road up ahead and let's make one more turnout," he said.

"That's okay with me," I replied. I drove up the side road until we came to a good hollow, stopping at a place that looked good as any. As we unloaded the hounds, I again noticed Amos and Deamon raise their heads into the air as if they smelled something. All three hounds left the road in a hard run. Amos opened almost immediately with a big bawl locate and was quickly backed by Deamon. Neither had opened on the ground but were both treed on their first bark. Tick never opened on this tree either and Casey was again shaking his head. They were treed close to the road and we walked in and leashed them. Tick was up on the tree when we arrived but was not barking. He was unsuccessfully trying to find scent. After shining the tree, another large coon was spotted near the top. We then walked back to the truck ready to call it a night. Casey said he had seen enough.

On the drive back to Casey's house we made a detour by the Bank to see what the flashing temperature sign read. The flashing sign read 8 degrees, but it was probably much colder on the mountain. I was amazed we had seen one coon much less three. As Casey was unloading Tick, he stated, "Tick is a good dog but I believe he couldn't smell those coon. Do you think that Amos and Deamon have more nose or more brains than Tick?" I looked at Casey and replied, "Honestly I don't know." As I drove away, Casey was still shaking his head.

In the months following our hunt, I saw Casey only a handful of times when he would visit or occasionally hunt a dog in the hunts for me. It would be many years before Casey and I would go on another pleasure hunt as he was soon married and I moved from the area. We eventually lost contact with each other and it would be 14 years before I would see him again. At that time, we would turn a good English hound loose on the same mountaintop at precisely the same place we had cut Amos and Deamon loose so many years before. This hunt would be the last hunt I went on with Casey and the last time I would see him.

One cold morning in 2004, only a few months following our last hunt, I received some very sad news. Casey was dead. One of the guys working on our construction crew informed us of the tragedy. Upon hearing the news, my heart sank to my feet and I became very sad. I moped around the remainder of the day thinking back on some of our past adventures. Casey had traveled across the country with me when he was only a child. We had been on some good hunts; both pleasure and competition. As the day slowly advanced, several thoughts from the past came to mind. My thoughts roamed to a time only a few days after our hunt on that cold winter night with Amos and Deamon. Casey had come by my home to borrow a dog to hunt with friends in another state. I told him to go out to the kennel and get whatever he wanted and I'd be out soon as I got my shoes on. As I walked towards the kennel, Casey was walking back towards me leading three Grand Nite Champions. I was slightly shocked because I thought he only wanted one dog. I guess he saw the shock on my face and quickly said, "Don't worry. I'll take good care of them." He then gave me the reason for taking each dog. I only smiled and replied, "Sounds like a good idea to me. I know you will take care of the dogs. You always have."

My mind then drifted back only a couple months to our last hunt together. This hunt was unplanned and happened only by accident. It was around 11 PM and I was going to make a turnout with a nice

English hound called Dual Grand Champion, PKC Champion, NKC Nite Champion, AKC Nite Champion Posted Land Swamp Dancer. I hoped to tree a quick coon or two then go in as I had a job to complete the following morning. I stopped at a small Quik Stop to get gasoline and as I was pumping gas Casey walked up and asked, "What are you doing?" It had been 14 years since I had seen him and I was slightly stunned. As I recovered from the surprise, I said, "'Going to turn this old dog loose." He then asked, 'Where are you going to hunt? Are you going by yourself?" "Yeah, I'm going to hunt alone and haven't yet decided where I'll go. Do you want to come along?" I asked. "If you'll run me by my house to get my hunting equipment, I know a good place in that direction to hunt, too," he said. "Sounds good to me. Let's go," I said.

After a detour by Casey's home, we drove to the top of the mountain to the same location where we had turned Amos and Deamon loose all those years before. Dancer was cut off the ridge into the hollow, where he swiftly struck with a big bawl and made quick work of a good track. We walked along the side of the ridge to Dancer's tree, which was only a short distance from the road. Dancer was treeing hard with a good, clear, fast chop and had a coon that was quickly spotted. Dancer didn't need coon put out to him so the coon was left to run again. Upon walking back to the road, Dancer was cut into the hollow on the other side and had another track going in minutes. This track ended with another coon seen.

We had treed two coons in only a few minutes and decided on one more drop. After moving to an area with a creek running through it where the terrain had flattened considerably, Dancer was once again released. He swiftly had another track going, ran it into the country

235

and seemed to be barking treed, but not exactly right. We walked in towards Dancer's tree and he left as we approached, only to go a short distance and tree or bay again. Once again he left as we approached. He was running his prey in the creek bed which had high banks on each side and quickly ran out of hearing range.

Following a drive around to where the creek crossed a small country road, we stopped and heard Dancer once again. He appeared to be baying along the creek bank. He was behind a house and neither Casey nor I knew who lived there. I drove up the road a short distance to a gated field, stopping at the gate to listen. Dancer was directly across the field, not moving, but steadily barking; yet he wasn't treed solid but baying. I advised Casey to stay with the vehicle while I walked in to retrieve Dancer. As I came near him he shut up and I couldn't get my hands on him. Becoming aggravated,

I walked back to the vehicle and sat down. I advised Casey that Dancer had ran off as I got near. About that time he began to bay again.

By this time I had decided to wait until daylight and let the landowner know what we were doing on his land as Dancer was directly behind his house. Casey asked, "What do you think Dancer is doing or running?" After thinking a few seconds I answered, "I believe he is messing with a coyote, probably a female in heat. I think he is baying it along the high creek bank. It is only playing with him."

I then dozed off for a short time and awoke to Casey opening the door. He had Dancer on the lead and also had a big smile on his face. He said he walked in to him with the light off and as he came very close he flipped the light on. "As I flipped on the light, the beam hit Dancer and a scrawny old coyote, just as you thought. Dancer cowered down and I caught him and the coyote ran off!" He exclaimed.

On the drive back to Casey's I told him that Dancer had never messed with a coyote before but sometimes dogs do strange things. We began talking and Casey said he was having a difficult time in his life, with some problems. It was a very troubled time for him. As he was getting out of the truck, I gave him my phone number and advised him to call if he wanted to go hunting or if he needed anything or anyone to talk to. I never heard from him.

I'll always remember Casey asking the question after our cold winter hunt with Amos, Deamon and Tick. "Do you think they have more nose or more brains?" And the serious look he gave me when he borrowed the three Grand Nite Champions and said he would take care of them. I'll also remember the smile he had on his face as he woke me from a sleep to say he had Dancer on the leash.

While still only a young man, Casey departed this earth way too early in life, a tragic act, leaving behind family, friends and loved ones.. With this thought in mind, "More Nose or More Brains?" is dedicated in his memory.

COMPETITION OR PLEASURE
24

On a cool winter Saturday evening, as I stood at the kennel contemplating competition hunt, my friend Stephanie pulled into the driveway, got out of the car and walked around to the kennel.

"Hey! Looks like you're going hunting tonight. I just came by to see what you were doing. Maybe I'll go hunting with you," she stated. "I'm thinking about going to a competition hunt, but you can come along if you want," I replied. "I want to hunt a dog myself, not just go along. I want to learn how to handle the dogs in the hunts too," she retorted. "I want to hunt Hawk as he is my favorite."

"Hawk is already Champion, a Grand Nite Champion, and he was only hunted in the larger hunts where there will be competition. There probably will not be another Grand Nite there as this is a smaller hunt, but maybe hunting alone you could learn to call your dog correctly before you hunt against competition. I'll give the coon club President a call and see if they have someone to judge and guide you," I responded. "Oh goody! I've wanted to try my hand at handling one of the dogs!" She exclaimed.

Following a brief conversation with the club President I found there would be several members present to guide and judge. There was also the possibility there would be another Grand Nite Champion or two in attendance to make a complete cast. Needless to say, Stephanie was elated. She had been going on a few pleasure hunts with me and liked the fun and excitement of an enjoyable hunt with good hounds. Stephanie liked a big Blue hound called Champion, Grand Nite Champion Uchtman's Southern Blue Hawk Jr., a good looking, big mouthed, broke hound that handled good and treed coons. I had purchased Hawk Jr from Gary Uchtman of Missouri, at the time, with intentions of studding him out and using him as a cross on my other hounds. Hawk would be the perfect hound for Stephanie to begin her competition hunting career with.

I was going to hunt a young hound sired by my Dual Grand Champion Moyer's Blue Chubbs called Champion, Nite Champion Nation's Blue Chubbs Jr.. I also owned Chubbs Jr 's grand sire Dual Grand Champion Davis' Blue Scooter and his grand dam Nite Champion Gregory's Blue Scat. Jr. had inherited a little from all of his good ancestors. He was an extremely hard going, big hunting hound that got by himself a lot and was very good about having a coon in the trees he made. He was an uncommonly good looking, 60 pound, dark blue hound that ran track with a loud hound bawl and treed with a short, loud bawl. He also stayed put under any kind of tree pressure. I wanted to finish Jr. to Dual Grand and possibly stud him at a later date.

With the deadline for the hunt fast approaching, we loaded our equipment along with the hounds and began the drive toward the clubhouse. Upon exiting the interstate highway we pulled into a truck plaza for gasoline and snacks. As I filled the truck with gas Stephanie went inside to purchase snacks and returned just as I finished filling both tanks. I asked her to pull the truck away from the gas pumps while I went inside to pay for the fuel. On returning to the pump area I was saddened to see Stephanie had pulled away from the pump and rubbed the curb with the right rear wheel causing the valve stem to be jerked from the wheel. We would be lucky to make the entry deadline even if we only changed the tire.

"Well at least we're at a place to get the tire fixed," I said to a very sorrowful Stephanie. "I don't think we'll make the deadline but we can go hunting anyway, it won't be a total loss," she replied.

The tire was fixed in record time but to avoid rushing to make the deadline, or possibly missing it by only minutes, we opted to enjoy a pleasure hunt. I wanted to turn the hounds loose alone and then together, the objective being for the two hounds to get a little hunting alone and for Stephanie to better learn their mouths for when she did get to competition hunt. With this thought in mind we drove back in the direction of home and some choice coon hunting territory.

Our first drop was made from a small dirt road directly onto the creek bank, with only Hawk released. Hawk went only 100 yards before he opened with a loud screaming locate bawl and immediately began to tree with a chop and bawl. We stood and listened to him for 10 minutes before proceeding to the tree; a large hardwood with a coon sitting in the top. Stephanie leashed Hawk and gave him a little praise before we returned to the truck. Coon season was open and we would have gave Hawk the coon but because of our intentions to go to the competition hunt the rifle had been left at home. We would have the coon to run again at another time.

After moving a couple miles Chubbs Jr. was cut loose on the opposite side of the road, he left the lead in a hard run looking for Mr. Ringtail. Thirty to forty minutes passed without hearing a bark before the tracker was checked to determine Jr.'s location. He had crossed over the road far in front of us; we drove in that direction stopping at intervals to listen for his loud bawl mouth. Jr. had an extremely loud, carrying, hound mouth that could be heard a long distance. On the third stop we heard him trailing in a deep hollow, barking only occasionally but drifting with each bark. Driving further to the top of the ridge we stopped to listen at a point near where he had last barked. He proved to be directly in front of us and running to catch; we could sit, listen and enjoy some good track work from our location high upon the ridge. Listen and enjoy is exactly what we did and it wasn't long until Jr. threw a big houndy locate bawl and shortened it down to a short bawl; he wasn't going any further.

The walk into Jr. took longer than anticipated as he was far deeper than he sounded. Following the lengthy walk, we arrived to find him stretched high on the side of a very large white pine. Jr. was leashed back and the tree shined, but nothing was seen. As we started to walk away Stephanie yelled, "Here it is." She was becoming very good at finding coon eyes in a difficult tree. I felt as if I hadn't looked hard enough as the coon was in plain sight, but that's the ones that are sometimes overlooked. Jr. was given a little praise and led back to the truck to prepare for a turnout with both hounds. Following a short drive, both Hawk and Chubbs Jr. were cast into a deep hollow from atop the ridge.

I had run and treed many coons in that hollow over the years and had never failed to strike a track when hunting there. Same as always the hounds had a good track going within 10 minutes with Jr. opening first and Hawk joining in. Nothing sounds better than hearing a couple of big mouthed hounds run a red hot track in the hills. The loud bawls were echoing off the surrounding hills and hollows making it sound as if there were far more than only the two hounds. The hounds ran the track down the hollow almost out of hearing and we drove closer to better hear what was happening. Hawk was giving more mouth than Chubbs Jr. as the two pushed the track from the hollow into the flat bottom land; we sat atop the high ridge listening to some very good track work. The hounds put pressure on the animal once it hit the creek bottoms and it wasn't long until the big bawl locates from both hounds were heard.

If we had been competition hunting the hound getting first tree would have been determined by the handler who made the call first because the hounds located at almost the exact moment. Both hounds immediately went to treeing after only one locate bark, Hawk with a bawl and chop and Chubbs Jr. sounding a lot like his sire with a short bawl. After listening to the treeing hounds for a few minutes, we drove close as possible and walked in to them, finding them treed on a big hardwood on the creek bank. Both hounds were leashed back and the tree shined. The coon was soon spotted lying in a fork high in the tree. The animal did not want to look at the light but his body could be seen along with his tail hanging down from the fork. I was glad that we didn't have the rifle with us as that old coon had run a good race and it is coons such as that one that I prefer to leave to run again. Following a little praise the hounds were led a little ways from the tree and released onto the creek.

When hunting the hills after making a tree, I usually like to move to another area if possible as it seems when you move to an area that hasn't been hunted the coon tree quicker and easier - maybe not always but many times. In the hills where the coons are not plentiful you might turn the dogs off one tree and they could go a long distance before striking another track thus using more time. In this instance cutting Hawk and Chubbs Jr. off the tree and back into the same area was a mistake. They got deep in the country and into some rough cutover and soon had an old bad track going that took some time to sort out and put a tree on. · The two hounds trailed the track out of hearing and treed it before we were able to get in position to hear them. Even then they were deep in some rough country that required a lot of hard walking; so rough that it could cause a beginning coonhunter to want to quit before they were started good.

Following a substantial period of time, we arrived at the tree, scratched and bruised by the rough terrain, briars and undergrowth, only to find the two hounds treed on a den. The hounds were given a little praise anyway but would remain on the leash until we got back to the vehicle. It had been a real chore getting to the treed hounds and would be even harder trying to lead them back through the tangled mess. After another considerable period of time and some careful maneuvering we arrived back at the truck thoroughly worn out. It is times like these that make a coonhunter realize how much they really love and appreciate the sport. We were finished for the night and I surmised that it would be Stephanie's last coon hunt but I was mistaken. Ensuing a week or so for the scratches and cuts to heal, Stephanie was ready to hunt again and also prepared to try a little competition hunting.

Many nights were enjoyed in the woods with Chubbs Jr. and I regretted that he wasn't campaigned in some of the larger hunts as he could have won his share. He was a natural coon treeing hound, but ran his share of off game when real young which only helped to improve his tracking ability. He was hard headed and difficult to completely break from off game, but once accomplished he was a good solid hound at a young age. I sold Chubbs Jr. as a young hound for a good price and sometimes wished I had kept him, but a person can't keep them all.

Hawk Jr. stayed in my kennel for only a short period of time but we enjoyed some good hunts with him. The opportunity was not given to raise pups from him or breed him to any outside females. A couple ads were ran on him and several calls received to breed to him but we no longer had him as he was stolen from the dog box at a RQE event in Murphy, North Carolina. Hawk was never recovered and it was probably a good thing that I never found anyone with my hound. Hawk was a big, good looking hound that would catch your eye. He had a loud mouth and treed lots of coon. He possibly could have helped the Bluetick breed as his great sire

Grand Nite Champion Uchtman's So. Blue Hawk did, but that's

something   that'll   never   be   known.

OPENING NIGHT, THE SEASON BEGINS
25

The day was extremely nice and the approaching night promised to be even better. It was the first night of raccoon season. The point in time was October 15, a special date, opening night of the season in our locality for long as remembered and also my birthday. I always tried to put aside this night to be enjoyed in the woods with friends and good hounds. As I impatiently sat awaiting sunset and darkness to roll in, I drifted back in time. Many good hunts were relished on this night from childhood into adulthood. There had been many good hounds, most had come and gone, only a select few stayed until the end. My ruminations were disturbed by the voice of my longtime friend Bren- da. "I want to take John Kidd along with us tonight," she said.

I smiled and asked, "What else do you want to take?" Brenda had a tendency to want to keep every pup we raised and every dog that came through the kennel. "Well, how many are we going to hunt? I'd like to take Lucky and you can take Snapper," she replied.

Grinning even wider I said, "That's exactly what I wanted to hunt." It really didn't matter what we hunted but she had picked a couple top hounds and I was content with her choices. I was surprised she hadn't said, "All of them."

As dusk settled in, we walked to the kennel, leashed John Kidd, Lucky and Snapper and loaded them into the dog box. We grabbed a few snacks, the cooler and extra clothes that might be needed. Our intentions were to hunt all night or most of it. We were going to hunt as many different turnouts as possible, some of them pretty rough. We hunted where the hounds had to hunt for a coon; I never hunted off coon feeders. On the drive to the hunting area I thought about the three hounds we were going to hunt.

John Kidd was a tough, dark colored English Redtick pup that we had raised. He had run loose around the house until he began running and treeing; he was then kenneled and his night hunt training started. He would run and tree a coon alone and had already split treed at eight months old. He was bred to make a coondog with his sire being Grand Nite Champion Raef's Big John. His pedigree contained other greats up close such as Dual Grand Champion Sugar Creek J.R., Dual Grand Champion Pinehill True Boy, Grand Nite Champion Raef's Freckles, Grand Nite Champion Raef's Red Rusty, Grand Champion, Nite Champion Paxton Abernathy and Dual Grand Champion Penny's Kentucky Kojak. His pedigree was full of not only top winning competition hounds, but balanced coon treeing hounds as well. John Kidd never acted like a puppy and was making a good hound. He would go hunting alone or in company, had a big bawl mouth on track and treed with a hard, loud chop.

Lucky was a three year old Treeing Walker, his registered name being Dual Grand Champion, A.C.H.A. Nite Champion Gordon's Lucky Striker. He was a 55 pound, streamlined, blanket backed, red headed hound with good feet, legs and a good head and ears. He was built to move, and that he could do. His breeding consisted of Paul Gordon's breeding from Kentucky going back to Grand Nite Champion, A.C.H.A. World Champion Bellars Striker. Lucky was a completely balanced hound with a cold nose and brains to use it. He was a one way, fast track dog with a big bawl mouth on track and a hard, loud chop on the tree. He treed coon not just trees; he treed what he struck and stayed put once treed. I liked him. Lucky was purchased from Mit Elliott, Dawson Georgia; I purchased him before he was two years old. He was a Show Champion and was finished to Grand Show, Grand Nite and A.C.H.A. Nite Champion after coming to my kennel.

Snapper was a three year old English Hound. His registered name was Dual Grand Champion, A.C.H.A. Nite Champion, N.K.C. Nite Champion Big Time Snapper. He was sired by Grand Nite Champion Snow's Tree Jammer by World Champion Hayes Hardtime Speck. Snapper was a 55 pound Redtick hound with a light blue frosting on his back and sides. His looks would draw your eyes to him. He was a tight made hound with good feet and legs, a big flat head with good ears and dark intelligent eyes. Snapper was a tightly wound live wire that would quickly get deep, get struck and treed with a coon, yet he did not overshoot tracks. He was a cold nosed, completely balanced, one way fast track dog that ran a track with a bawl and chops and treed with a hard, loud chop. Snapper was a split treeing fool, a radical tree dog that was very accurate and stayed put. He was purchased from Harry Snow of Rome, New York; and was already Dual Grand and N.K.C. Nite Champion when he came to my kennel. I finished him to A.C.H.A. Nite Champion.

The night was cool and dark as we prepared to make our first drop from a power line into a large, heavily timbered section of woods. All three hounds were cut onto a small stream that crossed the power line and ran several miles before running into a larger creek. A good track was struck almost immediately with Lucky opening first, followed by Snapper and John Kidd. The hounds ran the track deep into the section, turned and came back across the power line into a hardwood covered swamp land. Snapper fell treed on the edge of the swamp first. The locating bawls of Lucky and John Kidd followed, on a separate tree another 100 yards farther into the swamp. We walked into Snapper and quickly found his coon, leashed him at the tree and proceeded on to Lucky and John Kidd's tree, which also contained a coon. We gave Lucky and John Kidd their coon and then Snapper was given his. These two coons would probably be the only coon we took on this night unless something exceptional happened, as we did not kill all coons we treed, even in season. The hounds were led back to the vehicle and loaded, we then moved to another location.

The next drop was at a church surrounded by timber, mostly pines; one quarter mile behind the church yard there were beaver ponds and swamp land. All three hounds left the lead in a hard run, along a trail that led to the beaver swamp. John Kidd swiftly struck with a big bawl, trailed around for a couple minutes, located and treed with a loud, solid chop. He was still in the pines and received no backing from the other two hounds. We walked to his small pine and swiftly spotted a possum. Following a brief scolding, John Kidd was sent on his way. This was the first possum he had treed while hunting.

We soon heard Snapper strike deep in the beaver swamp. He was joined by Lucky and John Kidd. The track was good and the hounds worked it out of the swamp, down the creek and across a pasture into the distant ridges. We walked back to the vehicle, drove to the other side of the creek close as possible to the trailing hounds. The hounds were faintly heard, far back in a deep hollow. We drove around the ridge, stopped to listen and found all three hounds treed very near where we had stopped. Another coon was spotted in the tree and the hounds were once again leashed and led back to the vehicle, the coon was left to run again. A lot of time had been wasted on this turnout so we next moved to a couple of easy drops.

Following a short drive the hounds were cut in towards a small cattail filled pond. The pond was always a good place to strike and tree an easy coon. Lucky quickly struck; Snapper and John Kidd joined in and the race was on. We sat and listened to some good track work and pleasant hound music until the track was ran from the wooded area. The hounds crossed onto a small cut over mountain and treed in a den tree surrounded by rock cliffs; so much for the easy turnout. Regardless, we had heard a good race and it would have been hard to distinguish which hound had grabbed the tree first. After retrieving the hounds we moved to the next "easy spot."

The next drop was on a stream crossing under a seldom used dirt road. The stream ran through a long, narrow strip of hardwoods before running into the river. We released all three hounds onto a red hot track; they were struck before they left the lead and hastily finished the track. Snapper quickly exploded on a tree and was backed by Lucky and John Kidd. The hounds had run the track almost to the river bank and treed in an extremely large, vine and leaf covered tree with several visible holes in it. We leashed the dogs and thoroughly shined the tree without finding anything. As we walked back to the vehicle, we discussed where our next drop would be as our easy drops had not paid off. We decided on another church yard. It seems the coons are always around the church yards.

This area had clear, cold springs gushing from the ground in numerous places. The area across from the church was cutover with briars and water, water and more water. The area had timber on two sides and was a coon paradise. I had taken a visiting coon hunter from the North to this area a few months prior and he said, "Surely we aren't going to release the dogs into that mess. My hound has never seen anything like that."

Needless to say the area was very rough and hard on a hound. Most coon struck in the rough cutover did not tree on the few trees still standing, but ran into the timber to the left or right or crossed the road and treed behind the church. The hounds were released into the cutover on one of the streams and quickly had a track going. Lucky was first to strike with his big, clear bawl followed by the loud bawl of John Kidd. Snapper was not heard on this track.

Lucky and John Kidd worked the track through the rough cutover and into the heavily timbered woods to the right, almost out of hearing range. We drove closer, and as we stopped to listen Lucky came on a tree with a big locate and began to chop. He was backed by John Kidd and we walked into the tree. A coon was spotted high in the tree, the hounds were leashed and we headed back to the vehicle to look for Snapper.

We drove back to the church yard where the tracker was checked to determine Snapper's location. A weak signal was received from across the cutover. The tree switch was also going off but we couldn't hear him from that area. "I hope we aren't going to have to walk across that jungle," stated Brenda. "I think he may be treed in a hollow on the other side of the cutover. Maybe we can drive around," I replied. "If we can't get closer I'll walk in to get him from this side."

Driving around and into the parking lot of a commercial chicken farm we stopped to listen. Snapper was heard loud and clear and the walk to retrieve him began. He was treed at the end of a deep hollow which crossed the cutover. He had a big coon up a small tree. I quickly leashed him and we headed back to the vehicle as I didn't know who owned the chicken farm where we had parked the vehicle. We loaded Snapper and started for another turnout, back in the direction of home as it was getting late.

Our next drop was in an area called Dry Creek. The hounds once again left the lead in a hard run and soon had a track going. Lucky was first to find coon scent and was joined by Snapper and eventually John Kidd. Lucky and Snapper steadily drifted the track in one direction but very little was heard from John Kidd. The hounds worked the track until it could be run and John Kidd began to give mouth. The track was run a good distance and crossed the highway before we could head the hounds off. We drove across the highway and stopped to listen as the three hounds put pressure on the animal. It was going to be forced to tree or fight, and real soon.

After driving onto a side road and stopping at the creek bridge, we heard the hounds' running heads up along the creek bank. They would have to turn back or cross the small road we were on if something didn't give in a minute or so. Just as that thought occurred to me, Lucky gave a locate quickly followed by Snapper's dying locate. Both Lucky and Snapper were screaming on the tree, but no John Kidd. We heard him give a bawl or two but he wasn't on the tree. After a couple more bawls, he located and went to chopping on a separate tree. I grabbed the rifle and we began the short walk to the dogs. I was going to let John Kidd have his coon, if he had one and could stand the pressure and stay treed.

We arrived at Lucky and Snapper's tree first and leashed them at the tree. They were on a large leaf covered tree growing between the creek bank and the edge of a pasture. We didn't shine their tree but walked on to John Kidd, a couple hundred feet farther down the creek. John Kidd was on a willow tree, and he did have a coon that we promptly let him have. I felt if he could stay treed with all the noise the other two hounds were making that he deserved the coon. He was independent enough that he didn't just back the other hounds but picked a tree of his own. Lucky and Snapper also had a coon which we spotted from the pasture. Their coon was left to run again.

As we loaded the hounds, I decided to call it a night even though we had time for another turnout. I figured John Kidd would be going in with a good thought in his head. All dogs had looked good, even though John Kidd had treed a possum earlier but redeemed himself with a coon. Lucky or Snapper never made an off bark. Their performance would have made anyone proud.

The season's first night had been a good one, as was my birthday. Seeing John Kidd on that last tree alone was a great present. The hunt had been a good one and I was proud of the work performed by all three hounds Lucky, Snapper and John Kidd all joined the long list of hounds that had come and gone. Snapper was sold to Kerry Rooks of Fort Valley, Georgia, a coon hunter who has owned more good hounds than anyone I know. He was later resold to an English promoter, but only lived a short life. He died from an injury sustained while hunting.

John Kidd was said to have been lost by his handler before he had time to make his mark in the coonhound world. He was never recovered. I often wonder what type hound he would have finished into.

Lucky stayed in my kennel until he was five years old and was sold to some good coon hunting folks from Alabama after he struck

three tracks and treed three single coons while being hunted alone. I often wished I would have kept Snapper and Lucky but I had more hounds than could be hunted. Maybe I'll own more like them in the future.

HUNTIN' WITH THE REAL MCCOY
26

As I pulled off l-20 and into the truck plaza at Madison, Georgia I noticed an old friend out front of the restaurant, and drove over to say hello. It had been several years since I'd seen Michael T. McCoy, called Mike (The Real McCoy), but he was his same old jovial self; hadn't changed a bit. Mike smiled and said, "Long time no see old Buddy. What brings you over to this part of the country?" "Been over at the hunting camp in South Carolina, just stopped to eat and might even stay over for the night if a couple friends here in Madison want to hunt tonight," I answered.

"Looks like you're still coon hunting, guess you have the dogs in that box on the truck. Hey, why don't you come over to the house and I'll take you to some of the best coon hunting territory this area has to offer. Nobody hunts these spots and they're full of coon. Let's go inside and get a bite to eat and talk it over. I'm having a little cookout this evening at the house, but we can hunt soon as it gets dark." Cutting a fool Mike then quoted a line from Hank Williams Jr., "Come on over, I got the pig in the ground and the beer on ice, and all my rowdy friends are coming over tonight." Then adding a line of his own he jokingly said, "Soon as darkness comes we'll turn them old hounds loose and tree a coon or two before the morning light."

As we sat in the restaurant it took only a moment for me to take Mike up on the offer; I never turn down an opportunity to hunt some prime coon country. Mike only occasionally coon hunted but was a dedicated deer hunter, and much as he stayed in the woods I was certain he knew what he was talking about. "How far you live from here?" I asked Mike. "Not far, just a little ways in Putnam County. Got plenty of hunting there and over in Baldwin County too," He answered.

I followed Mike to his home, unloaded the hounds, gave them fresh water and allowed them to stretch then relax the remainder of the day. Following Mike's little get together, and as darkness approached we loaded the hounds and drove toward Murder Creek for our first drop. We would be hunting four good hounds, two Walkers, an English Redtick and a Bluetick; four hounds that would go hunting, get struck and get treed with the game.

The older of the two Walkers was Grand Nite Champion Smith's Ohio Rock, a Spring Creek Rock bred hound and a good one. Rock would get in the country quick, get struck and move the track swiftly to the correct tree, get hooked and stay put. Rock ran track with a loud chop and bawl, had a good locate and was a loud hard tree dog. I bought Rock from Creed Smith of Hamilton, Ohio; one of the good guys, now deceased. Creed's passing was a great loss to the coon hunting world. I bought several good hounds from Creed over the years and you could bet if you saw him at the hunts that he had a good hound on his lead.

The other Walker hound was Grand Nite Champion Logan's Wild Quick, a top hound sired by Grand Nite Champion Waggoner's Mr. Quick. He was a good hound that got in the country deep as necessary, quickly got treed with a coon and stayed put -regardless. Quick bawled and chopped on track and treed with a solid chop. Not only was Quick a good hound he was also a reproducer of many good hounds. I bought Quick from Jerry Winn and Rick Burnett who had promoted him quite a bit. Quick did a lot of winning for me in some of the larger hunts of the time.

The English Hound was Grand Nite Champion Nation's Captain Keno, a hound out of Al Gibson's breeding, that would leave the lead as if shot from a gun, quickly get struck and run every track to catch, locate fast and accurate and stay put on the tree. Keno ran track with a chop, squall and bawl, all high pitched and carrying; he was an outstanding tree dog that treed in excess of 130 barks per minute. Keno came out of Penny's English Kennels and had never been in a competition hunt when I purchased him. The Bluetick Hound was Champion Nite Champion Nation's Blue Chubbs Jr., a hard going young hound that hunted deep as necessary, got struck swiftly and drifted a track, quickly getting treed with a coon and stayed put. Jr. ran track with a big houndy bawl and treed with a short bawl, he would be treed alone every chance he got. Jr. was sired by my Dual Grand Champion Moyer's Blue Chubbs.

Our first drop was into a heavily wooded tract of land divided by Murder Creek, which ran through the center of the section. All four hounds were released into the timber, Rock went right, Quick and Jr. to the left and Keno busted a hole in the dark straight ahead. Keno was first to open, deep in the timber, he was moving, chopping and squalling as he got through the country. Nothing covered Keno, but Rock responded by striking a track of his own and rapidly putting a tree on it.

Mike and I stood listening to Rock tree for several minutes and began the walk to him. Quick and Jr. were not heard and Keno had gotten out of hearing range; we'd find them momentarily. As we walked into Rock's tree and saw him stretched high on a large hardwood Mike commented on Rock's treeing style. Stating, "Now that is a tree dog like I've never seen." As I leashed Rock back and shined the tree I said, "Yeah, and even better is this coon sitting in the tree."

We put the coon out to Rock, leashed him, and started the walk back to the truck to check the tracker for the other hounds location, Rock remained on the lead. Pinpointing the three hounds they were found to be in two different directions; Quick and Jr. together and Keno in the opposite direction. The drive to locate them began, with Quick and Jr. being the first to be found, and they were treed.

Driving close as possible we started the walk to them, we were able to follow a narrow trail almost to the tree. Quick and Jr. were both on the tree, another hardwood, which was hollow from the ground up. Quick stretched high on one side of the tree chopping loud and hard while Jr., belly laid on the other side of the tree steadily bawled. They were leashed back and the tree shined with nothing seen on the outside.

Leading the hounds from the tree Mike and I discussed the possibility of driving near Keno's location. Mike said the possibility of getting close as we did to Quick and Jr.'s tree was slim to none, but we could get within hearing range. Following a lengthy drive around the section we could, in fact, hear Keno blowing a tree down; he had crossed out of the large section of woods and into some rough territory. Driving near as possible the walk began.

As we walked toward the tree Mike remarked, "That coon was on his way to Macon, and if Keno had not gotten under him he would have made it too." "He might not have made it to Macon, but he made it half way for sure, and could have picked a route not so rough with a few roads," I replied.

After a good hour of hard walking we arrived at the tree, a small oak with a large coon perched in a fork near the top. Keno was sitting at the base of the tree shelling the barks out at an unbelievable rate. Mike put the coon out as I held Keno back, releasing him when the coon hit the ground. We then began the long walk back to the truck and another hunting area.

"I thought those Walker dogs were hard tree dogs but that Redtick can flat shell 'em out on the wood. Don't know how a dog can bark that fast and still breathe," Mike commented as we walked to the vehicle. "Where are we going to go next?" I asked Mike. "I'm going to take you to some of the best coon hunting you ever saw. We're going to Baldwin County, a place called Holenshed Swamp over near Toomsboro," a smiling Mike stated. I knew we were in for some really rough country by the way Mike was smiling, so I was prepared for it. Fifteen or twenty minutes later we pulled onto a rutted dirt road with good looking woods containing lots of mature hardwoods on both sides. "Not a bad looking place," I thought.

"Ain't nothing but deer, coons and hogs in here and it's rougher than a corn cob. The dogs are gonna have their work cut out for them; might even need armor to hunt in there," a grinning Mike stated.

"Nah, they're used to the rough stuff and if they're coons in there they'll tree them. Let's cut them loose and see what happens," I said. We cut all four hounds into the swamp and sat down to wait for a strike. Quick was first to strike with a chop and a couple bawls, deep in the swamp, opening only a few more times before loading up on a tree; he was alone and remained that way. With no roads to get closer to Quick, Mike and I began the walk to him. As we neared the tree we heard Keno and Rock much deeper, almost out of hearing range and running a track to catch. We walked in to Quick's tree, a large hardwood in knee deep water, leashed him back and shined the tree. Spotted a coon in the top of the tree, put it out to Quick and led him from the tree. Walking a short distance we stopped to listen for the other hounds and heard nothing. Leaving Quick on the lead we decided to return to the truck and check the tracker to locate the other hounds.

"Do you think they ran the track out of hearing, or quit it? They could have taken it to the Oconee River, it runs behind the swamp. I don't think we could hear them from here if they were on the river. When we get back to the truck we can drive toward the river and listen," said Mike. We'll check the tracker to see which direction they're in; I'm not familiar with this country so I don't know where they could go to get out of hearing," I stated.

As we arrived at the truck we heard Jr. opening far in the distance and he was alone. "Yeah, there's one of the dogs and I think he's on the river, but I don't hear the others with him," Mike said. Checking the tracker we discovered that Keno and Rock were in the opposite direction and the tree switches were going off, so they were treed wherever they were. We drove back to the main road and began driving in the general direction of Keno and Rock, leaving Jr. to finish his track. After several stops we clearly heard the hounds and Mike knew exactly where they were. Driving to another dirt road we were able to get within a few hundred yards of the treed hounds. We swiftly walked to them, found both on a big oak, Rock on one side and Keno on the other; two real tree dogs with Mr. Ringtail sitting above them. A large boar coon was put out to them; they were then led back to the truck and loaded up. We needed to go back in the other direction and locate Jr.; an easy task as it turned out. Mike said we could drive near where we had last heard Jr., right to the river bank. We drove in that direction; stopping at the river we heard Jr. treed not over 100 yards from where we parked. Jr. was steadily bawling, telling us to come on and get this one. I leashed Jr. back as we arrived at the tree and began to shine a large vine covered tree that extended out over the river, quickly spotting a coon hiding in the tangled vines. I held Jr. as Mike put the coon out for him; the coon did not hit the water but fell onto the bank where Jr. made short work of it.

With all four hounds in the box we were ready to make one more drop. Mike said we could cut the hounds onto a small stream that fed the swamp and maybe get a track going where the dogs would work together. I thought to myself, "That's a big maybe."

Moving several miles to another dirt road we led the hounds to the edge of the woods to release them, but before being released all struck from the lead and were turned onto a red hot track. How lucky could we get? It was not often that all four hounds would be on the same track. The question was would they end up on the same tree? We sat back to listen to one of the best races I'd heard in a while; lasting close to an hour before a tree was put on the end of it. Very seldom do hunters hear dogs run a track in the manner that one was ran; hound music at its best. The hounds had covered a lot of ground, yet never left the swamp.

The night came alive with the ringing echo of the treed hounds; all on the same tree it appeared. We listened to them tree for several minutes before walking toward them; we were close as we could drive. The hounds were deep in the swamp but the walk wasn't too bad, much better than some of the places I'd been hunting in South Carolina the previous week. Approaching the tree we saw what would be a treat for any hunter who appreciates a tree dog, all four hounds were on an extremely large oak in knee deep water. They were all stretched high on the tree, no jumping, growling, face barking or bad habits; just four tree dogs doing their job and doing it right.

All hounds were leashed back and the tree shined, a big coon was spotted in a fork midway up the tree. Mike and I looked at the coon for a minute or so and decided not to take it. The coon had ran a good race and earned the right to run again; when a coon runs like that I prefer to let them live. Who knows, maybe the next hunters to hunt in the swamp ran the same coon and enjoyed a race like we did, if so, hopefully they too let the coon live.

We walked from the tree leading the hounds, well satisfied with their performance; we were finished for the night, the sky was beginning to lighten as we reached the truck. Our hunt had been a good one, it was the last hunt Mike and I went on and would be the last time the four hounds were hunted together, all four were soon sold, but more would replace them. Mike and I will one day cut the hounds loose again; there's never a dull moment when hunting with the Real McCoy.

Rock was sold to Dave Roberts of Kentucky and I'm sure he enjoyed many nights in the woods with him. Dave hunted Rock in the hunts and did quite well with him. Rock was a good hound, and if not for his age I wouldn't have sold him.

Chubbs Jr. was sold to Kerry Rooks while only a young hound. He was a good looking hound with a big mouth; a hound that would get deep in the country, get treed with a coon and stay hooked. I owned many of Jr.'s ancestors and really hated to let him go. I hunted Jr. hard but didn't promote him as he should have been promoted; he was a little different than many Blueticks, extremely hard going and tight on track.

Keno was a hound that went hunting hard as any hound and quickly got struck; maybe not always on a coon, but he would get treed off the track and have a coon in the tree. He treed the same on every tree, a fast machine gun chop that could be heard a great distance. Keno was sold to Jason Bullard who enjoyed him for several years before letting me have him back, as an old dog, on a deal for a younger Grand Nite Champion. I sold Jason several dogs over the years and he will have a good hound on his lead if possible.

Quick was a hard going hound that would get through the country and get treed with the coon. He was a good bred and good colored hound, a winner in the hunts that produced some top hounds that were also winners. Quick was sold to Charles Harrellson of South Carolina and was promoted as he should have been. Quick can be found in the pedigrees of many hounds today. I had too many hounds to invest the time and attention that Quick deserved.

I've owned some good hounds over the years and a few could not be bought at any price. I always looked for a better hound than I had on my lead and will always continue. Many of the good ones came from unknown hunters who lived way back in the country, and had worn out numerous pairs of boots training them. Some I raised and some were never seen in public, but should have been. If you have a top hound, show him/her off at the hunts it will be unforgettable enjoyment cherished into the future.

UGLY—THE FIRST AND THE LAST

27

The first "Pretty Boy Ugly" was a big, coon treeing English Hound. He was tri colored, and had a big red head, long calico ears and a predominantly white body with blue and red ticks. When he came into my ownership he had no registration papers with him, but was soon single registered as an English Hound. He had been coon hunted, and hunted hard for hides only - he was never entered in a competition point hunt before or while I owned him. His original name was not Ugly, but that would become the name on his registration papers. He would receive the name we called him the first night we saw him in the woods. My hunting Buddy Ronnie and I cut him loose in a large section of bottom land and he quickly struck and treed a coon. As we walked into the tree he was treeing loud and hard, on arrival at the tree Ronnie said, "That dog might be Ugly but he is sure pretty stretched out on the side of that tree." I smiled and replied, "Yep, Pretty Boy Ugly."

This big Ugly hound came from Raymond (Sonny) Edwards of Salem, Indiana. I was told about this hound by Raymond Watts of Jeffersonville, Indiana. Raymond stated, "Sonny has a good hound, he's not much to look at but he trees a lot of coons and you can buy him reasonable."

I have bought a lot of good hounds from these two coon hunters; they have owned some good ones. Two top hounds that come to mind when I think of these two coon hunters are NKC World Champion, Dual Grand Nite Champion Watts' Little Blue and Tree Screaming Tree Power, the hound that came to be known as Dual Grand Nite Champion Hobbs' Tree Screaming Rock. Blue and Rock were two great hounds that would later be owned by my good friend Leonard Hobbs of Tennessee - the man who introduced me to these two Indiana coon hunters.

Ugly stayed with us for one season, he was a lot of fun to hunt. He never trailed a track, he either ran them or just fell treed; and stayed put. Ugly barked very little on the ground but was an excellent lay-up dog and a hide hunters dream. Ronnie and I hunted him hard during the coon season. The coons he treed helped us to win the yearly poundage hunt at the local club.

Even though Ugly was a coon treeing fool he was not the type hound I liked to hunt. He was soon put up for sale and sold in Northern Illinois. He made a hide hunters dream come true. As far as I know he was never entered in a point hunt by his new owner, even though he could have won. Most coon he treed were shut outs - he was alone 90 percent of the time. He was an accurate coon treeing coon dog and that was all he was used for.

The second "Pretty Boy Ugly" unlike the first would get the opportunity to compete on the competition circuit and make his mark. He was a registered Treeing Walker and his name was already "Ugly", only it didn't have the Pretty Boy before it. His registered name was Good-Bad-Ugly; he was sired by the renowned reproducing hound, "Grand Nite Champion Hardwood Buster." He was an ugly colored hound until one saw him on the wood, and then as Ronnie had said about the original Ugly, "He sure was pretty stretched out on the tree."

I learned of Ugly through a friend who stated he knew of a good, broke "coondog" that was for sale. At that time we were hunting the competition hunts really hard and I didn't need another hound. My friend continued to talk and said the hound would be good to hunt pups or young dogs with and even use to try dogs. He said the hound was solid broke from off game and was a tree dog deluxe. He went on to say the hound was a Walker, he was located in our State and that I should at least go look at him in the woods.

After thinking about the hound for a few days I phoned Ugly's owner Mitson (Mit) Elliott of Dawson, Georgia; and asked a few questions before making arrangements to come see him in the woods. Neither the price nor anything further was discussed. I had mostly Bluetick and English Hounds in my kennel at the time, but would hunt a one eyed spotted donkey if it would tree coons and do it right. It was my intentions to buy the dog to hunt young dogs and pups with if he was suitable for such. I had no desire to get another hound for the hunts.

Early on the day of our planned hunt I loaded Dual Grand Champion Moyer 's Blue Chubbs, a solid broke Bluetick hound and headed out for Dawson, Georgia. Dawson is located in the Southern part of the state, 20 miles or so from Albany, past home of the Winter Classic. I wanted to see the Walker hound go alone and with company; that was why I carried Chubbs along. We had been using Chubbs to hunt pups with; he ran nothing but coon and did not have a growl in him. Chubbs treed with his feet on the tree and was perfect to check a hound for any sort of ill disposition. He didn't run trash and didn't fight but would tell on a dog that did.

I had never met Mit Elliott before and had only spoken to him on the phone one time. On arrival at Mit's introductions were made and he began to tell me a little about the Walker hound named Ugly. He also stated that the little hound would do his own talking soon as it got dark. I liked what Mit said and would soon learn that he was a man of his word; a finer more likable Gentleman you'll never meet.

Sure as the sun set and darkness rolled in Mit let the little hound speak for his self. As we loaded the Walker into the box I looked him over very good. He was a three year old, 55 pound tight made hound with a good head and ears. He had good feet and dark colored eyes, only his color could be considered ugly and it wasn't that bad. His head was off colored, and his body mostly white with a few black spots but no ticks.

I always watch a new hound close and what caught my eye was his actions, he was very calm, did not jerk on the leash or growl when loaded into the box with Chubbs. He seemed to listen like a well behaved child; a trait I would see more of as the night progressed.

The first drop was made with Ugly being released alone from the road into a thick, flat section of woods. I watched as he left the leash, paying no attention to the dog remaining in the box, he calmly hit the woods and never looked back. It took some time for him to find a track, but he soon struck a track he had to work. I noticed that he had a high pitched mouth that carried well, a chop and tenor bawl on track. He was deep when he struck and we moved a little closer to better hear what he was doing. The area he was working in was dry and thick but he steadily worked the track in one direction, located a tree with a distinctive locate, turning it over to a ringing machine gun chop. Mit stated that he was going no further, with that we listened to him tree for a while and began the walk to him.

Ugly was farther in than first thought and I noted how well his voice carried as we walked to him. Walking in to the tree I observed the little Walker hound stretched high on the tree, not jumping, gnawing or moving. I also noted that he was treeing just as hard as when he had first made the tree, not over heating or overly excited. The tree was overgrown with vines, moss and leaves. After pulling a few vines the coon was spotted sitting amongst the tangled mess. Mit then snapped a short leash onto Ugly's collar and dropped it onto the ground and told Ugly to load up. Ugly followed along as we returned to the truck, never leaving the light.

The second drop, only Ugly was released once again; he went hunting same as the first drop and soon had a track going. He did a good job on that track too, quickly putting a tree on the end of it. We drove close as possible to the tree and walked in from there. He was on a large tree this time and had another coon that was rapidly spotted. I was admiring the white hound stretched high on the side of the tree when Mit suddenly said, "Come here Ugly." The little hound shot off the tree and stood beside him, he then said, "Ugly back on the tree," and he was right back up on the tree. Mit then walked over and snapped the leash on him and said, "Load up"; and that is what he did. Mit went on to say that Ugly could be called off a track or tree and that he would obey you better than most people's children.

As we were driving away from the area I told Mit I would now like to see Ugly go with Chubbs. We were on the edge of a big wooded section and Mit said, "Stop here and cut them loose." I watched how Ugly responded to being released with another hound. He paid no attention to Chubbs, he went one way and Chubbs the other.

Chubbs was first to open on this turnout and trailed for 10 minutes before Ugly joined him. I think the track was colder than Ugly preferred but soon after he joined in the track came to an end with Chubbs getting a big locate out of his mouth before Ugly came on the tree. We listened to the pair tree for a while before driving right to the tree, a large pecan tree in a grove. This coon was immediately spotted as I watched both hounds up on the tree, no head slinging, chewing or growling. A big bawl mouthed Bluetick standing on the tree letting us know he had the game with a short, loud bawl, standing alongside him the ugly colored Walker was treeing so hard you would have trouble counting the barks. We made another drop, listened to the two hounds work together and put another coon up that we also seen. With this turnout I told Mit I had seen enough. I had a long drive back to my home and needed to get on the road.

As we pulled into Mit's yard he said, "Just pull back beside the dog lot." At this point I had not asked Mit the price he wanted for Ugly. He had, a few months earlier, ran a full page ad on Ugly in one of the magazines and included a price with the ad. I told him I could not give the asking price he had placed in the ad but that I had come to buy the dog if I liked him. I then asked what was the least he would take for Ugly, and stated that I would pay him right then if we came to an agreement. Mit considered this for a minute and gave me a price. I paid him right then and considered myself as receiving a good deal for the amount of enjoyment that Ugly would bring to friends, family and me.

The following week we hunted Ugly hard, alone, and with other hounds. He consistently treed coons without an off bark from him; he was broke from off game and an accurate stay-put pressure tree dog. We began to use Ugly to hunt pups with and also used him as a check dog. If Ugly was not opening on a good track with other dogs he was hunted with you could be assured it was not a coon track they were running.

After the first week I received a call from Mit making sure I was satisfied with Ugly and to see how he was doing. He said if I didn't like him that I knew where I had gotten him and to bring him back. We were pleased with him and figured he would pay for himself as a pup starter and check dog. Little did we know that he would soon hit the competition circuit.

The leaves were off and the hunting good; the Georgia State Championship was coming up in a few days. I was hunting a couple hounds getting them ready for the hunt and had a young handler, really not much younger than me, who lived at my home getting a couple hounds ready also. I had spent a small fortune in entry fees on "Earl", the young handler and it was finally paying off - he had started winning a high percentage of his cast.

Earl had been handling the Bluetick hound that would come to be known as AKC World Champion, Grand Nite Champion Coz' Sparetime Spanky. I had purchased Spanky from Russ Downing of Wisconsin; an honest hard hunting coon hunter that has never been given the credit he deserves for the great Blue hound. Spanky was only a Nite Champion when I purchased him and Earl had finished him to Grand Nite Champion, while putting the finishing touches on him. Earl had all intentions to hunt Spanky in the Georgia State but at the last minute decided to take Ugly instead.

The first night of the State hunt Earl came in with a first place win and overall high scoring dog with Ugly. This was Ugly's first competition hunt to be entered in. The second night of the hunt Earl and Ugly repeated their performance with another first and overall high scoring dog. Ugly would be the Georgia State Champion for that year and have a good story written about him in The Georgia Outdoors Magazine. After the hunt Earl said he had proven that Ugly could win in competition and went back to hunting Spanky. He never hunted Ugly in another hunt.

Ugly's registered name was "Grand Nite Champion Nation's Pretty Boy Ugly" prior to finishing his competition career in my kennel and being sold. The smallest hunt he was ever entered in while I owned him was the Georgia State. He went from nothing to Grand Nite in all of the larger hunts. He was handled by Earl

Lockard, Vernon Holt and Randy Leonard on his way to Grand. He finished fourth in the Purina race in 1989, behind his half brother Grand Nite Champion Hardwood Dan owned by Paul Sheffield. I owned the second and third and fourth place winning hounds, Spanky was second, Grand Nite Champion Logan's Wild Quick was third, and Ugly completed the top four.

Ugly was not a top competition hound, he could not handle the long distant hauling to the hunts. He did not hunt well when he drew hounds that ran trash, but what permitted him to win was his ability to tree coons. He treed coons that could be seen and stayed put once he was treed. Ugly also produced some good hounds; most that he produced when I owned him were not competition hunted. I did however own one offspring from Ugly that was competition hunted, this hound was known as "Grand Nite Champion Nation's Hardwood Rolex"; a hound that would do a lot of winning. Rolex would later place in the final cast of the UKC World Championship with his new owner. Ugly and Rolex were sold as a package deal to a Walker promoter whom I hope did well with the pair. I was thankful to Mit Elliott for allowing me to own Ugly, Rolex and a few other top Walker hounds. The hunts with these hounds were good memories that stay with me until this day.

LOUISIANA SATURDAY NIGHT
28

The loud, carrying bawls of the four hounds could be heard resounding across the water as they worked the first track of the night deeper into the swamp; all four had exceptionally loud mouths used just right. The Black hound had struck the track soon after being released into the murky waters of the Atchafalaya basin. Immediately following his loud bawl the Black hound was joined by two Redtick hounds and a fine young Bluetick. They were taking the coon track deeper into the swamp as the large group of hunters stood listening to the swamp music.

This hunt on a cool, dark Saturday night was going to be a little different than most I'd been going on, in more ways than one. The terrain was different, in fact the State was different, the hunting companions weren't our regulars and the coons were thick as fleas on a stray dog. This Louisiana Saturday night would be different than what most consider a Louisiana Saturday night, no honky tonks, parties or Cajun bands. Nothing but some of the best coon hunting to be found in the swamplands of the South, some powerful young hounds and a couple of coon dogs; yes I said COONDOGS.

The day before this hunt I'd been home, in Georgia, when the phone rang and upon answering I heard the voice of Trey also known as the Parlanguah (swamp creature of Cajun folklore, half man - half gator), a friend from Louisiana say, "Hey my Friend! What the haps? Just wanted to brag a little about this blue pup; he is turning the crank like you never saw. This pup is so good you won't believe it. I sure wish you could come see him in the woods."

"Whoa, slow down a little and tell me about him. When do you want me to come for a hunt with him?" I asked. "Why don't you come on down today and we'll hunt tonight and tomorrow night. That way I don't have to tell you anything about Boogie; 'cause he'll do his own talking." "You got that my friend; I like to see a hound like that in the woods. Don't know if I can make it tonight but I'd like to come there tomorrow" I said. As our conversation continued I agreed to leave out for Louisiana sometime that day or night and be there the next day so we could hunt Saturday night.

A friend and I left out later that day for Louisiana, stopping off in Mississippi for the night and continuing on to Trey's home on Saturday morning. I took three hounds along, two fully trained broke hounds and one outstanding young hound. A Black & Tan and two English Redticks; hounds that could tree coons and make it look easy.

The Black hound was Grand Champion, Grand Nite Champion Hicks' Big Time Albert, a completely balanced hound from strike to tree. Albert was sired by Grand Nite Champion Oakchia Willie Boy and his dam was Nite Champion Thornhill's Hopeless. Albert was a good bred hound that reproduced some good hounds; he can be found in the pedigrees of many hounds today. Albert went hunting like a dog is supposed to, was a top strike dog, ran a track to catch and was an accurate, stay put, classy tree dog. He had a big bawl mouth on track, an outstanding locate and was a powerful, loud chop mouthed tree dog that could tree any kind of coon. Albert was a coonhunters coondog that was good in thick or thin coon. I bought Albert from Gene Hicks of Sweetwater, Tennessee for Vernon Holt to hunt in the competition hunts. Vernon had told me several times about Albert's coon treeing ability and said I should call Gene and ask about him. I had no idea that Gene would sell Albert when I did phone him, but after we spoke for a while he put a price on him and I bought him. Probably the only reason I was able to purchase him was because Gene also had Two Time Albert and Diamond Bill, two outstanding young hounds sired by Albert. I can also tell you that Gene Hicks is honest as they come and knows a coondog; Albert was good as Gene said and better.

The older Redtick was Grand Champion, Grand Nite Champion Nester's Red Boy Trailer, a top broke hound that went hunting good, got struck quickly and moved the track in the right direction with a big bawl mouth putting the correct tree on the end of it and staying hooked - regardless. Trailer was a loud chop mouthed tree dog that could also tree any kind of coon; he was as good alone as in company. Trailer was sired by Dual Grand Champion Dickey's Blue Boy Red, a hound out of the cross of the great Dual Grand Champion Beshears Blue Boy II (Junior), and Dual Grand Champion Indian Creek Wendy; all owned by R.F. (Roland) Dickey of Alabama. Trailer was a coondog and a reproducer that can also be found in many pedigrees today; he came to my kennel from Kerry Rooks.

The young Redtick was the hound that would come to be known as Grand Champion, Grand Nite Champion, and A.K.C. Nite Champion Nation's Red Boy Banjo; a top young hound. Banjo was a beautiful dark red colored hound, with not only looks but ability. He would go hunting alone or in company, was an outstanding strike dog that ran a track to catch with a loud bawl, had a big locate and was a loud, classy chop mouthed, accurate stay-put tree dog. Banjo had only been in the woods a couple times when I purchased him, but advanced at a rapid pace and was making a good balanced hound. I purchased him in November and he was hunted at the Grand American in early January, less than two months later, and placed in the top three both nights; he was one year old. Young hounds like Banjo were hard to find. Banjo was also sired by Dual Grand Champion Dickey's Blue Boy Red, maybe from the last litter sired by him.

The Bluetick called Boogie was a hound I had given to Trey when only a pup. He was sired by Grand Nite Champion Coz' Sparetime Spanky and his dam was Grand Nite Champion Russell's Blue Misty. I had owned several of Boogies ancestors, to include his sire and dam along with Misty's littermates Dual Grand Champion Moyer 's Blue Chubbs, Nite Champion Nation's Blue Buck and Bonnie. I also owned Misty's sire and dam, Dual Grand Champion Davis' Blue Scooter and Nite Champion Gregory's Blue Scat. Boogies pedigree was full of top hounds that treed coons' not just trees and also won in the hunts, not to mention they reproduced some good hounds. I would see that Boogie was a unique young hound that could have went far if he had been campaigned in the hunts. Trey used Boogie for one thing only and that was to tree coons and more coons. Boogie would go hunting alone or in company, he hunted with his head in the air yet got struck quickly, drifted a track and exploded on the tree. He was lightning fast at everything he did, and only improved with age. Boogie ran track with a distinguishing bawl and came on the tree with a screaming locate turning it over to a never ending chop, he was only one year old.

We pretty much had a convoy wanting to see the dogs go and we had proceeded to the swampland early. Our first drop had been minutes after darkness with Albert immediately striking a hot track; he was joined by the other three hounds and the track was now being taken into the swamp. The hounds split up, Albert and Banjo went one direction and quickly put a tree on their track. Albert located first with Banjo right behind him. Boogie and Trailer put an end to their track at almost the same time. Boogie exploded on the tree with a locating bawl that would make anyone take notice, and Trailer was only a split second behind him.

As Boogie located Trey grinned and said, "What you think about that locate? He is a tree dog too! No need to be in a hurry, let's go to the other dogs first and let Boogie and Trailer tree for a while. He'll only tree harder the longer he trees."

We proceeded to Albert and Banjo, found them treed on a cypress tree surrounded by ankle deep water. Both hounds were leashed back from the tree and the tree shined. A coon swiftly spotted and put out. We decided to lead the hounds on to Boogie and Trailer's tree as it was only a couple hundred yards away. Boogie and Trailer were treeing much harder than when they first treed, possibly because of our putting the coon out to the other two hounds. As we walked in to the tree it was found to also be a cypress surrounded by knee deep water. All hounds were leashed; a coon spotted high in the tree and put out to Boogie and Trailer.

The night was starting out really well; less than an hour and already two coon treed. Trey said we should keep the hounds on the lead and move to another area further down the bayou to avoid getting deeper in the swamp and into deep water. Wanting to avoid getting wet that early in the night all were in agreement and the move was made.

I told Trey I'd like to see Boogie go alone and on the next drop he was cut into the swamp all by his lonesome. He went hunting hard and in a hurry, quickly getting struck, drifting through the country, and coming on the tree with an explosive locate that anyone could call, then came the hard loud chops. We listened to him tree for several minutes before walking to him. As we arrived at the tree Boogie was found glued to its side; a picture of what a true slobber mouthed, belly rubbing tree dog should look like. Trey leashed Boogie back, showed me the coon, smiled and said, "He has been doing that since the first time he treed, I hunt him alone and he does the job he is supposed to do. He's young but he's good, don't need help and don't get none. What you think about him?"

I replied, "Cut him loose off this tree and let's see him go again."

Boogie was led a few feet from the tree and cut loose; he once again went hunting in a hard run. In only minutes he was struck, opened only a couple times and then came the explosive locate -

treed again. We walked in to find him glued to this tree also; picture perfect. Boogie had another coon up a small water oak, which was left to run again.

A smiling Trey said, "I told you he would do his own talking. Want to see him go by himself again?" "I've seen enough for now; let's cut him loose with the other hounds. I see he needs no help and is a tree dog, I also see traits from several of his ancestors. You should put him in the competition hunts, let people see what you have," I stated.

"Nope, he'll never see a competition hunt long as own him, and that will be a while 'cause he ain't for sale and never will be; I like him and don't need money. Besides where would I find another one like him?" Trey replied. I knew Boogie would never leave Trey's home as Trey was a man of his word; he said what he meant and meant what he said. Before the night was over I would know how good Boogie was and would liked to have taken him home with me but knew he would never leave Louisiana. Trey only wanted to show me how good the young hound was.

We walked back to the vehicles moved a short distance and cut all four hounds back into the swamp. Trey said the deer hunters often piled corn near the water's edge for the deer. The hounds were sent in the direction of the mounds of corn and soon had tracks going in several different directions. I knew we were about to have to do some serious walking when the hounds split in three directions. Trailer was first to come treed close to half a mile in the swamp, his loud chops did nothing to distract the other hounds from their tracks. As we started walking to Trailer's tree Albert let loose a big locate and began to chop hard as possible at least half a mile in the other direction. We decided to split up and go to both hounds, plus we still had Banjo and Boogie running a track behind us. Trey and a couple of the guys elected to go to Trailer while his cousin Cajun Mike, a couple other guys and me went to Albert.

As we arrived at Albert's tree we heard Trey and his group putting the coon out to Trailer. Our group stood and admired Albert stretched high on the side of a black gum tree barking well in excess of 100 barks per minute; he was a stylish tree dog that would draw ones attention and make any houndsman appreciate a tree dog. I started to leash Albert back and heard Cajun Mike yell, "Here is a big coon sitting low in da tree." We all looked at the coon and started walking from the tree as we didn't have the rifle to put it out. Albert didn't need a lot of coon put out to him anyway.

As we walked from the tree we could hear Banjo and Boogie both treed, and in the direction of the vehicles. We swiftly walked in their direction dropping Albert off at the vehicles and continuing on, arriving at the trees almost at precisely the same time as Trey and his group. Yes, I said trees as Banjo and Boogie were on separate trees less than 50 feet apart, both were treeing well over 100 barks per minute and both glued to their trees. I leashed Banjo at his tree and Trey leashed Boogie; the trees were shined and surprisingly both had coon in them.

"I knew Boogie could stand tree pressure but that Banjo can stand some too," said Trey. "Yeah, he'll stay treed and hasn't been hunted hard as Boogie or saw the amount of coon either. You know me, if they won't stay treed they can't stay at my house," I replied.

"I know that and I also know if they don't have coon in the trees that they don't stay there either, but that's the same here. I'm not going to walk to a bunch of empty trees. Glad I don't have that problem with Boogie. Let's put the coons out to them and move to a better place," Trey responded.

With all hounds loaded and our group ready to move to a "better place" I thought, "'Can it get any better than this; coon thick as ants in an ant hill." Trey said the coon weren't usually that thick but the areas we were hunting hadn't been hunted. With that said he then took us to his favorite hunting territory. As we drove along the narrow path of a road all that could be seen on both sides was swampland, stretching for miles and miles; a coon hunter's paradise, to say the least.

At the roads end all four hounds were once again cut into the swamp, Trailer, Banjo and Boogie quickly left the lead. Albert circled and crossed the road behind us, I shined the light on him as he crossed and noticed he had his head high in the air. Immediately after leaving the road he threw one big locate and began chopping, loud and hard. The other hounds did not cover him but started a red hot track of their own, putting a tree on it in only minutes.

We walked toward Albert shining the tree as we approached and spotted a large coon sprawled on a limb near the top of a leafless tree. I leashed Albert, looked at the coon and assumed it had been up there for a long time probably getting a little sun earlier in the day. Trey wanted to put the coon out to Albert but I didn't think he needed it so it was left to run again.

Leaving Albert on the lead we continued on to the other treed hounds; all three were on the same tree, another cypress in thigh deep water. All were leashed back and the tree shined, a coon spotted and put out to the hounds. We then walked a short distance from the tree and cut the hounds back into the swamp; a decision that turned out to be the wrong one.

A track was struck by Banjo, only seconds after he was released, he was joined by the other hounds. The track was worked farther into the swamp until the hounds were almost out of hearing range, as we made an attempt to stay close as possible. The water was getting deeper and the hounds deeper in the swamp, at places the water was waist deep and hard to navigate. Just as we thought they were going to get away from us I heard Albert throw a big locate and the swamp then came alive with the echo of treeing hounds.

As we attempted to get nearer the treed hounds the water continuously became deeper until it was chest deep. The hounds were still at least one quarter mile from us and the water was becoming even deeper, it was determined that we weren't going to get to them unless we did a lot of swimming and that was totally out of the question. We were already in water much deeper than was safe. I have always been very careful where the possibility of injury could be involved, and in this situation the chance of one losing their life was very possible. It wasn't worth someone receiving an injury, or even worse, trying to get to the treed hounds; we possibly could have gotten to the tree and then again maybe not. Following a brief discussion with Trey, it was determined that we would return to the vehicles, go to a nearby hunting camp and borrow a small flat bottomed boat which could be used to go to the tree.

After procuring the small boat it was decided that Trey and I would go in and retrieve the still treeing hounds. The hounds had been treed for a good period of time and we wanted to get to them quick as possible; we didn't know if the hounds were having to swim or were able to get up on the tree. Either way they had been treed for a considerable amount of time and were sure to be tiring. The boat had a slow moving electric motor as a power source, but with our help using paddles we arrived at the tree in record time as daylight crept in.

On arrival at the tree we found the hounds were on a small island, all four on the same tree, they were leashed and the tree looked over; no light needed, and yes they had another coon. I was surprised that Trey didn't want to put the coon out to the hounds; he was ready to get out of the swamp too. The hounds were given a little praise, loaded into the boat and received a free ride back to the vehicles. I had seen enough of the swamps for one night and was ready to get some rest. Our hunt was a good one overall with the exception of the hounds getting into the deep water. We treed a lot of coons and saw some good dog work. I would hunt the swamps with Trey numerous times following this hunt and watch Boogie develop into a top hound over time. I would also come to know why Louisiana is considered a Sportsman's Paradise.

I would liked to have owned Boogie but he never left Trey's home, never was entered in a competition hunt, but treed loads of coon over his lifetime. Trey later told me that he never permanently registered Boogie and that he still had the green pup registration papers on him, still in my name. He used Boogie for only one purpose and that was to tree coon and enjoy in the woods.

I liked Albert as he was the type hound I like to hunt, a completely balanced hound from strike to tree but because of circumstances I later sold him to Andy Mathis of South Carolina. I'm sure Andy enjoyed Albert in the woods as much as I did. Hounds like him are not often for sale, he was a good one.

Trailer was also a good hound, he wasn't quite as quick a strike dog as Albert or Banjo, but he would make you like him. He needed no help of any kind and would get treed with a coon that could be seen. Hounds like him were few and far between. Trailer later went back to Kerry Rooks.

Banjo was sold when only 18 months of age; he was burning the competition hunts up. He was a special hound at a young age but sometimes the price becomes too high to ignore. Banjo was a balanced hound and I'm sure he only got better with age; he was also a good one. Banjo was sold to Jimmy Pierce, Eddy and Bob Parker.

HUNTIN' THE SUWANNEE 29

The state of Florida is not only a great state for tourism but is also home to some very good coon hunting. The vast farmlands, river bottoms and swamps of Northern Florida are home to an abundant coon population. The orange groves of middle Florida also have an ample supply of coon. Farther south the treacherous and immense swamps of the Everglades, with its hard running coon possesses some very good hunting. With all things considered the Suwannee River basin of north Florida has some of the best hunting in the state. The Suwannee originates from the Okefenokee swamps of South Georgia and empties into the Gulf of Mexico.

While taking time off to do nothing but hunt and fish I enjoyed almost a year of coon hunting and fishing on the Suwannee River and other parts of Florida. Permission was obtained from various farmers and landowners to coon hunt on their land, with only one stipulation, and that was they wanted the coon killed if we were allowed to hunt their land. With Florida's warm climate the hides aren't very good even in the winter, but what little they bring pays for a little dog feed. Some of the coons were also given to the land owners who barbecued them.

At the time I had retired from competition hunting; something that I would later regret because of the ability of two of the hounds I hunted. I hunted five hounds during this time but a considerable amount more time was invested in two of the hounds. The two hounds were Grand Nite Champion Clear Creek Jammin' Jim and Nite Champion Long Creek Smoken' Toby. I hunted these two hounds 187 nights straight, rain, winds, lightning or temperature made no difference. They were hunted alone and together, they went hunting and treed coons somewhere when they were cut loose; regardless of the weather or terrain. Needless to say they saw plenty of coons. Long Creek Smoken Toby was a young Black & Tan that came out of Minnesota. I had heard about the young hound for some time but didn't know his owner. 'While attending the Grand American in South Carolina I ran into Alan Kalal, the Walker man, and he was telling me about Toby; he had regularly hunted with him. Alan said Toby was a tough young hound that stayed split treed and could win in the hunts. Toby was one and a half years old at the time, a Nite Champion with four wins toward Grand Nite Champion. Alan gave me Toby's owners name and phone number. The following week I spoke to Toby's owner and negotiated a deal for Toby. I never finished Toby to Grand Nite and often felt bad because of that; he should have been Granded. I learned of Grand Nite Champion Clear Creek Jammin' Jim a few weeks later while attending the N.K.C. World Hunt in Lake City, Florida. Timothy

Ball, another Walker man told me he knew of a good two year old Blue English Hound that I should buy. The hound was Jim, and he was owned by Sondra and Brent Beck of Oklahoma. I told Gary Van Meter of Alabama, who was handling dogs for me at the time, about Jim and he drove to Oklahoma, tried him and brought him back. Jim was raised and trained by the Beck's and already Grand Nite Champion.

Both Jim and Toby were bought with all intentions to put them in the competition hunts, but I never had the opportunity to put either in a hunt; something that I strongly regretted. I can take no credit for getting the hounds to the point they were when purchased, but I sure put some finishing touches on them. Hounds such as these deserved to be in the hunts, and before the eyes of the public, where hunters could see the quality and ability instilled within and know that their breeders and trainers are dedicated hunters and hounds persons.

Both these hounds were loud mouthed, hard, accurate stay-put pressure tree dogs, even at a young age. For several months after I purchased Toby and Jim they were only pleasure hunted by different handlers. That Summer and Fall I began to pleasure hunt the two hounds across the Southlands. Both hounds steadily improved with age and hard hunting.

Toby had to be broken off possums and armadillos, but he ran no other off game. Toby hunted hard and fast with his head up and could cover more ground in a shorter period of time than any hound I had seen; he was action packed. He was a tight mouthed hound that loved to split tree, a lay-up specialist and said by many who hunted with him when he was fine-tuned, to be a high powered Walker in a Black dog's skin. Toby was different from most dogs I hunted as I like a completely balanced dog that gets quickly struck and gives mouth on track. Over time, Toby became an outstanding strike dog that struck quickly but tightened up once struck, ran a good track to catch and drifted a bad track like it should be done; he was a lightning quick locator that had his coon. He was a tree dog that absolutely would not pull. He bawled and chopped on track and was a hard chop mouthed tree dog; a hound like Toby is hard to beat. I liked him.

Jim gave no problem on off game of any sort. Jim was a hard going, balanced hound that could take an old bad track and put a tree on the end of it with a coon that could be seen. Jim took his tracks as they came, hot or cold and put trees at the end with coon in them. Jim would please any coon hunter who appreciated a coondog. Jim ran track with a big bawl and treed with a hard, loud chop and stayed put.

When hunted together these two hounds would wear a tough coon hunter down on a long all night hunt, and you can bet that I came in at daylight many a morning ready to hit the bed. The last night these two hounds were hunted together in Florida was on and around the Suwannee River; they really looked good. I thought to myself that I should have been hunting both in the hunts as I felt; at that point, they were capable of winning any hunt, anywhere.

Toby was coming three years old and Jim had already turned three, both were good as they would ever be. This hunt followed over 6 months of hunting both hounds without missing a night, and putting an untold amount of coon out to them. Both hounds were tough as boot leather. The first drop Toby was cut loose from the road into a slough running into the river. I looked at my watch as I cut Toby loose; five minutes passed before he exploded on a tree, after opening only a few times on the ground. He was ¼ mile to the left, in the opposite direction of where he had been turned loose. I drove close as possible and walked in to him, finding he had an extremely large coon up a very small tree. The coon was put out to him; he was then led back to the vehicle and loaded up. It was now Jim's turn to show his ability alone.

After driving several miles to a primitive camping area on the banks of the Suwannee, traveling far as the road would allow, Jim was released onto the river bank. The small rutted road ran parallel with the river for easy access if Jim treed in the southern direction, Jim quickly struck a track, opening with a good loud bawl and moving the track away from the river. He ran the track hard for 10 minutes taking it south, away from the campgrounds and crossing the small road. The track was going into a populated area containing several homes, where people whom I did not know lived. As luck would have it, Jim threw a big locate and began to tree with a loud solid chop; he was directly behind one of the houses. I hurriedly started in that direction.

I walked to the tree, leashed Jim and shined a large moss covered tree, soon spotting a coon hiding in a clump of the Spanish moss. Just as the coon was spotted a man walked from the house and came to the tree to see what was going on. I explained that I was coon hunting and that Jim had been turned loose near the campground and ran the coon there and treed it. After showing the coon to the man, he advised that I should go ahead and take it and any others I might happen to tree. He said raccoons had been getting into his garbage and were a nuisance. I let Jim have the coon, and started back to the vehicle, prepared to turn both Jim and Toby loose together.

Moving to an area with a low lying bog which extended from the river, crossed under the road, and ran into a large section of woods both hounds were released into the wooded area. The bog was one of the first places to flood when the river was up, but always had standing water in it. Also, it was one of the few places the owner did not care if the coon were taken or not, so most were left to run again. Toby was first to open with a loud chop and bawl followed by Jim's loud bawl, they were pushing the track hard. The track was rapidly taken out of hearing range.

Upon driving around both hounds were found treed solid, Jim chopping hard and steady, Toby chopping fast and loud. The area the hounds were treed in contained several sink holes filled with water, which I shined as I walked passed. These sink holes would fill with water when the river overflowed and would often have gators in them, passing by one I spotted the glowing red eyes of a couple gators and picked my pace up. The hounds were in the edge of the bog on a live oak surrounded by 2 feet of water. I shined the area for gators, leashed the hounds and shined the tree, spotting a coon high in the tree, retrieved the hounds and walked from the bog to move to another area.

The next drop was made from the road onto a small stream that ran beside a peanut field. Jim turned and crossed to the other side of the road while Toby crossed the field and struck a hot track along the fence line. Toby was extremely intelligent and when hunted somewhere he had hunted before he always knew where to strike a coon. He ·had struck and treed many coons along the fence line he

291

was running in and this track would be no different. He drifted down the fence line opening accordingly, then located and began treeing well over 100 barks per minute. Once Toby located he did not move and he missed very few coon. I drove close as possible and walked in to him, spotting the coon as I walked in to the tree. I let him have the coon, leashed him and started back to the vehicle to try and find Jim.

Once back at the truck I checked the tracker and found the direction Jim was in and began to drive that way, stopping occasionally to listen. I finally heard Jim on the edge of a large cutover near the river; he was trailing toward the dirt road I was on. I pulled to the top of the rise and sat on the tailgate listening to Jim work the track through some rough territory. He trailed up a drainage ditch, crossed the road in front of where I was parked, crossing onto an unattended tree farm. The lanes between the rows of pines were overgrown with briars and small palmettos; it was rough. Twenty five minutes from the time I heard Jim trailing the track he located and began to chop hard and steady. I drove close as possible and started the difficult walk in to him, finally arriving at a vine covered pine on the edge of the drainage he had been trailing along. I swiftly spotted the coon and let Jim have it, leashed him and headed toward the truck. There was still time to make a few more turnouts.

I loaded Jim into the box and started to get into the truck when I looked down near the front wheel and saw a large rattlesnake, coiled up. The snake saw or heard me about the same time and began to sing. I promptly found a large stick and killed the rattler, which measured 7 feet and had 13 rattlers and a button. I assumed it was too cool for snakes but after thinking about it I guess the snake sensed the heat from the trucks engine and crawled toward it. This was not the first snake I had killed in the area, including several more rattlers and a couple coral snakes. Yes, Florida has some good hunting but it also has lots of snakes and gators. Thinking nothing else of it I drove to a large wooded section on the Suwannee to cut Jim and Toby loose onto the riverbank once again.

Jim started down the river along the water's edge while Toby shot into the woods away from the river. Toby was first to strike deep in the wooded section; he was pushing the track hard, giving more mouth than normal. I thought I could drive closer to better hear him and attempted to do so. Following a drive to the other side of the section I heard Toby treed solid back in the wooded section and also heard Jim running extremely hard near where I had made the drop. I drove back to the river to find Jim had swum to the other side and treed; Toby was still deep in the section, also treed.

The Suwannee River is deep and wide, my light beam would barely reach the other side so I knew I would have to drive around to retrieve Jim. I then began swiftly walking to Toby. After a good walk I arrived at Toby's tree and spotted another coon in plain sight. He was treed on the rim of a half full sinkhole. I shined the light into the sinkhole and saw two red eyes shining back at me, quickly grabbed Toby and started back to the truck, leaving the coon to run again. I was afraid if I put it out that it would fall into the sink hole with the gator. I didn't want to take a chance of the gator having coon and dog for supper.

The area across the river where Jim was treed was not known, but I did know there was a road that paralleled the river on that side. It was a long drive back to the bridge and the road where Jim was thought to be located. After checking the tracker several times I was able to get within hearing range of him, but it was going to be a long walk in to the tree. The walk to the tree was indeed a long one walking in to the tree I spotted Jim stretched high on a large tree fifty feet from the river. Jim was leashed back and the tree shined and found to be a den, full of holes. Nothing was seen on the outside. I started back to the truck thinking that of all the nights hunted on the Suwannee we had treed very few dens. As Jim was loaded into the box I knew there would not be another drop that night, I was tired and had a long trip ahead of me the next day. Toby and Jim had treed more coons in one night but I'd never had to walk that far to them before; this was my last night of hunting the Suwannee.

Toby and Jim were hunted hard for the next year in a number of different States; they treed coons and looked good wherever hunted. Both of these hounds did not like strangers when I first acquired them, but Toby soon became friendly with everyone and Jim only leery of certain people. Both wanted to please their handler when unleashed and would bust their heart to do so. When either of these hounds opened on track they were expected to put a tree on the end of it and have a coon; this was the norm not the exception, just like the dogs with which I had grown up hunting. I'm sure they did not need all of the coons killed to them, but to hunt some of the areas the coon had to be taken. Many dogs get tight on track the more coons killed to them but it only made Jim hunt harder and Toby hate coon and want to tree more.

I enjoyed hunting both, and spent many long memorable nights in the woods with only Jim, Toby, me and a lot of memories. As I think back I wish they had been hunted in some of the larger hunts. I believe they could have won big but I'll never know. Neither hound lived a long life, both hounds were given to my eldest Son, only a youngster at the time; they proved to be too much for him to handle. He did hunt them and tree lots of coon with them, but they were too much too soon. Jim died of natural causes not long afterwards and ironically Toby was killed by a gator while being hunted in the swamps of South Carolina.

CATFISH, CORNBREAD AND COONHUNTING
30

Occasionally, a person wants to take time off to relax, enjoy the great outdoors and live life in general. Nothing is more relaxing than a day of productive fishing followed by a night of coon hunting with friends and good hounds. If in an area where fish can be caught and plenty of coons treed, it could be a sportsman's dream come true. Certain areas of South Carolina contain both good fishing and an abundant coon population. I, along with several friends have spent an abundance of time hunting and fishing in such an area; just taking it easy and enjoying the great outdoors.

Bob Williams and I spent over a month fishing the Santee Cooper reservoir and various fishing holes in the swamps by day, and hunting many of the surrounding swamps by night. One of our favorite areas the "Four Hole Swamp" near Holly Hill was home to very good fishing and excellent coon hunting. We would often set up camp near the swamp, fish most of the day and hunt all night. Bob would fry the fish over an open flame, cook cornbread in a cast iron skillet and occasionally barbecue a coon. It didn't get much better than this.

On this particular day we started early, getting a little cat fishing in on the Santee Cooper; and doing quite well at it. Later in the day we fished the swamps for bream and again did exceptionally well. As late evening approached a few friends came around and Bob began frying fish and his special cornbread. Following a large meal we prepared for a night of hunting in the swamps with good hounds and good friends. The day had been great so far and if the night was anywhere near as good it would be remembered far into the future. Our hunting party would consist of Tommy, Cliff, Bob and I and we would be hunting Grand Nite Champion Clear Creek Jammin' Jim, Grand Nite Champion Briar Creek Molly B, Pete the Drifter and Tree Screaming Billy.

Jim was four year old blue English, a completely balanced hound that ran track with a loud bawl and treed with a hard loud chop. Jim was a broke hound that took his tracks as he came to them, hot or cold, it didn't matter as he could tree any kind of coon. Jim was a hard going very accurate hound that stayed put when he treed; he was a good hound. Jim was sired by Nite Champion Hamilton's

Blue Boy Ten, a Dual Grand Champion Beshear's Blue Boy II (Junior) bred hound.

Molly B was a four year old English Redtick; she had placed in the top twenty of the U.K.C. World Championship and was past U.K.C. World Champion English female. Molly was also a balanced hound and completely broke from off game, she ran track with a loud clear chop and an occasional bawl and treed with a loud solid chop. Molly was also accurate and stayed put when she treed; she was a pleasure hound deluxe. Molly was from Jim Ridge's Briar Creek breeding.

Pete was a four year old blue English hound that had never been in a competition hunt. Pete was a broke hound that ran every track to catch with a loud bawl and treed with a short bawl. Pete was broke from off game and was an accurate stay-put tree dog; just an honest coon treeing hound that was good to hunt pups with. Pete was sired by Duckett's Pistol Pete, another Beshears Blue Boy II bred hound.

Billy was sired by Jammin' Jim and his dam was Molly B, he was only a pup, but one of the rare ones. Billy was blue in color, ran track with a screaming bawl, came on the tree with an outstanding locate and treed with a machine gun chop. He would split tree and hold his tree with a coon that could be seen. Billy ran and treed the first night in the woods; he was progressing at an astonishing rate for his age. He could only be faulted in one way and that was his size; he was a small hound weighing maybe 40 to 45 pounds.

We usually hunted one area of the swamp early then moved farther and hunted another section late, if time permitted. When hunting deep in the swamp there was no driving around when the dogs treed because there were no roads, we walked to the dogs and sometimes never moved from the first section. The large section contained miles of swampland and lots of coon; the hounds often stayed split treed, causing much walking.

Our first drop was from a field road on the back side of the field, directly into the swamp. All four hounds were released into the swamp and swiftly had a track going. Jim was first to open followed by Billy, Pete and Molly. Pete drifted to the left running to catch; Billy and Molly joined in taking the track along the edge of the swamp before exploding on a tree. Molly was first to tree followed by Billy and Pete. Jim continued deeper into the swamp and picked a tree of his own as we walked toward the other treed hounds. It would be a while before we could get to Jim's tree. We were able to walk the field road we had drove in on to Molly, Billy and Pete's tree, they were treed on a large leaf covered tree at the edge of a field. All three had done a good job on the track and looked good on the tree. Molly was stretched high on one side treeing hard and steady, Billy was glued to the other side treeing hard as a dog possibly could, and Pete was standing at the base of the tree steadily bawling. All three were leashed back and the tree shined, a coon quickly spotted and put out to the hounds. To avoid keeping the hounds on the lead, after walking a short distance all three were once again released back into the swamp in the direction of the still treeing Jim.

Jim's hard, loud chops were heard echoing off the water deep in the swamp, telling us to come get this one. The chances of the other hounds covering him were slim, because they were sure to strike another track before reaching him; and that they did. Billy was first to strike followed by Molly and Pete, taking a bad track in the opposite direction of Jim's tree. Our hunting party then split up, with Bob and Tommy following Billy, Molly and Pete, while Cliff and I continued walking toward Jim. We luckily managed to maneuver around and get to Jim's tree without getting wet, but it took some time. Jim was leashed to a smaller tree and his tree shined, a large leaf covered water oak; unable to find anything we began to walk away. One last effort to locate the coon was made by Cliff as we walked from the tree, and as often is the case, the animal looked at the light and continued to look. Our intentions had been to let Jim have the coon, but since we had already walked a short distance from the tree I did not want to walk him back to the tree and then put the coon out to him. Jim had been hunted hard and had plenty of coons out to him and really didn't need it anyway, and besides we would probably tree more that night with all hounds on the tree. Jim remained on the leash as we walked toward dry ground and the still trailing Molly, Pete and Billy.

We clearly heard the other three hounds still working their track, but a good distance from our location. We swiftly walked in that direction. Their track was poor or possibly in swimming water, as they were having a difficult time with it. As Cliff and I came nearer and spotted the lights of Bob and Tommy we proceeded to where they stood. By this time the track had pretty much played out.

With our party back together and Molly, Pete and Billy's track almost diminished Jim was released in their general direction. No sooner had I released Jim than Billy squalled out repeatedly as if something had hold of him. It was thought he had caught something on the ground but this was not the case as he then began to tree. The other hounds hastily backed Billy and our group walked toward the treed hounds.

On arrival at the tree, a leaning snag in knee deep water with a large coon sitting atop it, we held the hounds and put the coon out, releasing them when it hit the water. I don't know if Billy had caught the coon in the water before it climbed the tree or if he was only excited, but he surely was squalling like something had hold of him. He really hated a coon and was developing into a good hound; I felt good about his future. We then walked from the tree back in the direction of the field road before releasing the hounds to hunt farther around the water's edge. Jim was first to find scent and gave mouth accordingly, he was joined by Molly, Billy and Pete, in that order. The hounds smoked the track out of the swamp quickly coming treed under a large dozer pile at the water's edge. The hounds did not want to come from under the tangled mess but were finally caught and leashed. Having all hounds on the lead we decided to move to a new location farther around the swamp.

Arriving at the new area all hounds were once again released into the swamp, going deep before a track was struck. Molly was first to give mouth followed by Jim, Billy and Pete on a seemingly good track. The hounds worked the track through deep water before Billy peeled off to the right, let out a screaming locate and began to tree. The other hounds continued on into the swamp chopping and bawling as they swam and occasionally found scent on water or a tree. We walked to Billy and found him treed on a small tree in thigh deep water, the tree was leafless and empty, but regardless he was treeing 130 plus barks per minute. This was one of the first 'for sure' slick trees Billy had made; he was given a slight scolding, taken off the tree and sent on his way.

The other hounds were now far in the distance and moving at a better pace. Billy joined the other hounds as the track really picked up and a tree was soon made. Jim was first to locate, followed by Molly, Pete and Billy; they were quite a distance into the swamp. We began the walk to the treed hounds and some walk it was, through deep moving water that was difficult to negotiate. Following an hour of laborious walking, and finally arriving at a tree in waist deep water with all four hounds on it; we leashed the hounds and took a much needed break before shining the tree. A coon was spotted sitting in a fork halfway up the tree, but it was left to run again. The coon had traveled a great distance through the swamp and then ran a good race after the hounds got up on it; the coon had earned the right to live and run again.

We were deep in the swamp and there was no way we were going to cut the hounds back into the swamp in that area. Not only were we soaking wet, we were a long, long walk from our vehicles. We started the long walk back toward the vehicles leaving the hounds on the lead. It took over an hour and a half before reaching the field road we were parked on; Tommy and Cliff said they were finished for the night and headed for home. Bob and I slowly drove along contemplating on another drop and decided to cut the hounds loose one more time. After all we couldn't get any wetter than we were and we had nothing else to do. A coonhunter always cuts the hounds loose one more time.

We decided to hunt a wooded area on the outskirts of the swamp where there were roads and the water would not be too deep. All four hounds struck from the lead as they were released onto the bank of a small creek flowing through the woods. Pete and Billy went one direction as Jim and Molly scorched their track the other direction. The hounds were able to run on solid ground now and we heard some good track work by the four hounds. Billy's screaming locate once again pierced the night as he grabbed the tree away from a hard running Pete. Bob and I sat listening to Jim and Molly trail out of hearing while Billy and Pete let us know they had reached the end of the line. We would be able to drive closer to Billy and Pete and possibly even Jim and Molly if they got treed before reaching the swamp.

Driving to the other side of the section we were able to get within a quarter from Billy and Pete. We parked and hurriedly walked to them, shined the tree, spotted a coon, gave both a little praise and led them back to the vehicle.

Checking the tracker and pin pointing Jim and Molly's location, we then drove to the next road over and stopped almost on top of the two treeing hounds. The hounds hadn't made it into the swamp and were treed on dry ground along the roadside. I walked to the tree and leashed both hounds as Bob yelled, "Here the coon is." Bob had spotted the coon from the road without leaving the vehicle. I gave both hounds a little praise and led them back to the vehicle; loading them into the box as daylight began to roll in. Our hunt had been a decent one even though hunting the swamps is sometimes rough, we had enjoyed it.

I enjoyed hunting Jim, Molly, Pete and Billy as all were hounds that gave no aggravation of any kind. A coon would be seen in most trees they made and they treed most tracks they struck. Not long after this hunt while being kept at a friend's home Billy's kennel was left unlatched; loose and roaming the neighborhood he was hit by a vehicle and killed.

Disgusted because of losing Billy; I then gave Jim to my eldest son Michael. He hunted him only a short period of time and was unable to enjoy him very much as he died of natural causes soon after he got him. Seems the good ones sometimes die young. I gave Molly and Pete to Bob, free of charge, as he had a soft spot for both. I don't know what Bob did with Pete but Molly died of a twisted stomach while still owned by him. Bob and I spent many nights following some good English hounds over the years and he remained a friend and devoted English follower until the end. Hopefully he enjoyed Molly and Pete as much as I did.

TREE POWER—YOUNG AND BLUE
31

The stillness of the night was shattered by the strange, high pitched bark of the young Bluetick Hound called "Quick," when he gave mouth on coon scent. The track he struck was old and Quick struggled to get it up and running, but he steadily moved it in one direction. The more mouth he gave on track the louder and clearer his voice became. He worked the track through some rough terrain including a good sized beaver swamp, a patch of cutover timber and then run the track into a good bottomland. He began to put pressure on the animal; it was either going to have to climb or make a stand on the ground - and soon. Quick's voice was now at full volume, it had changed from a high pitched squeal when he initially struck the track to a loud bawl, given sparingly, as he ran the track to catch. Upon approaching the river the dark blue hound suddenly threw his head into the air, gave a big locating bawl and began to chop loud and hard. He was letting the hunters know to come get this one as it had reached the end of the line.

Our hunting party stood listening to the loud, clear chops of the treeing hound. They were relishing the sound of the hard treeing young hound and knowing that he had treed a bad track without needing help. But would he have a coon in the tree? It was our first night in the woods with Quick; he was only a one year old but had already built a reputation for himself.

We slowly walked in the direction of the treed hound, listening to the loud ringing chops reverberate off the surrounding hills. As we walked into the tree we saw Quick was stretched high on the side of a large oak on the riverbank; and yes there was a coon sprawled on a limb high in the tree. He was leashed back from the tree and given a little praise for the outstanding job he had done on the bad track. He was then given his just reward in the form of a large boar coon, which he rapidly dispatched. Our party then returned to the vehicle, leaving the proud young hound on the leash. We were going to move to another area and see how he performed there.

Quick's registered name came to be Nite Champion Nation's Wild-N- Blue Mr. Quick. He came from the kennel of Mackie Manns of Indiana, who did an outstanding job starting the young hound. Quick was sired by Grand Nite Champion Manns' Wild-N Blue Spanky, a son of Grand Nite Champion A.K.C. World Champion Coz' Sparetime Spanky; a hound I owned that won many of the larger hunts, including the 1991 A.K.C. World Hunt. Quick had the breeding behind him to tree coons and do it in style. All he needed was to be put into the woods to reach his full potential; he would get plenty of hunting if he stayed in my kennel.

Our next drop would be from atop some rolling ridges with plenty of small, clear streams running through the hollows. Quick was released directly onto one of the small streams; he went hunting immediately. He hunted about fifteen minutes and returned without making a bark. Quick had not been hunted alone prior to that night, but he had already treed one coon alone, and I was sure he would tree more. He needed to hunt a little deeper to strike a track, so he was sent back into the woods; this time he went deep into the section and soon had a track going.

The track he was running was much better than the first one and he moved it swiftly through the country, drifting and bawling only occasionally. Living up to his name he made quick work of the track and his locating bawl was soon heard, followed by the hard loud chops. He was treed solid. Quick was deep in the section of woods and there was no roads or paths to get closer to him; so the walk began.

On arrival at the tree we found Quick stretched high as possible on the side of a large pine. He was leashed back from the tree and another coon was found high in the tree. Quick was once again given a little praise, but not the coon; it was left to run again because coons were not plentiful in the area. He shouldn't need every coon he treed anyway. As we walked from the tree a member of our hunting party said he would like to see how Quick operated with another hound. Following a brief discussion we made the drive back to his house to get an older, well trained hound named "Blue Boy". We would now see how Quick compared to a top hound.

It was decided we would hunt several smaller tracts of land that contained coon and other game. We would be better able to keep up with the hounds, and possibly tree a coon on every drop. The first drop was made from a farm lane onto the edge of a pond consisting of several acres. The shallow end of the pond had a growth of cattails which was home to an abundance of frogs, minnows and crawfish - a good source of food to draw coon to the area. Both hounds hunted in the direction of the cattails and both were soon struck in on a hot track, but swiftly split up. Quick went one direction and Blue Boy the other. Neither track lasted very long; Blue Boy was first to locate a tree with a long drawn out bawl before the heavy, houndy chops began. Quick followed suit, swiftly making a tree of his own. We listened to the two treeing hounds for several minutes, determining that both were going to hold their tree; proving that they could stand tree pressure neither hound pulled from their tree. After a short walk to Blue Boy's tree, he was leashed back from the tree and a small coon spotted. Blue Boy was given a little praise and led to the tree Quick was treeing on. His coon was left to run again.

As we walked into Quick's tree, which was not much more than a bush, a small coon was spotted sitting low in the tree. Quick was looking at the coon and treeing extra hard. He received a little petting and then he and Blue Boy were led back to the vehicle. His coon was also left in the tree. We wanted to move to a different area to make another drop, hopefully a fast one with both hounds on the same track.

The night was cool and it was getting late, we hoped the dogs would strike a good track - one they would work together on. We decided to hunt an area of pasture land surrounded by patch woods; we had treed many coons there in the past. Both Quick and Blue

Boy were cast from a field road towards a cattle feeder and immediately struck a track. Blue Boy was first to open with a thundering bawl and was joined by Quick with his squealing squall. The hounds worked the track across the pasture and into a patch of woods, Blue Boy bawling loud and clear and Quick's mouth clearing to a good bawl also. They worked together as one and soon had the animal up and running. They crossed from one patch of woods into another and rapidly run out of hearing range. Most coons we treed in that area did not run very far as a rule, but this one was an exception. This old coon was what would be called a traveling salesman; he was getting gone.

We hurriedly walked back to the vehicle to check the tracker and pinpoint the location of the hounds. Having discovered the general direction of the hounds we proceeded to drive in that direction, stopping at intervals to listen for the hounds. Topping a high ridge and hearing the hounds in a deep hollow we realized they hadn't run the track far as we assumed. We sat on the ridge and listened to some good track work as the two hounds ran the coon to catch. Blue Boy was giving good mouth on the track but Quick had tightened up and was attempting to catch the animal or make it climb. The old coon must have sensed the young hound gaining ground because it soon climbed a tree. Quick located the tree as he was coming into it and immediately went to chopping. Blue Boy took a moment to settle on the tree; he was making sure the coon hadn't tapped the tree.

Our little group listened to the treeing hounds for several minutes before slowly walking to them. The hounds were stretched high on the side of a large hardwood letting the world know what time it was. It took only a few seconds to find a very large coon sitting in a fork high in the tree. Both hounds were given a little praise and the big coon left to run again. It is coons that run the way that old coon ran that help to develop a good track dog, not to mention the enjoyment bestowed on the persons listening to the hounds run such a track.

We witnessed some good track work and heard a couple of good tree dogs on the wood that night. We called it a night after the last tree; it was all for that night but many more would follow. I hunted Quick alone the majority of the time and he needed no help of any kind. He treed what he struck and was very accurate; you would see a coon or a den at the end of his tracks. He was a good young hound, but like many before him he did not stay at my kennel until the end.

ROWDY

32

Rowdy was not his given name but a nickname, which he had earned early in life. He was small in stature when growing up and many times had to fight to be right. So he grew up with the belief that "might was always right". Thus, by his rowdy ways the moniker was given him and followed him throughout life. Rowdy was born tough but with age and through hard physical labor he developed into a really tough individual. He met all challenges head on. Rowdy was born and reared in the hills, the third of five children - all boys. As he was growing up there never seemed to be enough to go around and everyone was expected to pull their own weight. There was little industry and few jobs to be had, but Rowdy worked odd jobs and helped the family. He saved what remained, even at a young age. He was intent on getting an education and leaving the hills to make his fortune.

Rowdy eventually became well educated; this came to be because of his father's constant teachings about the need for education. He was educated in academics as well as trade school and possessed street smarts as well. He knew that education to the highest level was a path toward a better life for him. With these learned skills he became self sufficient.

Rowdy's father was a mountain man who knew little of the life outside the hills where he was born, reared and lived his life. He owned a small garage, doing mechanic work and building dirt track cars for the local racers. He also manufactured a little corn whiskey to help support his family, and occasionally built cars used by the whiskey runners to haul their wares. He did his best to support his family, but sometimes things were hard. He wanted better for his sons and made certain, even in hard times, that they received the education needed.

Growing up, Rowdy and his brothers enjoyed the traditions of mountain living, with hunting being part of the culture. They hunted game for the dinner table and the pelts were sold for extra money - nothing was wasted. Most mountain families owned a hunting dog of some sort - a hound or cur that would tree squirrels or possums or most anything that climbed a tree. Rowdy's family was no different and had several hounds around the house that were used for hunting small game.

In his spare time Rowdy hunted all game that could be consumed or their pelts sold for cash. He enjoyed hunting with hounds and trained several pups to conform to his hunting needs. Rowdy attacked his training efforts with a passion, bordering obsession; a zeal he exhibited in everything he did. Hunting with hounds was Rowdy's favorite pastime and one of the few things he would miss when he departed the mountains for gainful employment.

As time passed, Rowdy's older brothers departed the hills for valid employment in the trades they sought. Rowdy would soon follow, as he was skilled in many trades and waiting only for a suitable opportunity. Rowdy was soon offered a good paying union job working as a steel worker hanging steel on large high rise buildings. Even though schooled for better jobs, the pay was excellent and the benefits even better, he would get to see the country as his crew traveled from city to city.

Rowdy was young and wild when he began his new job, and having never seen the sights of the big cities, he was intrigued. The majority of Rowdy's coworkers were rough, tough young men from the city, but Rowdy was equally tough, only in a different sort of way. The crew would work all week long and hit the Honky Tonks and Juke Joints every weekend. Rowdy's first couple years with the crew was wasted on such activities. He became to be known as a barroom brawler who started no trouble but would finish it - someone not to be antagonized. Two years into the job Rowdy began to settle down, move up in rank and save every penny he made. He was going to earn his fortune and find an easier life. He was also beginning to miss life in the hills, especially the hunting. Rowdy continued to work hard as the years passed, and he advanced to engineer; his bank account had also begun to grow. Rowdy had invested wisely in certain stocks and was now beginning to see some positive results. Hopefully, in a few more years he could return home and start a business of his own.

Rowdy and his crew were now working in one of the bigger cities in Kentucky, erecting a large building. They were joined by coworkers from the area, some who were good ole country boys. While one day having lunch a new worker mentioned he had been coon hunting the night before. Hearing this, Rowdy joined the conversation and was invited along for a hunt the coming weekend.

The weekend seemed slow in coming, with Rowdy eager for it to arrive, anticipating the upcoming hunt. He had not realized how much he missed hunting until "Ray" the new coworker began discussing hunting and hounds. When the night of the hunt finally rolled around Rowdy was a little nervous because it had been so many years since he had been to the woods with a hound.

Ray came by and picked Rowdy up for the drive to the home of his Uncle Wayne, the hunter they were to hunt with. On further questioning Ray informed Rowdy that his Uncle Wayne owned two coondogs. On arrival at Wayne's home introductions were made and the hounds looked over before being loaded into the box for the short drive to the woods. During the drive to the hunting area Rowdy asked a few questions about the hounds, such

as their breeding, age, type of mouth, etcetera. Wayne explained that he had raised and trained the hounds which were both registered English - a male and a female. "Rock" was a four year old tri-colored hound with a red head and legs and a blue back. The female "Blondie" was a light colored three year old redtick. Wayne stated that both were out of old time local breeding and that Rowdy's other questions would be answered in the woods.

314

The area they were going to hunt was rolling hills heavily wooded with hardwood timber. The two hounds were released into the woods along a drainage ditch and quickly struck a track. Rowdy was awed by the volume of the two hounds; they had extremely loud bawl voices. Rowdy noted that the hounds steadily drifted the track and did not hang up, or bog down. They ran the track into the tree and located with distinguishing locates and began to tree with loud ringing chops. The hunters walked to the tree, leashed the hounds, spotted the coon and quickly dispatched it.

After the first tree Rowdy realized how much he missed hearing the hounds run and tree. Before the hunt ended he would again be hooked. Four more coons were treed before the hunters decided to quit for the night. Rowdy thanked Ray and Wayne for allowing him to come along on the hunt. He then asked if he could start joining them on their weekend hunts. Ray and Wayne replied, "Sure." Rowdy, Ray and Wayne hunted the remainder of the season, becoming very good friends as time advanced. Rowdy also came to admire Rock and Blondie because of their coon treeing abilities. He wished he lived where he could own another hound.

With their current construction job coming to a close, Rowdy and his crew would soon be moving to the next job. Rowdy was going to miss hunting with Ray and Wayne when he moved on. He would be fortunate if he could find hunters in the next city they were scheduled to work.

With only a couple days remaining on the job a drastic situation occurred. Rowdy was severely injured in an "on the job" accident, not of his doing, but caused by faulty equipment. The injuries sustained by Rowdy were life threatening, and career ending. He was hospitalized for many months before recovering enough to get back on his feet. The only good thing about Rowdy's accident was he had good insurance. The company that manufactured the faulty equipment, along with the company he worked for were attempting to negotiate a settlement with him.

While hospitalized Rowdy was visited by friends and family. Ray and Wayne visited on occasion and conversed of their hunts. Wayne informed Rowdy that he had bred Blondie to Rock and offered him the pick of the litter when released from the hospital. Rowdy promptly accepted the offer as his plans were to possibly move back to the hills and work with his father while recuperating. His father had offered him a very lucrative sounding partnership in his growing garage business.

Rowdy's oldest brother had done well for himself; he was living in Michigan and working in the automotive industry as a supervisor. He also did a little hunting with hounds. He asked Rowdy to come stay with him until fully recovered. He offered Rowdy a well paying job that involved no physical labor, a job he could perform while recuperating and still earn a good income. He also told Rowdy he had kennel space for a couple more hounds and that there was a heavy coon population in the area he lived. This was the deciding factor that influenced Rowdy to relocate to Michigan, at least until he fully healed. He would then make his move back home to the hills.

Rowdy was released from the hospital, and before leaving for his brother 's home, he visited Ray and Wayne. The pups from Rock and Blondie were ready to go, and he received his pick as promised by Wayne. Rowdy did not pick the best looking pup but the one that

316

attracted his attention. The pup was redtick with a light blue saddle on his back. What really drew Rowdy's attention were the dew claws on the pup's hind legs. Many of the mountain dogs he hunted in his youth had dew claws and this brought back memories. Wayne stated, "That is not the best pup, but he is your pick and hopefully he will make you happy." Rowdy let Wayne know how much he appreciated the pup and began the drive to his new home.

Once settled in, Rowdy slowly began working his new job. He looked forward to the day he could begin to hunt again. He was still having trouble getting around but was improving by the day. With therapy and hard work he would heal 100%, he hoped.

About one month after moving to Michigan, Rowdy had not officially named his new pup. He still called him pup but that was about to change. One evening when he returned home from work Rowdy found his pup steadily barking in the kennel. He walked to the kennel to see what the problem was and saw the neighbor s house cat up a small tree beside the kennel. The pup was standing on the kennel fence barking with a loud steady chop, looking directly at the cat. Rowdy thought that he sounded like a drum beating a steady beat; so "Drum" became the pups' name. Little did he know that with time Drum would develop into not only a coondog but a reproducer of top coondogs. Drum would be the foundation male of Rowdy's line of English hounds and would cross with most anything he was bred to.

As the months flew by Rowdy continued his therapy and walked the woods daily with Drum. This was accomplishing two things; he was getting stronger and it was allowing Drum to become familiar with the sights, sounds and smells of the wilderness. He and Drum were now ready to attempt a real hunt at night.

With coon season beginning the next day, Rowdy's brother and a local hunter were going to hunt opening night and invited Rowdy to come along and bring Drum. On the first turnout Drum left the leash with the other hounds and never looked back. The hounds quickly struck and treed a good track. As the hunters walked to the tree they heard a strange hound come on the tree with a series of loud long bawls. Each bawl became a little shorter until it was a heavy, solid chop that almost drowned the other hounds out. On their arrival at the tree the hunters were astonished at the sight they saw. Drum was sitting at the base of the tree looking straight up and never missing a bark - and what a mouth he had. The hounds were tied back, the coon spotted and dispatched, and the hounds allowed to wool it a little. It seemed Drum could not get enough of this newly discovered animal. Rowdy praised Drum and smiled to his brother and the other hunter. He was ready to turn the hounds loose again.

After walking away from the tree, the hounds were again cut loose, Drum immediately went hunting with them. They soon struck and Drum joined in on the track. He opened with a loud, screaming bawl; a voice that should have been heard on a hound twice his size. He split from the other hounds and took his track into the country, located a tree with a series of bawls, eventually shortening it down to a loud, heavy chop. He pulled the other hounds to his tree with his loud tree mouth. The hunters spotted the coon as they walked in to the tree. Drum was again sitting at the base of the tree and not missing a bark. This coon was also put out to the hounds and they were again cut back into the timber.

At the end of the hunt, eight coons had been treed and seen, or taken, and Drum ran track on all but the first. He treed on every tree, and after the first tree, he made several split trees alone. Rowdy and his brother had hunted many young hounds and pups in the past but had never seen the likes of Drum. Drum took to treeing coons like a duck to water. After only a few hunts he was as good alone as in company. He was independent and did his thing even at a young age. Only a small amount of discipline was required to break him from unwanted game.

Through other hunters Rowdy heard of a reputable breeder who had a top young English female that was for sale. A time was set to hunt the female, and after two nights of seeing her run and tree coons, Rowdy purchased her to go along with Drum.

The female was a well-bred Redtick with a loud squall bawl mouth on track, a one bark locate and a hard chop mouthed, accurate tree dog. Rowdy named the female "Daisey"; she would develop into a top coondog and reproducer. Daisey would come to be the foundation female of Rowdy's breeding program.

Rowdy was as near 100% as he ever would be. He still carried a slight limp, and would carry it for life, but he could get through the woods as good as anyone. He was fortunate to have healed as well as he had. He was thinking about moving back to the hills and taking his father up on the partnership at the garage. He would think on it for a day or two.

The decision was made for Rowdy a couple days later when he received a call from his attorney, informing him of a settlement in the suit filed over his accident. The settlement was such a large sum that it, along with his other savings and investments, would allow him to be financially stable for many years. He never dreamed the settlement could have reached the amount he would finally receive. It could not have come at a better time. He was moving back to the hills and taking two up and coming young hounds with him. He could not have been happier.

Part Two

****

Rowdy had actually been homesick for the hills for some time, but he was pleased to have spent the time in Michigan with his brother. The hunting was better, as well as easier, and he was able to put coons out to Drum and Daisey. Both hounds were doing an outstanding job in the woods and Rowdy hoped they would continue the good work in the rough hills he was about to subject them to. The mountains would either make them or break them, he was looking forward to finding out which. Rowdy was anxious to get home, but decided to make a slight detour to visit with his friends Ray and Wayne. He wanted to hunt for one night and show them how well Drum was developing. After all he would not have the hound if not for Wayne's generosity. He also wanted them to see his female Daisey in the woods.

Ray and Wayne were pleased to see Rowdy and were amazed at the progress he had made health wise. They both surmised that he would never hunt again following his accident, but here he was ready to hit the woods. He had to be the most determined, and strong willed person either had ever known.

As nightfall approached Ray, Wayne and Rowdy loaded their hounds for the hunt. Wayne was taking only Rock and Blondie; his littermate to Drum would be left at home. Rowdy loaded Drum and Daisey, eager to see how they compared to Rock and Blondie. They were going to hunt one of their favorite hunting areas. Rowdy knew there were coons in this area; he only hoped that his hounds would perform as they had in Michigan.

The hounds were cut into the woods on a small stream and very quickly struck a track. The track was a good running track and the animal was treed in only minutes. All hounds were on the same tree; Rock had located first, followed by Drum, Daisey and Blondie. As the hunters walked in to the tree they saw Drum sitting at the base of the tree doing as he always did not missing a bark. The other three hounds were up on the tree, looking straight up, and treeing every breath. Wayne and Ray were impressed with Drum and Daisey's treeing style, and especially their volume. They quickly spotted the coon, and then led the hounds a short distance from the tree before releasing them to hunt further.

Drum and Daisey had been hunted hard, they were accustomed to doing it alone, this time they got to themselves and rapidly put a coon up a tree. They were backed by Rock, as well as Blondie, and the coon spotted. Ray and Wayne were beginning to realize what Rowdy meant when he said his hounds were doing "pretty good." The hounds were cut loose one more time and a split track was struck. Rock and Drum trailed one direction and Daisey and Blondie in another. Rock and Drum ended their track on split trees, Drum had a coon and Rock had a den tree. Daisey and Blondie's track also ended on a den tree, without a coon being seen. The hunters quit for the night after this tree, as Rowdy wanted to be on the road early and needed a little rest.

Before Rowdy departed, Ray and Wayne bragged on Drum and Daisey. They also told Rowdy once he was settled in the hills and the season opened they would like to visit and hunt for a week or so. Wayne told Rowdy that Drum was doing better than any of his littermates, and he had the loudest mouth of any hound he had heard sired by Rock. He was going to make the cross between Rock and Blondie again, soon as possible. As Rowdy drove away Ray and Wayne commented that Rowdy was one dedicated hunter and was doing an outstanding job with the two young hounds. They looked forward to hunting in the hills with their friend and his hounds.

Rowdy was overjoyed to be home, his true home where he had spent the early years of his life. His family and friends who remained in the hills were also glad he was home. Rowdy moved back to the home place with his family until he could find a place of his own. He was also going into a partnership with his father at the garage. His father's garage had grown into a thriving business that was more than he could handle alone at his age. With only one of Rowdy's brothers remaining in the hills, and a business of his own to attend, he was unable to help much. It had been hard on their father. Rowdy was going to pitch in and relieve his father of a large portion of the work.

The garage had been a family business for many years with Rowdy's father operating it and his father before him. Over the years they had serviced the local automobiles, and built engines and cars for stock car racers as well as whiskey runners. With modern times, the whiskey business was all but an extinct thing of the past, but the racing industry was booming. Rowdy's father had taken advantage of this by building some of the best race cars and engines to be found, he had earned a reputation for these services. This reputation had brought much work, as well as growth. His business had made him a wealthy man; something he had worked hard for without ever leaving the hills. He was thankful Rowdy was home to help pull the weight.

Rowdy was settling in and reacquainting himself with old friends and neighbors. He wanted to request permission to hunt some of his old hunting grounds. He was ready to turn Drum and Daisey loose where the terrain was rough and the coon hard to tree - a true test for a hound. Rowdy's father and brother still owned tree dogs, and they did a little night hunting when time permitted. They still had the same old mountain stock they had owned when Rowdy left so many years before. Rowdy hoped to show them he had also brought home some good tree dog stock.

With permission obtained to hunt several large tracts of land he had hunted as a youngster, Rowdy loaded Drum and Daisey and headed for the woods. He wanted to hunt them alone at first. The area he planned to hunt was mountainous and rough, something that neither of his young hounds had been introduced to as of yet. The coon population was much thinner than where his hounds had been hunted. The deer population was also heavy, though, probably no heavier than where they had been hunted. Rowdy had taken the time to thoroughly break both hounds from off game and felt they would give no problems.

Rowdy cut the two young hounds up a deep hollow and sat down to wait. He had faith that they would tree coons and do it in style. An hour passed and Rowdy had heard neither hound, he then became restless. He began to walk in the direction the hounds were released, angling up the ridge toward the crest. Once he topped the ridge he heard the hounds in the hollow on the opposite side; they were treed. He walked to the tree, leashed both hounds back and began looking for the coon. Rowdy promptly found the coon, gave the hounds a little praise, led them a short distance from the tree and released them back in the direction he had come.

Rowdy walked the top of the ridge where he could hear the hounds if they struck again. He didn't have to wait long, after only a few minutes, Daisey struck with two long squall bawls followed by a screaming bawl from Drum. The hounds worked the track, drifting and giving just enough mouth, moving back in the direction Rowdy had parked the vehicle. Both hounds shut up for a few seconds when suddenly the silence of the night was pierced by a series of loud locating bawls from Drum. Daisey quickly covered him with a screaming locate and turned it over to a ringing chop. Rowdy sat down and listened to the loud mouthed hounds voices reverberate off of the surrounding mountains before beginning the walk to them. Rowdy walked in to the tree, leashed the hounds back and swiftly found the coon. He then led the hounds toward the truck. Yes, they would tree coons in the rough old hills. After that night Rowdy did not miss a night in the woods for many weeks. He was going to have Drum and Daisey polished for the upcoming season.

Rowdy continued to work hard at the garage throughout the summer and hunt nightly, sometimes with his father and brother. Both Rowdy's father and brother were impressed with Drum and Daisey's ability, as were the other hunters who had the pleasure to hunt with them.

Many of the old mountain dogs were coondogs, but even at their young age Drum and Daisey held their own with whatever hunted with. In short time it became known that Rowdy owned two top hounds. With talk of the two hounds escalating, the locals soon wanted to breed their females to Drum. They had either witnessed or heard of the overpowering mouth and outstanding ability of the young hound, and his looks wasn't bad either

A couple weeks before the opening of coon season, Rowdy had a streak of good fortune. The farm adjoining his family's old home place came up for sale and Rowdy was able to negotiate a deal for it. This would be the ideal place for him to start and expand his kennel business and eventually start a family of his own. There was good hunting out the back door and plenty of state land surrounding the property. The deal was closed and Rowdy settled in within a month.

Hunting season was in full swing; both Drum and Daisey were finely tuned. Rowdy was ready to have his friends come for a hunt. He phoned Ray and Wayne and invited them to come visit and hunt for a week or two. Arrangements were made, and they arrived the following week bringing along a surprise for Rowdy.

As Ray and Wayne drove into the small town where Rowdy lived, they observed the scenery and said, "This is really pretty country but these mountains sure look rough." They looked forward to turning their hounds loose in the rough terrain. Wayne had brought Rock, Blondie and Pete, a littermate to Drum. They had also brought along a young blue English male that was ready to be hunted. He was a gift for Rowdy. Rowdy was happy to see his friends, he was long overdue for a week or two of nothing but hunting and enjoying the companionship of his friends. Wayne and Ray unloaded the hounds and placed them in the kennels Rowdy had prepared for them. When they came to the young blue English hound Rowdy said, "Now that is a fine looking hound. What will he do and how is he bred?"

Wayne replied, "His sire is a good hound called Little Blue and his dam is some of the same breeding as Rock and Blondie. He has never been hunted but has run loose on the farm and anything he knows he learned on his own. He has an outstanding mouth and is ready to be hunted hard. Oh yeah, he is the surprise that we brought for you, and if he turns out he should be a good outcross on pups from Drum and Daisey."

Rowdy wanted to breed Daisey when she came in season, he would now have something to work with while she was with pups.

Rowdy, Wayne and Ray hunted hard for two weeks and treed coons in style every night. Wayne and Ray were astonished at the different types of terrain Rowdy put them in. He had rough mountains with fast running streams, river bottoms and even some beaver swamps. The coon population was not as good as their part of the country, but the hunting was very good. A hound trained in this part of the country should tree coons anywhere turned loose.

Wayne's hounds had performed very well, even Pete his young hound had treed a coon or two off to himself. Drum and Daisey had looked best of all and put trees at the end of their tracks with coons the majority of the time. Rowdy had finished Drum and Daisey into top hounds, Wayne and Ray hoped he would do the same with the young blue hound they had given him.

Soon after Wayne and Ray departed for home, Daisey came in season and was bred to Drum. During this time Rowdy began to hunt the young blue hound his friends had given him. The young hound had run loose and learned on his own, he was farther along than Wayne and Ray implied. The first night in the woods he ran and treed coons with Drum. Rowdy called the hound "Young Blue", but would name him appropriately after seeing him do something of importance, something that would give the name some meaning. Thirty days into Young Blue's hunting career he was coming along in leaps and bounds, he would soon earn his registered name. Young Blue was an outstanding track drifting dog that ran every track to catch, sometimes putting long distances between each bark. Rowdy thought that Young Blue being the great drifting track dog he was deserved an appropriate name and permanently named him "Drifter," a name that suited his style.

As Drifter developed, he would go hunting every time released; his hunting style was a little different than Drum and Daisey. He hunted as deep and hard, but completely covered the ground around where he was released, he did not overshoot tracks. He was a good strike dog with a booming bawl on track, had a good nose and track speed, a quick accurate locator as well as a powerful chop mouthed tree dog that stayed put. He also treed a lot of lay-up coon. Rowdy liked and enjoyed hunting Drifter; he was a welcome addition to his kennel.

Daisey delivered her pups as scheduled, having nine nice healthy pups, some redtick, some bluetick and a couple tri-colored. These pups would be just right to start the next hunting season. Rowdy was keeping a male and a female for himself; the remaining pups would be started and sold to hunters wanting a good started hound. As the pups aged, Rowdy began to expose them to the elements and picked the two he would keep. These pups would come to be named Doc and Dixie because of their attachment to a couple of Rowdy's close friends. The pup called Doc would jump upon and show his affection to the local vet when receiving his immunizations and worming, thus earning his name. The female pup showed the same affection with Rowdy's close friend and future wife Dixie, so she was named in her honor.

Rowdy continued to hunt hard in the off season keeping Drum, Daisey and Drifter in hunting condition and looking forward to the opening of raccoon season. When time permitted, he walked the woods with his pups, noting their actions and how they adapted to the woods and surroundings. He looked for any undesirable traits the pups might show or possess. The pups were exposed to tree game and off game alike. They would know what game they were expected to run and tree once their night hunting began.

Once the season opened, Rowdy's friends Wayne and Ray would be coming back for a week or two of hunting. In the meantime, Rowdy hunted nightly watching the progress of Drifter and his pups. Drifter had become a great track dog that could take the hard tracks and make them look easy - he was a keeper. Doc and Dixie had also taken to treeing coons very easily and were both naturals, needing very little correcting or disciplining. Rowdy was proud of his hounds and looked forward to showing them in the woods. His friends would be arriving for their planned visit in only a few days. Rowdy could hardly wait.

Part Three

****

Rowdy hunted hard the first two weeks of the coon season, awaiting the arrival of his friends, and fine tuning his hounds. Drum, Daisey and Drifter were polished and his pups Doc and Dixie were treeing coons alone. The whole litter of pups by Drum and Daisey were performing exceptionally well. Counting Doc and Dixie seven of the nine pups would run and tree. alone. Two were not performing at a satisfactory level, but Rowdy would give them a little more time to prove their worth. By seasons end he would know what he had. The pups that turned out would be sold and the ones that didn't would be culled. Rowdy would not pass a useless pup off on another. He culled and culled hard and his efforts would surface in his breeding program as time passed. His non-reluctance to cull would be seen in the literal bone yard on the hillside behind his home.

Wayne and Ray arrived as planned for their two week stay with Rowdy. Their yearly hunts would become an annual event for the three friends. It was a time to catch up on old times and compare dog power. Wayne had brought Rock, Blondie and Pete his littermate to Drum. Wayne advised Rowdy that Pete had finished into a top hound, one of the better hounds he had owned. He also said he had made the cross between Rock and Blondie again, but all pups had been sold to local hunters. He thought there possibly could be another Drum or Pete in the litter; he just didn't have the patience to start another pup. Rowdy showed Wayne and Ray his pups by Drum and Daisey, he told them "Doc" and "Dixie" were the two he was keeping. Wayne couldn't take his eyes off Doc; he said Doc was one of the finest looking hounds he had ever laid eyes on. He asked Rowdy what the young hound would do in the woods and as always Rowdy said, "He is doing pretty good." When they came to Drifters kennel they asked how he was doing, and Rowdy repeated, ''Pretty good." Wayne knew they would see for themselves when they hit the woods. Rowdy would not brag on a hound.

As darkness settled in they loaded Drifter, Doc, Rock and Pete and headed to the woods for their first drop. Their plans were to hunt the mountains the early half of the night, with intentions of making a couple turnouts. If all went well they would then switch hounds and hunt Drum, Daisey, Dixie and Blondie the remainder of the night.

The first drop was made from an old logging road high on the mountainside. The hounds were released into a hollow running to the bottom of the mountain. A hot running track was struck and Drifter quickly revealed his great tracking ability. The other three hounds were forced to give less mouth on track just to run with him. Drifter easily located the tree ahead of Doc, Pete and Rock, but they swiftly backed him. Doc located the tree with the same series of extremely loud bawls as his sire Drum, with volume to match. On the trek into the tree both Wayne and Ray commented that Doc sounded identical to Drum when he located a tree. When they arrived at the tree they would see that he also possessed the same treeing style. The hounds were leashed back, the tree shined and a coon quickly spotted and given to the deserving hounds.

The hunters then moved to the base of the mountain to make another drop. The hounds were released onto a small stream surrounded by cutover timber and dozer decks. All hounds went hunting and soon had another track going. Doc split from the other hounds and suddenly exploded on a tree. The other three hounds continued on through the country, trailing almost out of hearing range before making a tree of their own. On arrival at Doc's tree the hunters spotted a coon and let him have it. Wayne stated, "I'm impressed. I would put some time in on a young hound like that."

The hunters then began the long walk toward the other hounds, and found they also had a coon up their tree. The hounds were led back to the vehicle from this tree. It was time to switch the hounds, Drum, Daisey, Dixie and Blondie would be hunted the remainder of the night. The hounds all looked good, treeing several more coons, and as daylight neared both Wayne and Ray noted that Rowdy's other young hound "Dixie" was no joke either.

As the first week turned into the second Wayne and Ray had seen some good dog work from Rowdy's hounds, and Wayne's were operating to perfection as well. Rowdy hunted a couple of the other littermates to Doc and Dixie that looked good too. Ray became fond of one of the pups called "Drummer Boy," he liked his looks, mouth and style. He would sure like to own him. Wayne could not get Doc off his mind, he was a young hound like he had always wanted to own.

The day that Wayne and Ray were to depart for home came too soon. They had enjoyed the hard hunting but couldn't understand how Rowdy always seemed to get the full potential from all his hounds. Drum, Daisey and Drifter would make any hunter proud, and the pups were better than some finished hounds they had hunted with. One thing was for certain, Rowdy's breeding program was advancing in the right direction. Both Wayne and Ray looked forward to seeing the young hounds Rowdy would be hunting in the years to come. Rowdy had patience to work with and finish a young hound, including knowledge to properly train them. He never ceased to amaze them.

As the hunters were saying their goodbyes Rowdy said to Wayne and Ray, "You know I would not have Drum and Drifter if not for you guys, now I'm going to return the favor." He told Wayne that he had all intentions to keep Doc for himself but had decided to let Wayne have him. He told Ray that he was giving him Drummer Boy, and hopefully he would make a hound that pleased him.

Rowdy knew Wayne and Ray would finish the two young hounds, he also knew they would appreciate them. He had wanted to keep Doc but he really needed to put his time into females for his breeding program. Dixie was coming along and would be bred to Drifter at a later date. He also intended to breed Daisey to Drum again soon as she came in season.

Wayne and Ray were pleased to receive Doc and Drummer Boy as gifts from Rowdy, even though it came as a total surprise. They hoped to finish both into top hounds and return the following year to show Rowdy their progress. They discussed how well Drifter had developed, he was as good a track dog as either had ever seen and a tree dog deluxe to go with it. They also discussed the pups Drum was reproducing, not only from Daisey but from local females bred to him as well. Drum was a coondog and a reproducer that was acknowledged by others. Time would tell how great a reproducer he would become.

After Wayne and Ray had departed for home Rowdy continued to hunt hard, putting time into Dixie and the remaining pups. Dixie was a sensible young dog that had everything a hunter could ask for in a hound. She treed lots of coon, liked to split tree off to herself and was a very accurate tree dog. She would be a great asset to his kennel. At the close of season all but two of the remaining pups were advancing well. Rowdy hastily culled the two; he had given them ample time to show their worth. The remaining pups with the exception of Dixie were sold to local hunters.

As spring turned into summer, Rowdy continued to hunt Drum, Daisey, Drifter and Dixie with good results. Daisey and Dixie came in season and Daisey was bred back to Drum. Dixie coming in season for the second time was bred to Drifter. The female pups from Drifter and Dixie would be used to cross back on Drum if they proved worthy of such.

With both Daisey and Dixie bred, Rowdy put some hard enjoyable hunting on Drum and Drifter. He was getting the two ready for the coming coon season. His friends Wayne and Ray were to arrive early this year and Rowdy was going to show them that his hounds were once again finely tuned. There was nothing like a little friendly rivalry. Little did he know that they were going to show him that their hounds were also polished like new chrome.

One month prior to Wayne and Ray's arrival Daisey and Dixie gave birth to their pups. Daisey delivered eight nice pups and all survived. Dixie delivered seven pups, but raised only four with one female surviving. Rowdy planned to keep a female from each litter for future breeding purposes. He knew that top blooded, reproducing females would carry his line of hounds forward into the future. He would breed for ability first and foremost.

When Wayne and Ray arrived opening day of coon season Rowdy was surprised that they had brought only Doc and Drummer Boy. Rowdy asked how the two young hounds were doing. Using one of Rowdy's lines Wayne and Ray replied, "Pretty good." Rowdy knew that the two young hounds had developed into beautiful hounds for sure. He looked forward to seeing them in the woods that night.

Rowdy then proudly showed Wayne and Ray his two liters of pups. He explained his plans to keep a female from each litter. He had several to choose from in Daisey's litter but had no choice in Dixie's litter as there was only one female. The female he kept from Daisey's litter was a brightly colored redtick and would be called, "Red Dawn." The pup from Dixie's litter was redtick with a blue back and dew claws; she would be called "Dolly." Both would develop into coondogs, with Dolly being a superb reproducer and dam of Rowdy's future studs.

Prepared for the hunt Rowdy, Wayne and Ray loaded their hounds. Rowdy was hunting Drum and Drifter, Wayne and Ray had Doc and Drummer Boy. Rowdy had hunted Drum and Drifter hard during the summer and fall; he would soon see that his friends had put some hard hunting on their hounds too. After an all-nighter and at first signs of daylight the three hunters walked from the woods. Rowdy smiled to himself, he now knew what his friends meant when they stated their young hounds were doing, "Pretty good." The two young hounds had given Rowdy's hounds a run for the money. They along with their litter mates and other Drum sired hounds in the area were acknowledgment of Drum's ability to reproduce his likeness or better.

At the end of their two week stay Rowdy, Wayne and Ray were three exhausted hunters, from hunting every night all night. On occasion they hunted with the locals and their Drum sired hounds, and became even more impressed. The hunters had walked much more this year than in previous years as the hounds were split treed on most trees they made. They had treed more coons this year too, even with the young hounds. They knew they had some dog power and were glad to show it. As Wayne and Ray drove away they thought, "Next year won't be long in coming - it couldn't get much better.

Rowdy had been impressed with Doc and Drummer Boy, his friends had hunted them until their full potential surfaced. They were good and reminded him of Drum when he was young. After Wayne and Ray were gone Rowdy continued to hunt nightly with some of the local hunters. He was putting the finishing touches on Dixie and looking forward to starting the new pups as they aged. As the months flew by Rowdy slowly began exposing his pups to the woods and elements. They were a fine group of pups; their hunting career was to begin soon.

The pups were just right for a little corn field hunting, all but one of the pups started quickly. Rowdy focused most of his spare time on the pups, putting a little extra time into Red Dawn and Dolly, the two he was keeping. Red Dawn had earned her name for her bright color, almost as bright as the morning sun rising over the mountain tops. Dolly received her name because of an attachment to a small ornamental doll owned by Rowdy's close friend Dixie. Dolly possessed the loudest mouth Rowdy had ever heard on a female, she also inherited Drifters tracking ability. She was a stay put, radical tree dog to top the package off. Red Dawn was a lot like her dam Daisey, a sensible one bark locator that improved with every trip to the woods.

The coon season had come and gone. Rowdy's friends Wayne and Ray had come for their yearly hunt, and Rowdy had hunted only his young females and Dixie. Wayne and Ray brought only Doc and Drummer Boy; they were once again amazed at the ability of Rowdy's young hounds. At seasons end Rowdy culled any of the young hounds not progressing well, or ones having flaws. The remainder of the two litters excluding Red Dawn and Dolly were sold to local hunters. Rowdy now had hunters waiting in line to purchase his young hounds. He was not into breeding the hounds for the money, but wanted only to put quality young hounds in the hands of tough hunters.

As spring began Rowdy and his longtime sweetheart Dixie were married. Dixie, by this time, had graduated school earning her veterinarian license, and she also enjoyed hunting and raising pups. Their plans were to keep a couple more females from their next litter, and continue to increase their kennel size. Their goal was to eventually own eight or ten top reproducing females. Drum was their primary stud, but Drifter was also proving to produce quality pups. Rowdy felt that if a hound produced good quality hounds from most females bred to he was a reproducer, Drum had proven he would cross on all bloodlines he was bred to. There were pups all around the area from different bloodlines that were doing an outstanding job in the woods.

Of all the hounds Rowdy had raised, Dolly was his favorite up to this point. She had it all -the total package. Rowdy would be mating her with Drum soon as possible. He was going to keep a female and two males from her litter for himself. With time the two males would replace Drum, that is, if they turned out. Red Dawn and Dixie would be bred to Drifter and a female from each litter kept to cross back on Drum. Maybe there would be another Dolly from one of the litters.

As time passed Rowdy's plans came together. Several of the tough young hunters in the area were helping start and train young hounds. Dolly had been bred to Drum and produced a nice litter of pups, of which Rowdy kept a female and two males as planned.

The female was redtick and came to be called "Dot" because of large red spots that covered her body and looked to be painted on. Dot finished into a coondog and become a part of Rowdy's kennel for future breeding purposes.

The two males were redtick with a blue frosting on their backs, both had dew claws. They started young and finished quickly. They were two of the hardest hunting hounds Rowdy had ever seen, and earned their names in the woods. They would be called "Zigzag" and 'Ricochet" because of their hunting style. They quickly and

337

completely hunted the area where released, shooting around as if shot from a gun. Because of the ability shown by these two great hounds Rowdy came to not only demand but expect when a hound of his located and treed for it to stay put and have game up the tree. This was the rule not the exception.

Rowdy and Dixie eventually started a family of their own with twin sons coming first, followed by another son and a daughter later on. Their breeding program grew, and in time Rowdy's sons would be old enough to hunt and carry the tradition to the next level. Zigzag and Ricochet replaced Drum and were thought by many to be even better than their great sire. They advanced forward carrying Rowdy's breeding efforts into the future. With success there always comes jealousy and animosity from some, but Rowdy ignored it all, knowing that in the end despite our differences we are all the same.

FOOD FOR

THOUGHT

33

As a hunter and outdoorsman who has been associated with hounds and hunting all my life, I now often contemplate on all the changes that have occurred in the years I have been involved. The style of hunting has changed along with the type of dog, equipment, dog boxes, advertising, transportation, hunting areas and numerous other things. I often wonder if my grandchildren or great grandchildren will even be able to experience the thrill of hearing a hound run and tree game. Will there be anywhere to hunt? Will the organizations that are against hunting have bills passed to prohibit it? Will some of these organizations have bills passed that prohibit the breeding of dogs? Will all firearms be banned? These are only some of the things that could very well come to be, and should be considered in ones thoughts.

I remember when I was growing up that a person could hunt most anywhere without trouble from anyone. The farmers wanted the coon, deer and other game thinned out because they often did damage to their crops. The land owners didn't mind people hunting on their land if the hunters took care not to damage property, fences, roads, etc.; in fact they were glad to be rid of nuisance game and would many times go hunting with you. One didn't have to worry about someone who only owned half an acre coming out and shooting their treed dog for no reason other than not knowing what it was doing or because they didn't want it around. Things have sure changed in this day and time.

When I was very young we would drive to one area, turn the dogs into the woods and walk with them, usually hunting only one large wooded section without moving to another location. There usually were no roads to get closer if the dogs treed deep or got out of pocket; you simply walked to them, sometimes very long distances. Many times only one or two coons were treed or maybe even none. Today you could go to these same areas where roads have now been built, turn loose and tree a quick coon, move to the other side of the section and tree another coon. The roads being built through the large sections of timber cut back on available timber to hunt but made it more accessible to reach the treed dogs, thus less time to get to the tree and move to another area. I have treed four or five coons in a large section of woods by moving from one drop to the next after making a tree.

In younger years when we hunted this same tract of land on foot we would walk many miles and maybe tree a coon or two. Are there more coons in these areas today? Could the dogs today be better? Is the new way better than the old way? I suppose there could be arguments for both ways.

In the past we treed coon in areas where it was said there were no coon but we were hunting a coondog that treed coon anywhere turned loose, when the dog struck we expected him to tree the track, and when he treed we expected to see a coon up the tree. This was the norm and not the exception with all coon hunters who hunted a "coondog". How many coons per night could a dog like that have treed if it had only been spot hunted as many people hunt in this day and time. Could the quality of the hunt have been better in those days or possibly even the fellowship?

What about the tracking ability of dogs today, is it the same as thirty years ago, or even fifty years? Has the nose been bred out of the dogs of today? Do hunters want their dogs to make more trees or tree more game in a shorter period of time? Do they want dogs that give less mouth on track or only run hot tracks? What about mouth, can a chop mouthed dog run a track faster than a bawl mouthed dog? I have heard this said by some, in theory they believe it takes a dog longer to bawl than to bark with a chop on track. What if the chop mouthed dog barks 100 times in a space of 100 yards and the bawl mouthed dog drifted and only barked once in the same 100 yards.

Maybe only certain breeds today can still trail or run an old bad track and put a tree on the end of it with a coon or other game that can be seen. Or could it be that only certain bloodlines within the breeds still have the ability to trail an old bad track with adequate speed, in the right direction, and put a tree on the end of it where game can be seen. Did the dogs of old cut, drift and slash on a track as many now do? There has been many changes in the way our hounds are now bred.

What about treeing ability, do dogs locate a tree faster now than they did decades ago? Are the dogs of today as accurate as they were in years past? Will dogs stay treed for as long a period of time as they did years ago? Did the dogs of the past stand the tree pressure that dogs will stand today? What about aggressiveness around the tree, are dogs more aggressive today than in the past? Do dogs tree harder now than in the past? Do dogs of today tree more dens, or trees where game could be, but is not seen, than the dogs of yesteryear did?

What about the winding dog, or dogs that hunt with their heads in the air, could they have birddog in their bloodlines or are they just faster hunters that need not put their nose to the ground? Are dogs of this type hot nosed or can they strike a cold track, work it up and put a tree on the end of it with the game in the tree?

Can dogs learn certain abilities from other dogs? An example of this is maybe a poor strike dog being continuously hunted with an outstanding strike dog. Will the poor strike dog learn from the top strike dog, possibly where to look for a track, or maybe not to bypass tracks, hot or cold? What about hunting an average locating dog with a fast and accurate locator? Can the average locator learn from the quick locator or is this determined by the amount of brains possessed by the dog or a trait bred within?

Will an outstanding hybrid reproduce top dogs, and if so, for how many generations into the future will the offspring continue to reproduce top dogs? If the hybrid does reproduce will it also reproduce when crossed on dogs of other breeds? Is breeding the best to the best a sure way to get offspring that develop into top dogs? What about breeding dogs within their family, or line breeding them on a certain dog within their lineage for certain traits, will this always work or possibly increase the chances for success? Old timers and the modern day breeder will see eye to eye on some aspects, yet argue over other things. What is right, or could a little of both be correct?

What about DNA analysis? It could possibly be one of the best things to come along. Knowing beyond a shadow of a doubt that the dog you are breeding to is positively from the bloodlines it is supposed to be from is definitely a plus. What about the dedicated breeder who has bred a certain line of dogs for a certain amount of years and suddenly sees a dog advertised at stud from this same lineage and becomes impressed with this dogs accomplishments and uses him in his breeding program. This breeder bred to the dog because he thought it was the same lineage he had bred for many years; even though he bred to an outside dog it was supposed to be of the same bloodlines of his dogs. A generation or two on down the road the breeder discovers that the dog he bred to was not from the lineage he assumed, but from totally unrelated bloodlines and the registration papers on the dog were incorrect. All the years of careful breeding to keep his lineage pure were taken away from the breeder just that quick. DNA can and will eliminate such a scenario. When breeding dogs that are DNA profiled there is no guesswork involved as far as the bloodline goes. Most reputable breeders have their dogs DNA profiled, if not, could there be a reason why not?

There is an enormous amount of new equipment on the market today, lights, dog boxes, tracking equipment, boots and clothing. I can remember when we hunted with a two cell flashlight or a 6 volt battery powered light and a lantern; the lantern was used as a walking light and the flashlight to shine the tree. At this period in time the person whom I hunted with used a carbide light and refused to use anything else.

The flashlights used an excessive amount of batteries but they did work to find eyes in a tree. The carbide light and lantern would also show eyes in a tree and some swore by them. As time passed the rechargeable miner light manufactured by several different companies became the light of choice. As time revolved the bigger and sometimes bulky higher voltage lights were heavily used and the light of choice. Some of these lights were powered by acid filled batteries which would leak and destroy your clothes. Eventually the heavy lights evolved into a more compact box light using solid batteries, and next came the belt lights. Most of the newer belt and box lights had a long service life and would hold a charge for a substantial period of time. In the last couple of years the technology has advanced to a greater degree with the LED lights and the length of time they will hold a charge. The size and weight have also drastically changed along with numerous other improvements. The light industry will continue to advance in the future, better quality, battery life, never needing bulbs or service of any kind. I can't imagine what will be in ten years.

Methods of hauling our dogs have also improved to an extreme. At one time our hunting dogs were hauled in the trunk of the car or homemade boxes. The industry advanced to boxes made of aluminum and other reinforced materials. Most boxes of today have adequate ventilation to keep a dog cool and avoid suffocation. I lost one of the best young hounds I ever owned to suffocation or overheating in a poor quality box, but I learned from this mishap. There are now hauling boxes that contain water outlets and other means of cooling. The industry has vastly improved over the years, and for the better. There are many reputable companies that manufacture and sell top quality boxes.

The ability to locate an out of pocket or out of hearing range dog is constantly improving as time advances. I remember when we would walk and walk trying to find a dog that had gotten out of hearing. Often times we would drive many miles stopping to listen for a lost dog. Many times someone had picked the dog up and carried it home with them, and the owner would spend all night looking for the dog. One had to rely on someone who had found a lost dog to phone and inform them of such. There were no tracking devices back then, but as time passed and the telemetry systems became popular a lost dog was no longer a problem. The tracking systems made it so much easier to recover a lost or out of pocket dog. Many of the older tracking systems are still in use today, the receivers were good and the transmitting collars have been improved. There are all sorts of new tracking equipment today to include the GPS and also the combined GPS and remote trainer.

Technology has advanced at a rapid pace and will continue to advance in the future.

Years back if a dog ran off game the common way to correct it was to try and catch it in the act and whip it, hopefully, eventually breaking it from unwanted habits. Many times the hunter would have to drive around attempting to head the dog off when it crossed a road. With the e-collar much of the aggravation ended and the trash running dog became easier to control and retrieve. The e-collar also had many other corrective uses and became a useful tool for hunters and dog trainers. Not only are there top quality remote trainers today but as stated before there are now remote trainers combined with GPS technology, thus making training and retrieval much easier than in the past. If hunters of the 19th and early 20th century could see the advanced technology of today they would be shocked, even some hunters from later 20th century would have a surprise or two.

The method of transportation has also drastically changed with all the new types of vehicles on the market. In the "old days" people would put their dogs in the trunk or back seat of the family car and go hunting. People hunted in vehicles of all sorts. Then everyone wanted a four wheel drive, but it has now advanced to four door trucks with plush interiors and diesel engines. The price tags on some of these vehicles can well exceed fifty thousand dollars. I've seen people with a new expensive vehicle and a useless dog. It is always good to own a good vehicle and a good dog, but when both are not an option I'd rather have the good dog and the not so good vehicle.

The quality of hunting clothes and boots has improved to an unbelievable quality. When young I would bundle up in layers of clothes to keep warm in the cold weather, poor quality clothes for the purpose, at best. The clothes would often become ripped or torn by briars and would have to be discarded after only one night of hunting. In this day and time one can wear only thin layers and stay warm and dry as needed. Also much of the hunting clothes today are constructed with materials that are briar proof and moisture resistant. Such clothes can last for several years, and the price is very reasonable for the quality.

There are so many different boots on the market today that it would be hard to choose. Snake proof, water proof, lightweight and tough and also at an affordable price. When I was young I hunted all night every night if I could find someone to hunt with me. I went through lots of boots and my feet would sometimes hurt because of the poor quality of boot I wore. A family member said if I was going to hunt so hard that I needed a good boot to protect my feet; and this was true. She also said that my feet had to support me throughout my life and a good boot would take care of my feet. She purchased for me, at an astronomical price, what she assumed was the best boot on the market at the time. The new boot looked good and felt even better on my feet but lasted less than a month in the conditions that I used it. The boots were returned to the store where purchased because the sole had separated from the upper portion; they were replaced with a new pair. The new pair of boots lasted no longer than the first pair as they just weren't made for the rough wear and constant usage in water sustained in coon hunting. For many years thereafter I used a heavy rubber boot made specifically for coon hunting; it was heavy and tough. Then the coon hunting boot industry was revolutionized by a boot made by a coonhunter for the coonhunter. This boot was soon copied and from it many top quality boots have materialized. A good boot will take care of your feet and be an asset well worth the money in the end.

In younger years I patiently awaited the arrival of the hunting magazines at the first of the month. The magazines were full of advertised stud dogs and dogs, pups, equipment, etc. for sale. Years later I purchased, and sold many good dogs from ads in the magazines and bred many dogs to my studs; many friends were also made through the ads I later ran. The magazines also contained an abundance of good articles and stories; some very good reading. There is still a lot of dogs and equipment advertised today yet the volume is nowhere near what was once advertised.

Some advertisers of today have converted to the internet to advertise dogs, pups or whatever. There are still many people who are not familiar with the internet and who only get the magazines. Advertisement in the magazines is still worthwhile and will easily pay for itself many times over if you are selling a good product. The many who cannot, or do not, use the computer can then see what you have to sell or promote.

I am sure there are still many that look forward to the magazines coming out monthly, and you can be assured that if you are selling good dogs, pups, equipment, or advertising a dog at stud that the ads will promote business for you. New friends and acquaintances can and will be made through advertisement, with the bonus of promoting your stud or selling the dogs and pups you advertise. If you have good dogs or pups to sell or a stud dog to promote you should try running an ad or two. Also, if you have stories of good hunts or dogs of the past write an article about them and send it to the magazines, share the hunts with others; there are always people who enjoy hearing of good hunts with good dogs.

Yep, not all things are agreed upon by everyone but I'm sure there is some good in both the old and the new, but then again the old is in the past so one must prepare for the new and the newer. Just some thoughts to stimulate the mind and maybe bring back memories, there are many more but this is enough for now.

May all your hunts be the best and bring great happiness and pleasure.

ACKNOWLEDGEMENT

I would like to give thanks to the many people who have helped me with the hounds over the years. It would also not have been possible without the houndsmen who trained and promoted many of the hounds described within these stories, or without the handlers who handled for me. I must also thank everyone who sold me many of these hounds even though they did not want to let them go. Jerrell and Dustin Thomas helped me to train young hounds, and hunt and prepare many of these hounds for competition. They handled some in the hunts and both deserve a big thank you. I want to thank Raynor Frost, Jerrell Thomas, Joe Moyer and Terry Walker and all the staff at American Cooner and Full Cry for their contribution of photos. I must give credit to my brother Scott for all the help he has given me over the years. And last but not least all my friends who have stood beside me during the good times along with the bad. You all know who you are.

About the Author

Gregory Bart Nation grew up in the hills of North Georgia and has coon hunted all of his life, pursuing the wily raccoon across the United States and Canada. He has owned top hounds since only a child and as he became older he would always have a top hound on his lead. He enjoys pleasure hunting with good hounds and good friends and was not afraid to hit the competition circuit and show the world the type hounds that were in his kennel. Let the hound do the talking was and always will be his motto. He showed any hound in his kennel to anyone who wanted to see them go, either alone or in company.

Made in the USA
Lexington, KY
05 August 2018